# Weeve invites you to be part of something special.

Sign up for an account today and h~~
future of langua~~

www.

Upload books of your choice

Dynamically adjust translation difficulty

Real-time pronunciations

## Welcome to Weeve

Here at Weeve, we believe that traditional language education, with its painful memorisation, repetition and tedious grammar classes, have failed students around the world in their pursuit of learning a new language. Over 50 years of education research supports us on this. Studies show that the best way of encouraging language acquisition is reading and listening to engaging and accessible content. With that vision in mind, we created Weeve. Our method allows you to learn up to 20 words per hour in your target language – we are confident you'll never want to learn languages in any other way. Thank you for supporting us on this journey.

## How to Use Weeve

**Weeved Words**

The sentences in this novel have foreign words weaved into the English sentences. Introducing foreign words within the context of an English sentence allows our brain to form a contextual representation of that foreign word without needing to translate it. At the start of our books only a few words are translated, as you progress, getting lost in the world of fantasy, more and more translated words are added.

**Read - Don't Translate**

When you come across a foreign word weaved into a sentence resist the urge to translate the word back to English. Your brain will automatically do this at first, but with practice this skill can be mastered.

**Context is Key**

Read the foreign words as they are written and try to understand it in the context of the story. Translating disrupts the flow of the story, and it is these flow states where pleasure and language acquisition will occur. Don't worry about your speed of acquisition - trust the process.

**Go with the Flow**

Language acquisition is a subconscious process that happens when we read and listen to interesting things that we understand. All you have left to do is enjoy the story, try not to think too much about the words and you will acquire them faster.

## Vocab Tables

You will find vocabulary tables at the end of chapters - consider these milestones, showing the weaved words you have read during that chapter. Quickly double check you understand them and continue learning! These vocab tables also offer the International Phonetic Alphabet (IPA) phonetic pronunciation of the word.

# Weeve's Story

The idea for Weeve was born when Cian was having a bath and an apple hit him on the head. Four years ago, Cian spoke only English and decided to try and learn Portuguese. For two years he tried and failed to learn the language using the traditional methods available out there – flashcards, language learning apps, grammar lessons. Despite having over 5000 words memorised, Cian found his speech was still slow and his comprehension was poor.

Frustrated at his lack of progress, Cian began to research second language acquisition. The core message that research and academia has proven over the past 50 years is simple - *you only acquire language when you read and listen to content you understand.* The problem was that there is no option for beginners to get their hands on comprehensible input as they do not have the foundational knowledge required to jump into reading short stories and novels.

So, inspired by the evidence that bilingual students learn best in settings where languages are blended together, Cian began a six-month long journey of researching, trialling, and developing the first ever Weeve book (a Swedish version of *The Wheel of Time*). He pulled in Evan, who had had a terrible experience learning languages in school, and the two of them began developing the idea. As the first Weeve guinea pigs, the pair knew they were onto a winner when they were capable of learning their first 400 Swedish words with no effort, no memorisation and no pain.

The hunger for Weeve's products was evident from the launch of the first book, *Learn Spanish with Sherlock Holmes*, in July 2020. Since launch, Weeve have had an immensely exciting time. The collection has expanded to include eleven languages and has sold over 2500 copies. The Weeve team joined a Trinity student accelerator program, which connected them with Sinéad. Sinéad was a member of the judging panel at a start-up competition when she first came across the Weeve duo. It was love at first sight and just three days after the competition she was officially part of the gang.

The fourth member of our team, Oisín joined over the summer of 2021. A computer scientist determined to digitise the Weeve method so it can reach global scale. Currently working on an application that will allow for complete dynamic control over translations within your weeve.

The response to our Weeve books around the globe has been immense winning a number of awards like the LEO ICT Award and placing in Spark Crowdfundings top 100 most amibitious companies. With the founders appearing in the Sunday Independant's 30 Under 30.

Weeve wants to make languages ridiculously simple and accessible to everyone. We hope you enjoy it as much as we do, and stick around for our journey.

## Meet the Team

### Cian McNally

Cian is a Psychology graduate from Trinity College Dublin and a language learning enthusiast. In the past 4 years he has gone from speaking only English to being able to read many novels in Portuguese, Spanish and German, as well as short stories in Swedish and Italian. When he's not revolutionising the language learning industry, he is probably found playing chess or talking about how tall he is.

### Evan McGloughlin

Evan is a Neuroscience graduate from Trinity College Dublin and has a passion for learning and education. He runs a youtube channel where he attempts to make practical neuroscience accessible and entertaining. He always despised how languages were taught in school always thinking it felt very unnatural. When Cian came to him with the idea for Weeve it instantly resonated with him as a more natural and effective approach.

### Sinead McAleer

Sinead lives a double life – working in a bank by day and growing Weeve by night. After graduating from Computer Science & Business at Trinity College Dublin, Sinéad moved to London where she now leads our international office (aka a desk in the corner of her bedroom). She has a passion for start-ups, technology and vegan/vegetarian experimentation!

### Oisín T. Morrin

Oisín loves all things at the intersection of language and technology. This brought him to study Computer Science, Linguistics and Irish at TCD as an All-Ireland Scholar. Japanese, Irish and Python are his love languages, and he also dabbles in Korean, German and Scot's Gaelic. Outside of Weeve, Oisín can invariably be found with a new book in one hand and a coffee in the other.

## How to Have a Perfect Accent

You may have never seen the IPA before but it's the universal way to perfectly write pronunciations. The aim of the IPA is to provide a unique symbol for each distinctive sound in a language. You already know most of these symbols as they are letters in English. If you familiarise yourself with the other ~15 of these symbols you'll always be able to pronounce foreign words perfectly without having to learn more than 140 spelling rules.

# German Pronunciation Guide

The very first step of learning how to pronounce words in a new language is to learn how to use its International Phonetic Alphabet. We are going to focus on some of the German sounds that are inexistant in the English pronunciation and that you will need to be able to spot in the IPA and to understand when looking for the pronunciation of a specific German word.

Here are the unusual **consonant** related sounds which you will have to remember:

- /ç/: you can find this sound in words like <i**ch**> or <dur**ch**>. Think of it as an middle way between the /hju/ sound in the word <human> and the pronunciation of <sh>. v
- /x/ : it symbolizes sounds like the <**ch**> like <nach> and it is pronounced like the <ch> in 'loch ness'.
- <**j**>: it is pronounced just like a <y> in English.
- <**w**>: it is pronounced just like a <v> in English. Conversely, <v> is pronounced like an <f> in most words, but not always! Here, you need to pay attention to what the IPA says; whether the <f> or the <v> sound applies.
- <**s**>: it is pronounced like the <z> in <zebra> and you will also find it as a /z/ in the German IPA.
- <ʁ>: this is what you call a "voiced uvular fricative" and is the <r> that is used in French as well. This <r> is pronounced in the back of your mouth, where you would pronounce the letter <k>. The difference is that the letter <k> is voiceless, so to pronounce the German <r>, try pronouncing a <k> and adding voice to it!

Most IPA **symbols**, which looked different from normal letters, are used in English words, too:
- /d͡ʒ/: <**Dsch**ungel>, <**j**ungle>
- /t͡ʃ/: <Ma**tsch**>, <ma**tch**>
- /ŋ/: <si**ng**en>, <si**ng**>
- /ʃ/: <**Sch**rift>, <**sh**all>
- /t͡s/: <**z**aubern>, <ha**ts**>
- /ʒ/: <**G**enie>, <trea**s**ure>

The German language has very unique vowel sounds and the most important ones are what are called the **umlauts**:
- /oe/ is a symbol that you will find used for words like <öffnen> (short vowel with a double consonant after it, the vowel being called an umlaut) and it sounds similar to the <i> in <bird> or the <u> in <burn>. The long version of this umlaut is symbolized /ø:/ and can be found in <Österreich> for example.

- <ä> might look complicated but is actually pronounced the same as a short <e> in German, which is symbolized /ɛ/ and is also used in the English IPA. You find it in words like <bet>. While an <ä> pronounced like an /ɛ/ is found in words where it precedes two consonant letters, it's longer version can be found in words like <spät> (symbolized ɛ:) and pronounced like the <ai> in <hair>.

- The symbol /y/ brings together both the umlaut <ü> and the vowel <y> and they are pronounced somewhat like the <u> in <cute>, or <ew> in <grew>.

Talking about the umlauts, we briefly mentioned short and long vowels. The difference between short and long lies in the time it will take you to pronounce the vowel and the sound you make while pronouncing it will slightly vary as well.

The easiest way to figure out whether the vowel will be long or short is the look at the letters following it: the vowel will be short when succeeded by two consonants and it will be long if there is just one consonant or a vowel after it. Just like any rule, there are exceptions to it and the following-consonant-trick does not always work, which is why the IPA will tell you whether the vowel is long or short. In the IPA, **long vowels** are typically symbolized by a semi-colon:

| Letters   | Phonetic symbol | English | German    |
|-----------|-----------------|---------|-----------|
| a (short) | a               | cut     | Affe      |
| a (long)  | aː              | father  | Bahnhof   |
| e (short) | ɛ               | bet     | retten    |
| e (long)  | ɛː              | hair    | eben      |
| i (short) | ɪ               | sin     | bitte     |
| i (long)  | iː              | see     | spazieren |
| o (short) | ɔ               | got     | offen     |
| o (long)  | oː              | note    | Boot      |
| u (short) | ʊ               | foot    | rund      |
| u (long)  | uː              | moon    | Uhr       |

Here are a few more exceptions and final **unusual sounds** to remember:
- \<ai\> and \<ay\> are pronounced like the word \<eye\>, symbolized /aɪ̯/
- \<au\> is pronounced \<ow\>, symbolized /aʊ̯/
- \<äu\> and \<eu\> are pronounced \<oy\>, symbolized /ɔɪ̯/
- \<ie\> is pronounced like \<ee\>, symbolized /iː/

Book Publishing Details

Exclusive book publishing rights pertain to copyright ©Weeve 2022

Design, production, editing, and illustration credits:
Logo and Cover Design by Aaron Connolly

Cover and Interior Illustrations by Otherworld Creations, Leoramos
www.fiverr.com/Otherworlder
www.fiverr.com/Leoramos

Editing, production:
Weeve

Translation:
Laura O'Sullivan (Weeve Translator)
Elsa Gaffet (Weeve Translator)

Fonts:
Recoletta, Times New Roman, Tomarik

Publisher Address:
31 Millers Lane, Skerries, Co. Dublin, Ireland
Author Website:
https://weeve.ie/
Country in which the book was printed:
United States, United Kingdom

*All rights reserved. No part of this publication may be reproduced, distributed, or transmitted in any form or by any means, including photocopying, recording, or other electronic or mechanical methods, without the prior written permission of the publisher, except in the case of brief quotations embodied in critical reviews and certain other noncommercial uses permitted by copyright law. For permission requests, contact info@weeve.ie*

# ALICE
# ꟼ
# WONDERLAND

# Book 1

# 1

# DOWN THE RABBIT HOLE

**Weeve Reading Tip:** When you come across a foreign word weaved into a sentence resist the urge to translate the word back to English. Your brain will automatically do this at first, but with practice this skill can be mastered. Read the sentence as it is presented and try to understand it.

Alice was beginning to get **sehr** tired of sitting by her sister on the bank, **und** of having nothing to **machen**: once **oder** twice she had peeped **in** the book her sister was reading, **aber** it had no pictures **oder** conversations in it, "**und** what is the use of a book," thought Alice "without pictures **oder** conversations?"

So she was considering in her own mind (as **gut** as she could, for the hot day made her feel **sehr** sleepy **und** stupid), whether the pleasure of making a daisy-chain would be worth the trouble of getting up **und** picking the daisies, **als** suddenly a White Rabbit **mit** pink eyes ran close by her.

**Es gab** nothing so **sehr** remarkable in that; nor did Alice think it so **sehr** much **aus dem Weg** to hear the Rabbit say to itself, "Oh dear! Oh dear! **Ich** shall be late!" (**als** she thought it over afterwards, it occurred to her that she ought to have wondered at this, **aber** at the time it all seemed quite natural); **aber als** the Rabbit actually took a watch out of its waistcoat-pocket, **und** looked at it, **und** then hurried on, Alice started to her feet, for it flashed across **ihr Gedächtnis** that she had never before seen a rabbit **mit** either a waistcoat-pocket, **oder** a watch to take out of it, **und** burning **mit** curiosity, she ran across the field after it, **und**

1

fortunately was just in time **um zu sehen** it pop down a large rabbit-hole under the hedge.

In another moment down went Alice after it, never once considering **wie** in the world she was to get out again.

The rabbit-hole went straight on like a tunnel for some **Weg, und** then dipped suddenly down, so suddenly that Alice had not a moment to think about stopping herself before she found herself falling down a **sehr** deep **Brunnen**.

Either the **Brunnen** was **sehr** deep, **oder** she fell **sehr** slowly, for she had plenty of time as she went down to look about her **und** to wonder what was going to happen next. First, she tried to look down **und** make out what she was coming to, **aber** it was too dark **um zu sehen** anything; then she looked at the sides of the **Brunnen, und** noticed that **sie waren** filled **mit** cupboards **und** book-shelves; here **und** there **sie sah** maps **und** pictures hung upon pegs. She took down a jar from one of the shelves as she passed; it was labelled "ORANGE MARMALADE", **aber** to her great disappointment it was empty: she did not like to drop the jar for fear of killing somebody underneath, so managed to put it **in** one of the cupboards as she fell past it.

"**Gut!**" thought Alice to herself, "after such a fall as this, **ich** shall think nothing of tumbling down stairs! **Wie** brave **sie** will all think me at home! Why, **ich würde** not say anything about it, even **wenn ich** fell off the top of the house!" (Which was **sehr** likely true.)

Down, down, down. Would the fall never come to an end? "**Ich** wonder **wie** many miles **ich** have fallen by this time?" she said aloud. "**Ich** must be getting somewhere near the centre of the earth. Let me see: that would be four thousand miles down, **ich** think—" (for, **sehen Sie,,** Alice had learnt several things of this sort in her lessons in the schoolroom, **und** though this was not a **sehr** good opportunity for showing off her knowledge, as **es gab** no one to listen to her, still it was good practice to say it over) "—yes, that's about the right distance—but then **ich** wonder what Latitude **oder** Longitude **ich** have got to?" (Alice had no idea what Latitude was, **oder** Longitude either, **aber** thought **sie waren** nice grand words to say.)

Presently she began again. "**Ich** wonder **ob ich** shall fall right through the earth! **Wie** funny it will seem to come out among **den Menschen** that walk **mit** their heads downward! The Antipathies, **ich** think—" (she was rather glad **es gab** no one listening, this time, as it did not sound at all the right word) "—but **ich** shall have to ask **sie** what the name of the country is, wissen Sie. Please, Ma'am, is this New Zealand **oder** Australia?"

(**und** she tried to curtsey as she spoke—fancy curtseying as you

2

are falling through the air! Do you think you could manage it?) "**Und** what an ignorant little girl she will think me for asking! No, it will never do to ask: perhaps **ich** shall see it written up somewhere."

Down, down, down. **Es gab** nothing else to **machen**, so Alice soon began talking again. "Dinah will miss me **sehr** much tonight, <u>**ich sollte**</u> think!"

(Dinah was the cat.) "**Ich** hope **sie** will remember her saucer of milk at tea-time. Dinah my dear! <u>**Ich wünsche**</u> you were down here **mit** me! <u>**Es gibt**</u> no mice in the air, I'm afraid, **aber** you might catch a bat, **und** that's **sehr** like a mouse, <u>**wissen Sie**</u>. **Aber** do cats eat bats, **ich** wonder?" **Und** here Alice began to get rather sleepy, **und** went on saying to herself, in a dreamy sort of **Weg**, "Do cats eat bats? Do cats eat bats?" **und** sometimes, "Do bats eat cats?" for, **sehen Sie**,, as she couldn't answer either question, it did not much matter which **Weg** she put it. She felt that she was dozing off, **und** had just begun to dream that she was walking hand in hand **mit** Dinah, **und** saying to her **sehr** earnestly, "Now, Dinah, tell me the truth: did you ever eat a bat?" **als** suddenly, thump! thump! down she came upon a heap of sticks **und** dry leaves, **und** the fall was over.

Alice was not a bit hurt, **und** she jumped up on to her feet in a moment: she looked up, **aber** it was all dark overhead; before her was another long passage, **und** the White Rabbit was still in sight, hurrying down it. **Es gab** not a moment to be lost: away went Alice like the wind, **und** was just in time to hear it say, as it turned a corner, "Oh my ears **und** whiskers, **wie** late it's getting!" She was close behind it **als** she turned the corner, **aber** the Rabbit was no longer to be seen: she found herself in a long, low hall, which was lit up by a row of lamps hanging from the roof.

**Es gab** doors all round the hall, **aber sie waren** all locked; **und wenn** Alice had been all <u>**ganz unten auf**</u> one side **und** up the other, trying every door, she walked sadly down the middle, wondering **wie** she was ever to get out again.

Suddenly she came upon a little three-legged table, all made of solid glass; **es gab** nothing on it except a tiny golden key, **und** Alice's first thought was that it might belong to one of the doors of the hall; **aber**, alas! either the locks were too large, **oder** the key was too small, **aber** at any rate it wouldn't open any of <u>**ihnen**</u>. However, on the second time round, she came upon a low curtain she had not noticed before, **und** behind it was a little door about fifteen inches high: she tried the little golden key in the lock, **und** to her great delight it fitted!

Alice opened the door **und** found that it led **in** a small passage, not much larger **als** a rat-hole: she knelt down **und** looked along the passage **in** the loveliest garden you ever saw. **Wie** she longed

3

to get out of that dark hall, **und** wander about among those beds of bright flowers **und** those cool fountains, **aber** she couldn't even get her head through the doorway; "**und** even **wenn** my head would go through," thought poor Alice, "it would be of **sehr** little use without my shoulders. Oh, **wie ich** wish **ich** could shut up like a telescope! **Ich** think **ich** could, **wenn ich** only knew **wie** to begin." For, **sehen Sie**,, so many out-of-the-way things had happened lately, that Alice had begun to think that **sehr** few things indeed were really impossible.

There seemed to be no use in waiting by the little door, so she went back to the table, half hoping she might find another key on it, **oder** at any rate a book of rules for shutting **Menschen** up like telescopes: this time she found a little bottle on it, ("which certainly was not here before," said Alice,) **und** round the neck of the bottle was a paper label, **mit** the words "DRINK ME," beautifully printed on it in large letters.

It was all **sehr gut** to say "Drink me," **aber** the wise little Alice was not going to **machen** that in a hurry. "No, **ich** will look first," she said, "**und** see whether it's marked 'poison' **oder** not"; for she had read several nice little histories about children __die__ had got burnt, **und** eaten up by wild beasts **und** other unpleasant things, all __weil sie__ wouldn't remember the simple rules their friends had taught **sie**: such as, that a red-hot poker will burn you **wenn** you hold it too long; **und** that **wenn** you cut your finger **sehr** deeply **mit** a knife, it usually bleeds; **und** she had never forgotten that, **wenn** you drink much from a bottle marked "poison," it is almost certain to disagree **mit** you, sooner **oder** later.

However, this bottle was not marked "poison," so Alice ventured to taste it, **und** finding it **sehr** nice, (it had, in fact, a sort of mixed flavour of cherry-tart, custard, pine-apple, roast turkey, toffee, **und** hot buttered toast,) she **sehr** soon finished it off.

\* \* \* \* \* \* \*

\* \* \* \* \* \*

\* \* \* \* \* \* \*

"What a curious feeling!" said Alice; "**Ich** must be shutting up like a telescope."

**Und** so it was indeed: she was now only ten inches high, **und** her face brightened up at the thought that she was now the right size for going through the little door in that lovely garden. First, however, she waited for a few minutes um **zu sehen**, **ob** she was going to shrink any further: she felt a little nervous about this; "for it might end, **weißt du**," said Alice to herself, "in my going out altogether, like a candle. **Ich** wonder what **ich sollte** be like then?" **Und** she tried to fancy what the flame of a candle is like after the candle is blown out, for she couldn't remember ever having seen such a thing.

After a while, finding that nothing more happened, she decided on going **in** the garden at once; **aber**, alas for poor Alice! **als** she got to the door, she found she had forgotten the little golden key, **und als** she went back to the table for it, she found she couldn't possibly reach it: she could see it quite plainly through the glass, **und** she tried her best to climb up one of the legs of the table, **aber** it was too slippery; **und als** she had tired herself out **mit** trying, the poor little thing sat down **und** cried.

"Come, there's no use in crying like that!" said Alice to herself, rather sharply; "**Ich** advise you to leave off this minute!" She generally gave herself **sehr** good advice, (though she **sehr** seldom followed it), **und** sometimes she scolded herself so severely as to bring tears **in** her eyes; **und** once she remembered trying to box her own ears for having cheated herself in a game of croquet she was playing against herself, for this curious child was **sehr** fond of pretending to be two **Menschen**. "**Aber** it's no use now," thought poor Alice, "to pretend to be two **Menschen**! Why, there's hardly enough of me left um **zu machen** one respectable person!"

Soon her eye fell on a little glass box that was lying under the table: she opened it, **und** found in it a **sehr** small cake, on which the words "EAT ME" were beautifully marked in currants. "**Gut, ich** will eat it," said Alice, "**und wenn** it makes me grow larger, **ich kann** reach the key; **und wenn** it makes me grow smaller, **ich kann** creep under the door; so in jedem Fall **ich** will get **in** the garden, **und ich** do not care which happens!"

She ate a little bit, **und** said anxiously to herself, "Which **Weg**? Which **Weg**?", holding her hand on the top of her head to feel which **Weg** it was growing, **und** she was quite surprised to find that she remained the same size: to be sure, this generally happens **wenn** one eats cake, **aber** Alice had got so much into the way of expecting nothing **aber <u>ungewöhnliche</u>** things to happen, that it seemed quite dull **und** stupid for life to go on in the common **Weg**.

So she set to <u>**Werk**</u>, **und sehr** soon finished off the cake.

\* \* \* \* \* \* \*

\* \* \* \* \* \*

\* \* \* \* \* \* \*

5

# weeve
## Chapter 1

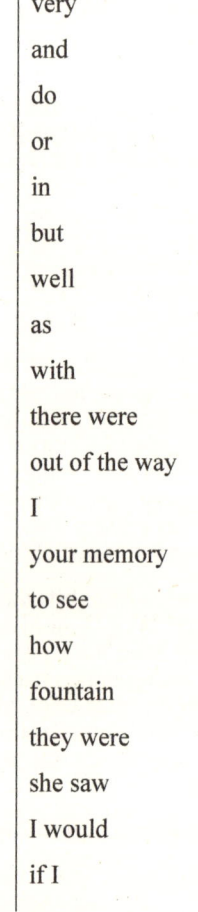

| German | Pronunciation | English |
|---|---|---|
| sehr | zeːə | very |
| und | unt | and |
| machen | maːxən | do |
| oder | odə | or |
| in | in | in |
| aber | abə | but |
| gut | gut | well |
| als | als | as |
| mit | mit | with |
| es gab | es gap | there were |
| aus dem Weg | aus dem vek | out of the way |
| ich | ix | I |
| ihr Gedächtnis | iːr geːdextnis | your memory |
| um zu sehen | um t͡su seːhən | to see |
| wie | viə | how |
| Brunnen | prunən | fountain |
| sie waren | ziː vaːrən | they were |
| sie sah | ziː saː | she saw |
| ich würde | ix vyədə | I would |
| wenn ich | vənn ix | if I |

# weeve
## Chapter 1

| German | Pronunciation | English |
|---|---|---|
| den Menschen | dən mənʃən | the people |
| ich sollte | ix soltə | I should |
| ich wünsche | ix vynʃə | I wish |
| es gibt | es gibt | there is |
| wissen sie | visən siə | you know |
| ganz unten | gan͡ts untən | at the bottom |
| auf | auf | on |
| ihnen | iːnən | them |
| die | diə | the |
| weil sie | vail siə | because they |
| ich kann | ix kan | I can |
| ungewöhnliche | uŋeːvøːnlixə | unusual |
| Werk | veək | work |

# 2
## THE POOL OF TEARS

**Weeve Reading Tip:** If you struggle reading the weaved words try reading the full sentence and ignore the fact you didn't understand the foreign word. Your brain will subconsciously process this word, using context to better understand it for the next time it appears.

"Curiouser **und** curiouser!" cried Alice (she was so much surprised, that for the moment she quite forgot **wie** to speak good English); "now I'm opening out like the largest telescope that ever was! Good-bye, feet!"

(for **als** she looked down at her feet, **sie** seemed to be almost out of sight, **sie waren** getting so far off). "Oh, my poor little feet, **ich** wonder **wer** will put on your shoes **und** stockings for you now, dears? I'm sure **ich** sha not be able! **Ich** shall be a great deal too far off to trouble myself about you: you must manage the best **Weise ihr könnt**;—but **ich** must be kind to **ihnen**," thought Alice, "**oder** perhaps **ie** won't walk **den Weg ich** want to go! Let me see: **ich** will give **ihnen** a new pair of boots every Christmas."

**Und** she went on planning to herself **wie sie würde** manage it. "**Sie** must go by the carrier," she thought; "**und wie** funny it will seem, sending presents to one's own feet! **Und wie** odd the directions will look!

Alice's Right Foot, Esq., Hearthrug, near the Fender, (**mit** Alice's love).

Oh dear, what nonsense I'm talking!"

8

Just then her head struck against the roof of the hall: in fact she was now more **als** nine feet high, **und** she at once took up the little golden key **und** hurried off to the garden door.

Poor Alice! It was as much as she could do, lying down on one side, to look through **in** the garden **mit** one eye; **aber** to get through was more hopeless **als** ever: she sat down **und** began to cry again.

"You ought to be ashamed of yourself," said Alice, "a great girl like you," (she might **gut** say this), "to go on crying in this **Weise**! Stop this moment, **ich** tell you!" **Aber** she went on all the same, shedding gallons of tears, until **es gab** a large pool all round her, about four inches deep **und** reaching half down the hall.

After **einiger Zeit** she heard a little pattering of feet in the distance, **und** she hastily dried her eyes **um zu sehen** what was coming. It was the White Rabbit returning, splendidly dressed, **mit** a pair of white kid gloves in one hand **und** a large fan in the other: he came trotting along in a great hurry, muttering to himself as he came, "Oh! the Duchess, the Duchess! Oh! won't she be savage **wenn ich** have kept her waiting!" Alice felt so desperate that she was ready to ask help of any one; so, **als** the Rabbit came near her, she began, in a low, timid voice, "**Wenn** you please, sir—" The Rabbit started violently, dropped the white kid gloves **und** the fan, **und** skurried away **in** the darkness as hard as he could go.

Alice took up the fan **und** gloves, **und**, as the hall was **sehr** hot, she kept fanning herself **die ganze Zeit** she went on talking: "Dear, dear! **Wie** queer everything is to-day! **Und** yesterday things went on just as usual. **Ich** wonder **ob ich** have been changed in the night? Let me think: was **ich** the same **als ich** got up this morning? **Ich** almost think **ich kann** remember feeling a little different. **Aber falls** I'm not the same, the next question is, **Wer** in the world am **ich**? Ah, that's the great puzzle!" **Und** she began thinking over all the children **sie kannte** that were of the same age as herself, **um zu sehen, ob** she could have been changed for any of **ihnen**.

"I'm sure I'm not Ada," she said, "for her hair goes in such long ringlets, **und** mine doesn't go in ringlets at all; **und** I'm sure **ich** can't be Mabel, for **ich kenne** all sorts of things, **und** she, oh! she **kennt** such a **sehr** little! Besides, she's she, **und** I'm **ich**, and—oh dear, **wie** puzzling it all is! **Ich** will try **ob ich kenne**, all the things **ich kannte**. Let me see: four **mal** five is twelve, **und** four **mal** six is thirteen, **und** four **mal** seven is—oh dear! **Ich** shall never get to twenty at that rate! However, the Multiplication Table doesn't signify: let's try Geography. London is the capital of Paris, **und** Paris is the capital of Rome, **und** Rome—no, that's all wrong, I'm certain! **Ich** must have been changed for Mabel! **Ich** will try **und** say '**Wie** doth the little —'" **und** she crossed her hands on her lap as **wenn** she were saying lessons, **und** began to repeat it, **aber** her voice sounded hoarse **und** strange, **und** the words did not come the same as they used to:—

"**Wie** doth the little crocodile Improve his shining tail, **Und** pour the waters of the Nile On every golden scale!

"**Wie** cheerfully he seems to grin, **Wie** neatly spread his claws, **Und** welcome little fishes in **Mit** gently smiling jaws!"

"I'm sure those are not the right words," said poor Alice, **und** her eyes filled **mit** tears again as she went on, "**Ich** must be Mabel after all, **und ich** shall have to go **und** live in that poky little house, **und** have next to no toys to play **mit**, **und** oh! ever so many lessons to learn! No, **ich** have **mich entschieden** about it; **wenn** I'm Mabel, **ich** will stay down here! It will be no use their putting their heads down **und** saying 'Come up again, dear!'

**Ich** shall only look up **und** say '**Wer** am **ich** then? Tell me that first, **und** then, **wenn ich mag** being that person, **ich** will come up: **wenn** not, **ich** will stay down here till I'm somebody else'— but, oh dear!" cried Alice, **mit** a sudden burst of tears, "**Ich** do wish **sie würden** put their heads down! **Ich** am so **sehr** tired of being all alone here!"

As she said this she looked down at her hands, **und** was surprised **zu sehen** that she had put on one of the Rabbit's little white kid gloves while she was talking. "**Wie** can **ich** have done that?" she thought. "**Ich** must be growing small again." She got up **und** went to the table to measure herself by it, **und** found that, as nearly as she could guess, she was now about two feet high, **und** was going on shrinking rapidly: she soon found out that the cause of this was the fan she was holding, **und** she dropped it hastily, just in time to avoid shrinking away altogether.

"That was a narrow escape!" said Alice, a good deal frightened at the sudden change, **aber sehr** glad to find herself still in existence; "**und** now for the garden!" **und** she ran **mit** all speed back to the little door: **aber**, alas! the little door was shut again, **und** the little golden key was lying on the glass table as before, "**und** things are worse **als** ever," thought the poor child, "for **ich** never was so small as this before, never! **Und ich** declare it's too bad, that it is!"

As she said these words her foot slipped, **und in** another moment, splash! she was up to her chin in salt water. Her first idea was that she had somehow fallen in the sea, "**und** in that case **ich kann** go back by railway," she said to herself. (Alice had been to the seaside once in her life, **und** had come to the general conclusion, that wherever you go to on the English coast you find a number of bathing machines in the sea, some children digging in the sand **mit** wooden spades, then a row of lodging houses, **und** behind

**sie** a railway station.) However, she soon made out that she was in the pool of tears which she had wept **als** she was nine feet high.

"**Ich** wish **ich** had not cried so much!" said Alice, as she swam about, trying to find **ihren Weg** out. "**Ich** shall be punished for it now, **ich** suppose, by being drowned in my own tears! That will be a queer thing, to be sure! However, everything is queer to-day."

Just then she heard something splashing about in the pool a little **Weg** off, **und** she swam nearer um **herauszufinden** what it was: at first she thought it must be a walrus **oder** hippopotamus, **aber** then she remembered **wie** small she was now, **und** she soon made out that it was only a mouse that had slipped in like herself.

"Would it be of any use, now," thought Alice, "to speak to this mouse? Everything is so out-of-the-way down here, that **ich sollte** think **sehr** likely it can talk: at any rate, there's no harm in trying." So she began: "O Mouse, **kennst du den Weg** out of this pool? **Ich** am **sehr** tired of swimming about here, O Mouse!" (Alice thought this must be the right **Weg** of speaking to a mouse: she had never done such a thing before, **aber** she remembered having seen in her brother's Latin Grammar, "A mouse—of a mouse—to a mouse—a mouse—O mouse!") The Mouse looked at her rather inquisitively, **und** seemed to her to wink **mit** one of its little eyes, **aber** it said nothing.

"Perhaps it doesn't understand English," thought Alice; "**Ich** daresay it's a French mouse, come over **mit** William the Conqueror." (For, **mit** all her knowledge of **Geschichte**, Alice had no **sehr** clear notion **wie** long ago anything had happened.) So she began again: "Où est ma chatte?" which was the first sentence in her French lesson-book. The Mouse gave a sudden leap out of the water, **und** seemed to quiver all over **mit** fright. "Oh, **ich** beg your pardon!" cried Alice hastily, afraid that she had hurt the poor animal's feelings. "**Ich** quite forgot you did not like cats."

"Not like cats!" cried the Mouse, in a shrill, passionate voice. "Would **Sie mögen** cats **wenn du wärst** me?"

"Well, perhaps not," said Alice in a soothing tone: "do not be angry about it. **Und** yet **ich** wish **ich** could show you our cat Dinah: **ich** think you'd take a fancy to cats **wenn** you could only see her. She is such a dear quiet thing," Alice went on, half to herself, as she swam lazily about in the pool, "**und** she sits purring so nicely by the fire, licking her paws **und** washing her face—and she is such a nice soft thing to nurse—and she's such a capital one for catching mice—oh, **ich** beg your pardon!" cried Alice again, for this time the Mouse was bristling all over, **und** she felt certain it must be really offended. "**Wir** won't talk about her any more **wenn** you'd rather not."

"**Wir** indeed!" cried the Mouse, **die** was trembling down to the end of his tail. "**Alswürde ich** talk on such a subject! Our family always hated cats: nasty, low, vulgar things! Do not let me hear the name again!"

"**Ich** won't indeed!" said Alice, in a great hurry to change the subject of conversation. "Are you—are you fond—of—of dogs?" The Mouse did not answer, so Alice went on eagerly: "**Es gibt** such a nice little dog near our house I should like to show you! A little bright-eyed terrier, you know, **mit** oh, such long curly brown hair! **Und** it will fetch things **wenn** you throw **sie**, **und** it will sit up **und** beg for its dinner, **und** all sorts of things—I can't remember half of them—and it belongs to a farmer, you know, **und** he says it's so useful, it's worth a hundred pounds! He says it kills all the rats and—oh dear!" cried Alice in a sorrowful tone, "I'm afraid **ich** have offended it again!" For the Mouse was swimming away from her as hard as it could go, **und machte** quite a commotion in the pool as it went.

So she called softly after it, "Mouse dear! Do come back again, **und wir** won't talk about cats **oder** dogs either, **wenn du sie nicht magst Wann** the Mouse heard this, it turned round **und** swam slowly back to her: its face was quite pale (**mit** passion, Alice thought), **und** it said in a low trembling voice, "Let us get to the shore, **und** then **ich** will tell you my **Geschichte**, **und** you will understand why it is **ich** hate cats **und** dogs."

It was high time to go, for the pool was getting quite crowded **mit** the birds **und** animals that had fallen **in** it: **es gab** a Duck **und** a Dodo, a Lory **und** an Eaglet, **und** several other curious creatures. Alice led **der Weg**, **und** the whole party swam to the shore.

# weeve

## Chapter 2

| German | Pronunciation | English |
|---|---|---|
| wer | və | who |
| weise ihr könnt | vaiese i:r kønt | wise you can |
| ie | iə | ie |
| einiger Zeit | aiəniçər t͡sait | some time |
| die ganze Zeit | di: gant͡se t͡sait | the whole time |
| aber falls | abər fals | but if |
| sie kannte | zi: kantə | she knew |
| ich kenne | ix kənnə | I know |
| kennt | kənnt | knows |
| mal | mal | times |
| mich entschieden | mix ənt͡ʃi:dən | decided me |
| wenn ich mag | vənn ix mak | if i like |
| sie würden | zi: vyədən | they would |
| ihren Weg | i:rən vek | your way |
| herauszufinden | he:raust͡su:findən | to find out |
| kennst du den Weg | kənnst du dən vek | do you know the way |
| Geschichte | ge:ʃixtə | story |
| sie mögen | zi: mø:gən | they like |
| wenn du wärst | vənn du veəst | if you were |
| wir | viə | weather |

13

# weeve
## Chapter 2

| German | Pronunciation | English |
|---|---|---|
| als würde ich | alsvyəde ix | as if I would |
| und machte | und maxtə | and made |
| wenn du sie nicht magst | vənn du si: nixt magst | if you don't like them |
| wann | van | when |
| der Weg | dər vek | the way |

# 3

# A CAUCUS RACE AND A LONG TAIL

**Weeve Reading Tip:** Bolded words represent words that have been translated into the target language. Bolded and underlined words/phrases represent the first incidence of the translated word/phrase in the text. We have included the most important underlined words and phrases in vocabulary tables at the end of each chapter to keep you on track.

**Sie waren** indeed a queer-looking party that assembled on the bank—the birds **mit** draggled feathers, the animals **mit** their fur clinging close to **ihnen, und** all dripping wet, cross, **und** uncomfortable.

The first question of course was, **wie** to get dry again: **sie** had a consultation about this, **und** after a few minutes it seemed quite natural to Alice to find herself talking familiarly **mit ihnen, als <u>hü sie sie gekannt</u>**, all her life. Indeed, she had quite a long argument **mit** the Lory, **der** at last turned sulky, **und** would only say, "**Ich** am older **als** you, **und** must know better;" **und** this Alice wouldn't allow without knowing **wie** old it was, **und**, as the Lory positively refused to tell its age, **es gab** no more to be said.

At last the Mouse, **die** seemed to be a person of authority among **ihnen**, called out, "Sit down, all of you, **und** listen to me! **Ich** will soon make you dry enough!" **Sie** all sat down at once, in a large ring, **mit** the Mouse in the middle. Alice kept her eyes anxiously fixed on it, for she felt sure **sie würde** catch a bad cold **wenn** she did not get dry **sehr** soon.

"Ahem!" said the Mouse **mit** an important air, "are you all ready? This is the driest thing **ich kenne**. Silence all round, **wenn**

15

you please! 'William the Conqueror, whose cause was favoured by the pope, was soon submitted to by the English, **die** wanted leaders, **und** had been of late much accustomed to usurpation **und** conquest. Edwin **und** Morcar, the earls of Mercia **und** Northumbria—'"

"Ugh!" said the Lory, **mit** a shiver.

"**Ich** beg your pardon!" said the Mouse, frowning, **aber sehr** politely: "Did you speak?"

"Not **ich**!" said the Lory hastily.

"**Ich** thought you did," said the Mouse. "—I proceed. 'Edwin **und** Morcar, the earls of Mercia **und** Northumbria, declared for him: **und** even Stigand, the patriotic archbishop of Canterbury, found it advisable—'"

"Found what?" said the Duck.

"Found it," the Mouse replied rather crossly: "of course **Sie wissen** what 'it' means."

"**Ich weiß** what 'it' means **gut** enough, **wenn ich** find a thing," said the Duck: "it's generally a frog **oder** a worm. The question is, what did the archbishop find?"

The Mouse did not notice this question, **aber** hurriedly went on, "'—found it advisable to go **mit** Edgar Atheling to meet William **und** offer him the crown. William's conduct at first was moderate. **Aber** the insolence of his Normans—' **Wie** are you getting on now, my dear?" it continued, turning to Alice as it spoke.

"As wet as ever," said Alice in a melancholy tone: "it doesn't seem to dry me at all."

"In that case," said the Dodo solemnly, rising to its feet, "**Ich** move that the meeting adjourn, for the immediate adoption of more energetic remedies—"

"Speak English!" said the Eaglet. "**Ich kenne nicht** the meaning of half those long words, **und**, what's more, **ich** do not believe you do either!" **Und** the Eaglet bent down its head to hide a smile: some of the other birds tittered audibly.

"What **ich** was going to say," said the Dodo in an offended tone, "was, that the best thing to get us dry would be a Caucus-race."

"What is a Caucus-race?" said Alice; not that she wanted much to know, **aber** the Dodo had paused **als ob** it thought that somebody ought to speak, **und** no one else seemed inclined to say anything.

"Why," said the Dodo, "the best **Weg** to explain it is to **machen** it." (**Und**, as you might like to try the thing yourself, some winter day, **ich** will tell you **wie** the Dodo managed it.)

First it marked out a race-course, in a sort of circle, ("the exact shape doesn't matter," it said,) **und** then all the party were placed along the course, here **und** there. **Es gab** no "One, two, three, **und** away," **aber sie** began running <u>**wenn sie wollten**</u>, **und** left off **wenn sie** liked, so that it was not easy **zu wissen**, **wann** the race was over. However, **als sie** had been running half an hour **oder** so, **und** were quite dry again, the Dodo suddenly called out "The race is over!" **und sie** all crowded round it, panting, **und** asking, "**Aber wer** has won?"

This question the Dodo couldn't answer without a great deal of thought, **und** it sat for a long time **mit** one finger pressed upon its forehead (the position in which you usually see Shakespeare, in the pictures of him), while the rest waited in silence. At last the Dodo said, "Everybody has won, **und** all must have prizes."

"**Aber wer** is to give the prizes?" quite a chorus of voices asked.

"Why, she, of course," said the Dodo, pointing to Alice **mit** one finger; **und** the whole party at once crowded round her, calling out in a confused **Weg**, "Prizes! Prizes!"

Alice had no idea what to **machen**, **und** in despair she put her hand in her pocket, **und** pulled out a box of comfits, (luckily the salt water had not got **in** it), **und sie** round as prizes. **Es gab** exactly one a-piece, all round.

"**Aber** she must have a prize herself, weißt du," said the Mouse.

"Of course," the Dodo replied **sehr** gravely. "What else have you got in your pocket?" he went on, turning to Alice.

"Only a thimble," said Alice sadly.

"Hand it over here," said the Dodo.

Then **sie** all crowded round her once more, while the Dodo solemnly presented the thimble, saying "**Wir** beg your acceptance of this elegant thimble;" **und, als** it had finished this short speech, **sie** all cheered.

Alice thought the whole thing **sehr** absurd, **aber sie** all looked so grave that she did not dare to laugh; **und**, as she couldn't think of anything to say, she simply bowed, **und** took the thimble, looking as solemn as she could.

The next thing was to eat the comfits: this caused some noise **und** confusion, as the large birds complained that **sie** couldn't taste theirs, **und** the small ones choked **und** had to be patted on the back. However, it was over at last, **und sie** sat down again in a ring, **und** begged the Mouse to tell **ihr** something more.

"You promised to tell me your **Geschichte, weißt du**," said Alice, "**und** why it is you hate—C **und** D," she added in a whisper, half afraid that it would be offended again.

"Mine is a long **und** a sad tale!" said the Mouse, turning to Alice, **und** sighing.

"It is a long tail, certainly," said Alice, looking down **mit** wonder at the Mouse's tail; "**aber** why do you call it sad?" **Und** she kept on puzzling about it while the Mouse was speaking, so that her idea of the tale was something like this:—

"Fury said to a mouse, That he met in the house, 'Let us both go to law: **ich** will prosecute you.—Come, **ich** will take no denial; **Wir** must have a trial: For really this morning **ich** have nothing to **machen**.' Said the mouse to the cur, 'Such a trial, dear sir, **Mit** no jury **oder** judge, would be wasting our breath.' '**Ich** will be judge, **ich** will be jury,' Said cunning old Fury: '**Ich** will try the whole cause, **und** condemn you to death.'"

"You are not attending!" said the Mouse to Alice severely. "What are you thinking of?"

"**Ich** beg your pardon," said Alice **sehr** humbly: "you had got to the fifth bend, **ich** think?"

"**Ich** had not!" cried the Mouse, sharply **und sehr** angrily.

"A knot!" said Alice, always ready **zu machen** herself useful, **und** looking anxiously about her. "Oh, do let me help to undo it!"

"**Ich** shall do nothing of the sort," said the Mouse, getting up **und** walking away. "You insult me by talking such nonsense!"

"**Ich** did not mean it!" pleaded poor Alice. "**Aber** you are so easily offended, **weißt du**!"

The Mouse only growled in reply.

"Please come back **und** finish your story!" Alice called after it; **und** the others all joined in chorus, "Yes, please do!" **aber** the Mouse only shook its head impatiently, **und** walked a little quicker.

"What a pity it wouldn't stay!" sighed the Lory, as soon as it was quite out of sight; **und** an old Crab took the opportunity of saying to her daughter "Ah, my dear! Let this be a lesson to you never to lose your temper!" "Hold your tongue, Ma!" said the young Crab, a little snappishly. "You are enough to try the patience of an oyster!"

"**Ich** wish **ich** had our Dinah here, **ich weiß, ich** do!" said Alice aloud, addressing nobody in particular. "She'd soon fetch it back!"

"**Und wer** is Dinah, **wenn ich** might venture to ask the question?" said the Lory.

Alice replied eagerly, for she was always ready to talk about her pet: "Dinah's our cat. **Und** she's such a capital one for catching mice you can't think! **Und** oh, **ich** wish you could see her after the birds! Why, she will eat a little bird as soon as look at it!"

This speech caused a remarkable sensation among the party. Some of the birds hurried off at once: one old Magpie began wrapping itself up **sehr** carefully, remarking, "**Ich** really must be getting home; the night-air doesn't suit my throat!" **und** a Canary called out in a trembling voice to its children, "Come away, my dears! It's high time **ihr** wart all in bed!" On various pretexts **sie** all moved off, **und** Alice was soon left alone.

"**Ich** wish **ich** had not mentioned Dinah!" she said to herself in a melancholy tone. "Nobody seems **zu mögen** her, down here, **und** I'm sure she's the best cat in the world! Oh, my dear Dinah! **Ich** wonder **ob ich** shall ever see you any more!" **Und** here poor Alice began to cry again, for she felt **sehr** lonely **und** low-spirited. In a little while, however, she again heard a little pattering of footsteps in the distance, **und** she looked up eagerly, half hoping that the Mouse had changed **<u>seine Meinung</u>**, **und** was coming back to finish his story.

# weeve
## Chapter 3

| German | Pronunciation | English |
|---|---|---|
| hü | hy: | hü |
| sie sie gekannt | zi: si: geːkant | she knew her |
| wenn sie wollten | vənn si: voltən | if you wanted |
| seine Meinung | zaiəne maiənuŋk | his opinion |
| und | unt | and |
| sie waren | zi: vaːrən | they were |
| mit | mit | with |
| ihnen | iːnən | them |
| wie | viə | how |

# 4

# THE RABBIT SENDS IN A LITTLE BILL

**Weeve Reading Tip:** Use vocab tables to check your knowledge and look at our pronunciation guides. Don't try to memorise the vocab tables - if you find you do not understand the vocab in the vocab tables, try re-reading the chapter and see if you can pick them up through context the second time round.

It was the White Rabbit, trotting slowly back again, **und** looking anxiously about as it went, **als ob** it had lost something; **und** she heard it muttering to itself "The Duchess! The Duchess! Oh my dear paws! Oh my fur **und** whiskers! She will get me executed, as sure as ferrets are ferrets! Where can **ich** have dropped **sie, ich** wonder?" Alice guessed in a moment that it was looking for the fan **und** the pair of white kid gloves, **und** she **sehr** good-naturedly began hunting about for **sie, aber sie waren** nowhere to be seen—everything seemed to have changed since her swim in the pool, **und** the great hall, **mit** the glass table **und** the little door, had vanished completely.

**Sehr** soon the Rabbit noticed Alice, as she went hunting about, **und** called out to her in an angry tone, "Why, Mary Ann, what are you doing out here? Run home this moment, **und** fetch me a pair of gloves **und** a fan! Quick, now!" **Und** Alice was so much frightened that she ran off at once in the direction it pointed to, without trying to explain the mistake it had made.

"He took me for his housemaid," she said to herself as she ran. "**Wie** surprised he will be **wenn** he finds out **wer ich** am! **Aber** I'd better take him his fan **und** gloves—that is, **wenn ich kann** find **sie**." As she said this, she came upon a neat little house, on

21

the door of which was a bright brass plate **mit** the name "W. RABBIT," engraved upon it. She went in without knocking, **und** hurried upstairs, in great fear lest **sie würde** meet the real Mary Ann, **und** be turned out of the house before she had found the fan **und** gloves.

"**Wie** queer it seems," Alice said to herself, "to be going messages for a rabbit! **Ich** suppose Dinah will be sending me on messages next!" **Und** she began fancying the sort of thing that would happen: "'Miss Alice! Come here directly, **und** get ready for your walk!' 'Coming in a minute, nurse! **Aber ich** have got **zu sehen** that the mouse doesn't get out.' Only **ich** do not think," Alice went on, "that they'd let Dinah stop in the house **wenn** it began ordering **Menschen** about like that!"

By this time she had found **ihren Weg in** a tidy little room **mit** a table in the window, **und** on it (as she had hoped) a fan **und** two **oder** three pairs of tiny white kid gloves: she took up the fan **und** a pair of the gloves, **und** was just going to leave the room, **als** her eye fell upon a little bottle that stood near the looking-glass. **Es gab** no label this time **mit** the words "DRINK ME," **aber** nevertheless she uncorked it **und** put it to her lips. "**Ich weiß** something interesting is sure to happen," she said to herself, "whenever **ich** eat **oder** drink anything; so **ich** will just see what this bottle does. **Ich** do hope it will make me grow large again, for really I'm quite tired of being such a tiny little thing!"

It did so indeed, **und** much sooner **als** she had expected: before she had drunk half the bottle, she found her head pressing against the ceiling, **und** had to stoop to save her neck from being broken. She hastily put down the bottle, saying to herself "That's quite enough—I hope **ich** sha not grow any more—As it is, **ich** can't get out at the door—I do wish **ich** had not drunk quite so much!"

Alas! it was too late to wish that! She went on growing, **und** growing, **und sehr** soon had to kneel down on the floor: in another minute there was not even room for this, **und** she tried the effect of lying down **mit** one elbow against the door, **und** the other arm curled round her head. Still she went on growing, **und**, as a last resource, she put one arm out of the window, **und** one foot up the chimney, **und** said to herself "Now **ich** can do no more, whatever happens. What will become of me?"

Luckily for Alice, the little magic bottle had now had its full effect, **und** she grew no larger: still it was **sehr** uncomfortable, **und**, as there seemed to be no sort of chance of her ever getting out of the room again, no wonder she felt unhappy.

"It was much pleasanter at home," thought poor Alice, "**als** one was not always growing larger **und** smaller, **und** being ordered about by mice **und** rabbits. **Ich** almost wish **ich** had not gone down that rabbit-hole—and yet—and yet—it's rather curious,

**weißt du**, this sort of life! **Ich** do wonder what can have happened to me! **Als ich** used to **lesen** fairy-tales, **ich** fancied that kind of thing never happened, **und** now here **ich** am in the middle of one! There ought to be a book written about me, that there ought! **Und wenn ich** grow up, **ich** will write one—but I'm grown up now," she added in a sorrowful tone; "at least there's no room to grow up any more here."

"**Aber** then," thought Alice, "shall **ich** never get any older **als ich** am now? That will be a comfort, one way—never to be an old woman—but then—always to have lessons to learn! Oh, **ich würde** not like that!"

"Oh, you foolish Alice!" she answered herself. "**Wie** can you learn lessons in here? Why, there's hardly room for you, **und** no room at all for any lesson-books!"

**Und** so she went on, taking first one side **und** then the other, **und** making quite a conversation of it altogether; **aber** after a few minutes she heard a voice outside, **und** stopped to listen.

"Mary Ann! Mary Ann!" said the voice. "Fetch me my gloves this moment!"

Then came a little pattering of feet on the stairs. Alice knew it was the Rabbit coming to look for her, **und** she trembled till she shook the house, quite forgetting that she was now about a thousand **Mal** as large as the Rabbit, **und** had no reason to be afraid of it.

Presently the Rabbit came up to the door, **und** tried to open it; **aber**, as the door opened inwards, **und** Alice's elbow was pressed hard against it, that attempt proved a failure. Alice heard it say to itself "Then **ich** will go round **und** get in at the window."

"That you won't!" thought Alice, **und**, after waiting till she fancied she heard the Rabbit just under the window, she suddenly spread out her hand, **und** made a snatch in the air. She did not get hold of anything, **aber** she heard a little shriek **und** a fall, **und** a crash of broken glass, from which she concluded that it was just possible it had fallen **in** a cucumber-frame, **oder** something of the sort.

Next came an angry voice—the Rabbit's— "Pat! Pat! Where are you?" **Und** then a voice she had never heard before, "Sure then I'm here! Digging for apples, yer honour!"

"Digging for apples, indeed!" said the Rabbit angrily. "Here! Come **und** help me out of this!" (Sounds of more broken glass.)

"Now tell me, Pat, what's that in the window?"

"Sure, it's an arm, yer honour!" (He pronounced it "arrum.")

"An arm, you goose! **Wer** ever saw one that size? Why, it fills the whole window!"

"Sure, it does, yer honour: **aber** it's an arm for all that."

"**Gut**, it's got no business there, at any rate: go **und** take it away!"

**Es gab** a long silence after this, **und** Alice could only hear whispers now **und** then; such as, "Sure, **ich mag es nicht**, yer honour, at all, at all!" "Do as **ich** tell you, you coward!" **und** at last she spread out her hand again, **und** made another snatch in the air. This time **es gab** two little shrieks, **und** more sounds of broken glass. "What a number of cucumber-frames there must be!" thought Alice. "**Ich** wonder what **sie** will do next! As for pulling me out of the window, **ich** only wish **sie** could! I'm sure **ich** do not want to stay in here any longer!"

She waited for some time without hearing anything more: at last came a rumbling of little cartwheels, **und** the sound of a good many voices all talking together: **sie entzifferte** the words: "Where's the other ladder?—Why, **ich** had not to bring **aber** one; Bill's got the other—Bill! fetch it here, lad!—Here, put 'em up at this corner—No, tie 'em together first—they do not reach half high enough yet—Oh! **sie** will do **gut** enough; do not be particular—Here, Bill! catch hold of this rope—Will the roof bear?—Mind that loose slate—Oh, it's coming down! Heads below!" (a loud crash)— "Now, **wer** did that?—It was Bill, **ich** fancy—Who's to go down the chimney?—Nay, **ich** sha not! You do it!— That **ich** won't, then!—Bill's to go down—Here, Bill! the master says you are to go down the chimney!"

"Oh! So Bill's got to come down the chimney, has he?" said Alice to herself. "Shy, **sie** seem to put everything upon Bill! **Ich würde** not be in Bill's place for a good deal: this fireplace is narrow, to be sure; **aber ich** think **ich kann** kick a little!"

She drew her foot as far down the chimney as she could, **und** waited till she heard a little animal (she couldn't guess of what sort it was) scratching **und** scrambling about in the chimney close above her: then, saying to herself "This is Bill," she gave one sharp kick, **und** waited **um zu sehen** what would happen next.

The first thing she heard was a general chorus of "There goes Bill!"

then the Rabbit's voice along— "Catch him, you by the hedge!" then silence, **und** then another confusion of voices— "Hold up his head—Brandy now—Do not choke him—How was it, old fellow? What happened to you? Tell us all about it!"

Last came a little feeble, squeaking voice, ("That's Bill," thought Alice,) "**Gut, ich** hardly know—No more, thank ye; I'm better now—but I'm a deal too flustered to tell you—all **ich weiß** is, something comes at me like a Jack-in-the-box, **und** up **ich** goes like a sky-rocket!"

"So you did, old fellow!" said the others.

"**Wir** must burn the house down!" said the Rabbit's voice; **und** Alice called out as loud as she could, "**Wenn** you do, **ich** will set Dinah at you!"

**Es gab** a dead silence instantly, **und** Alice thought to herself, "**Ich** wonder what **sie** will do next! **Wenn sie** had any sense, they'd take the roof off." After a minute **oder** two, **sie** began moving about again, **und** Alice heard the Rabbit say, "A barrowful will do, **erst mal**."

"A barrowful of what?" thought Alice; **aber** she had not long to doubt, for the next moment a shower of little pebbles came rattling in at the window, **und** some of **sie** hit her in the face. "**Ich** will put a stop to this," she said to herself, **und** shouted out, "You'd better not do that again!" which produced another dead silence.

Alice noticed **mit** some surprise that the pebbles were all turning **in** little cakes as **sie** lay on the floor, **und** a bright idea came **in** her head. "**Wenn ich** eat one of these cakes," she thought, "it's sure **zu machen** some change in my size; **und** as it can't possibly make me larger, it must make me smaller, **ich** suppose."

So she swallowed one of the cakes, **und** was delighted to find that she began shrinking directly. As soon as she was small enough to get through the door, she ran out of the house, **und** found quite a crowd of little animals **und** birds waiting outside. The poor little Lizard, Bill, was in the middle, being held up by two guinea-pigs, **die** were giving it something out of a bottle. **Sie** all made a rush at Alice the moment she appeared; **aber** she ran off as hard as she could, **und** soon found herself safe in a thick wood.

"The first thing **ich** have got to **tun**," said Alice to herself, as she wandered about in the wood, "is to grow to my right size again; **und** the second thing is to find **meinen Weg in** that lovely garden. **Ich** think that will be the best plan."

It sounded an excellent plan, no doubt, **und sehr** neatly **und** simply arranged; the only difficulty was, that she had not the smallest idea **wie** to set about it; **und** while she was peering about anxiously among the trees, a little sharp bark just over her head made her look up in a great hurry.

An enormous puppy was looking down at her **mit** large round eyes, **und** feebly stretching out one paw, trying to touch her. "Poor little thing!" said Alice, in a coaxing tone, **und** she tried hard to whistle to it; **aber** she was terribly frightened **die ganze**

**Zeit** at the thought that it might be hungry, in which case it would be **sehr** likely to eat her up in spite of all her coaxing.

Hardly knowing what she did, she picked up a little bit of stick, **und** held it out to the puppy; whereupon the puppy jumped **in** the air off all its feet at once, **mit** a yelp of delight, **und** rushed at the stick, **und** made believe to worry it; then Alice dodged behind a great thistle, to keep herself from being run over; **und** the moment she appeared on the other side, the puppy made another rush at the stick, **und** tumbled head over heels in its hurry to get hold of it; then Alice, thinking it was **sehr** like having a game of play **mit** a cart-horse, **und** expecting every moment to be trampled under its feet, ran round the thistle again; then the puppy began a series of short charges at the stick, running a **sehr** little **Weg** forwards each time **und** a long **Weg** back, **und** barking hoarsely all the while, till at last it sat down a good **Weg** off, panting, **mit** its tongue hanging out of its mouth, **und** its great eyes half shut.

This seemed to Alice a good opportunity to **machen** her escape; so she set off at once, **und** ran till she was quite tired **und** out of breath, **und** till the puppy's bark sounded quite faint in the distance.

"**Und** yet what a dear little puppy it was!" said Alice, as she leant against a buttercup to rest herself, **und** fanned herself **mit** one of the leaves: "**Ich würde** have liked teaching it tricks **sehr** much, if—if I'd only been the right size to **machen** it! Oh dear! I'd nearly forgotten that **ich** have got to grow up again! Let me see—how is it to be managed? **Ich** suppose **ich** ought to eat **oder** drink something **oder** other; **aber** the great question is, what?"

The great question certainly was, what? Alice looked all round her at the flowers **und** the blades of grass, **aber** she did not see anything that looked like the right thing to eat **oder** drink under the circumstances. **Es gab** a large mushroom growing near her, about the same height as herself; **und als** she had looked under it, **und** on both sides of it, **und** behind it, it occurred to her that she might as **gut** look **und** see what was on the top of it.

She stretched herself up on tiptoe, **und** peeped over the edge of the mushroom, **und** her eyes immediately met those of a large blue caterpillar, that was sitting on the top **mit** its arms folded, quietly smoking a long hookah, **und** taking not the smallest notice of her **oder** of anything else.

# weeve
## Chapter 4

| German | Pronunciation | English |
|---|---|---|
| als ich | als ix | than i |
| lesen | le:sən | read |
| sie entzifferte | zi: əntsifeətə | she deciphered |
| erst mal | eəst mal | for now |
| tun | tun | to do |
| meinen Weg in | maiənən veg in | my way in |
| ich | ix | I |
| sehr | ze:ə | very |
| aber | abə | but |
| oder | odə | or |
| als | als | as |

# 5

## Advice From a Caterpillar

**Weeve Reading Tip:** Translating words will make it more difficult to enter a flow state. This is where the natural process of language learning is most powerful. In this state your brain has the strongest ability to learn a language

The Caterpillar **und** Alice looked at each other for some time in silence: at last the Caterpillar took the hookah out of its mouth, **und** addressed her in a languid, sleepy voice.

"**Wer** are you?" said the Caterpillar.

This was not an encouraging opening for a conversation. Alice replied, rather shyly, "I—I hardly know, sir, just at present—at least **ich weiß wer ich** was **als ich** got up this morning, **aber ich** think **ich** must have been changed several **Mal** since then."

"What do you mean by that?" said the Caterpillar sternly. "Explain yourself!"

"**Ich** can't explain myself, I'm afraid, sir," said Alice, "**weil** I'm not myself, **sehen Sie**,."

"<u>**Ich sehe nicht**</u>," said the Caterpillar.

"I'm afraid **ich** can't put it more clearly," Alice replied **sehr** politely, "for **ich** can't understand it myself to begin **mit**; **und** being so many different sizes in a day is **sehr** confusing."

"It isn't," said the Caterpillar.

28

"**Naja**, perhaps you haven't found it so yet," said Alice; "**aber wenn** you have to turn **in** a chrysalis—you will some day, you know—and then after that **in** a butterfly, **ich würde** think you will feel it a little queer, won't you?"

"Not a bit," said the Caterpillar.

"**Naja**, perhaps your feelings may be different," said Alice; "all **ich weiß** is, it would feel **sehr** queer to me."

"You!" said the Caterpillar contemptuously. "**Wer** are you?"

Which brought **sie** back again to the beginning of the conversation. Alice felt a little irritated at the Caterpillar's making such **sehr** short remarks, **und** she drew herself up **und** said, **sehr** gravely, "**Ich** think, you ought to tell me **wer** you are, first."

"Why?" said the Caterpillar.

Here was another puzzling question; **und** as Alice couldn't think of any good reason, **und** as the Caterpillar seemed to be in a **sehr** unpleasant state of mind, she turned away.

"Come back!" the Caterpillar called after her. "**Ich** have something important to say!"

This sounded promising, certainly: Alice turned **und** came back again.

"Keep your temper," said the Caterpillar.

"Is that all?" said Alice, swallowing down her anger as **gut** as she could.

"No," said the Caterpillar.

Alice thought she might as **gut** wait, as she had nothing else to **tun**, **und** perhaps after all it might tell her something worth hearing. For some minutes it puffed away without speaking, **aber** at last it unfolded its arms, took the hookah out of its mouth again, **und** said, "So you think you are changed, do you?"

"I'm afraid **ich** am, sir," said Alice; "**Ich** can't remember things as **ich** used—and **ich** do not keep the same size for ten minutes together!"

"Can't remember what things?" said the Caterpillar.

"**Ach**, **ich** have tried to say "**Wie** doth the little busy bee," **aber** it all came different!" Alice replied in a **sehr** melancholy voice.

"Repeat, "You are old, Father William,'" said the Caterpillar.

Alice folded her hands, **und** began:—

"You are old, Father William," the young man said, "**Und** your hair has become **sehr** white; **Und** yet you incessantly stand on your head— Do you think, at your age, it is right?"

"In my youth," Father William replied to his son, "**Ich** feared it might injure the brain; **Aber**, now that I'm perfectly sure **ich** have none, Why, **ich** do it again **und** again."

"You are old," said the youth, "as **ich** mentioned before, **Und** have grown most uncommonly fat; Yet you turned a back-somersault in at the door— Pray, what is the reason of that?"

"In my youth," said the sage, as he shook his grey locks, "**Ich** kept all my limbs **sehr** supple By the use of this ointment—one shilling the box— Allow me to sell you a couple?"

"You are old," said the youth, "**und** your jaws are too weak For anything tougher **als** suet; Yet you finished the goose, **mit** the bones **und** the beak— Pray, **wie haben** you manage to **machen** it?"

"In my youth," said his father, "**Ich** took to the law, **Und** argued each case **mit** my wife; **Und** the muscular strength, which it gave to my jaw, Has lasted the rest of my life."

"You are old," said the youth, "one would hardly suppose That your eye was as steady as ever; Yet you balanced an eel on the end of your nose— What made you so awfully clever?"

"**Ich** have answered three questions, **und** that is enough," Said his father; "do not give yourself airs! Do you think **ich kann** listen all day to such stuff? Be off, **oder ich** will kick you down stairs!"

"That isn't said right," said the Caterpillar.

"Not quite right, I'm afraid," said Alice, timidly; "some of the words have got altered."

"It is wrong from beginning to end," said the Caterpillar decidedly, **und es gab** silence for some minutes.

The Caterpillar was the first to speak.

"What size do you want to be?" it asked.

"Oh, I'm not particular as to size," Alice hastily replied; "only one doesn't like changing so **häufig**, **wissen Sie**."

"**Ich weiß nicht**," said the Caterpillar.

Alice said nothing: she had never been so much contradicted in her life before, **und** she felt that she was losing her temper.

"Are you content now?" said the Caterpillar.

"**Gut, ich möchte** to be a little larger, sir, if you don't not mind," said Alice: "three inches is such a wretched height to be."

"It is a **sehr** good height indeed!" said the Caterpillar angrily, rearing itself upright as it spoke (it was exactly three inches high).

"**Aber** I'm not **gewöhnt daran**!" pleaded poor Alice in a piteous tone. **Und** she thought of herself, "**Ich** wish the creatures wouldn't be so easily offended!"

"You will get **gewöhnt daran** in time," said the Caterpillar; **und** it put the hookah **in** its mouth **und** began smoking again.

This time Alice waited patiently until it chose to speak again. In a minute **oder** two the Caterpillar took the hookah out of its mouth **und** yawned once **oder** twice, **und** shook itself. Then it got down off the mushroom, **und** crawled away in the grass, merely remarking as it went, "One side will make you grow taller, **und** the other side will make you grow shorter."

"One side of what? The other side of what?" thought Alice to herself.

"Of the mushroom," said the Caterpillar, just as **ob** she had asked it aloud; **und** in another moment it was out of sight.

Alice remained looking thoughtfully at the mushroom for a minute, trying **herauszufinden** which were the two sides of it; **und** as it was perfectly round, she found this a **sehr** difficult question. However, at last she stretched her arms round it as far as **sie würden** go, **und** broke off a bit of the edge **mit** each hand.

"**Und** now which is which?" she said to herself, **und** nibbled a little of the right-hand bit to try the effect: the next moment she felt a violent blow underneath her chin: it had struck her foot!

She was a good deal frightened by this **sehr** sudden change, **aber** she felt that **es gab** no time to be lost, as she was shrinking rapidly; so she set **ans Werk** at once to eat some of the other bit. Her chin was pressed so closely against her foot, that **es gab** hardly room to open her mouth; **aber** she did it at last, **und** managed to swallow a morsel of the lefthand bit.

\* \* \* \* \* \* \*

\* \* \* \* \* \*

\* \* \* \* \* \* \*

"Come, my head's free at last!" said Alice **in** a tone of delight, which changed in alarm in another moment, **als** she found that her shoulders were nowhere to be found: all she could see, **als** she looked down, was an immense length of neck, which seemed to rise like a stalk out of a sea of green leaves that lay far below her.

"What can all that green stuff be?" said Alice. "**Und** where have my shoulders got to? **Und** oh, my poor hands, **wie** is it **ich** can't see you?"

She was moving **sie** about as she spoke, **aber** no result seemed to follow, except a little shaking among the distant green leaves.

As there seemed to be no chance of getting her hands up to her head, she tried to get her head down to **ihnen**, **und** was delighted to find that her neck would bend about easily **in** any direction, like a serpent. She had just succeeded in curving it down in a graceful zigzag, **und** was going to dive in among the leaves, which she found to be nothing **aber** the tops of the trees under which she had been wandering, **als** a sharp hiss made her draw back **in** a hurry: a large pigeon had flown in her face, **und** was beating her violently **mit** its wings.

"Serpent!" screamed the Pigeon.

"I'm not a serpent!" said Alice indignantly. "Let me alone!"

"Serpent, **ich** say again!" repeated the Pigeon, **aber** in a more subdued tone, **und** added **mit** a kind of sob, "**Ich** have tried every **Weg**, **und** nothing seems to suit **sie**!"

"**Ich** haven't the least idea what you are talking about," said Alice.

"**Ich** have tried the roots of trees, **und ich** have tried banks, **und ich** have tried hedges," the Pigeon went on, without attending to her; "**aber** those serpents! There's no pleasing **ihnen**!"

Alice was more **und** more puzzled, **aber** she thought **es gab** no use in saying anything more till the Pigeon had finished.

"**Als ob** it was not trouble enough hatching the eggs," said the Pigeon; "**aber ich** must be on the look-out for serpents night **und** day! Why, **ich** haven't had a wink of sleep these three weeks!"

"I'm **sehr** sorry you have been annoyed," said Alice, **die** was beginning to see its meaning.

"**Und** just as I'd taken the highest tree in the wood," continued the Pigeon, raising its voice to a shriek, "**und** just as **ich** was thinking **ich** should be free of **ihnen** at last, **sie** must needs come wriggling down from the sky! Ugh, Serpent!"

"**Aber** I'm not a serpent, **ich** tell you!" said Alice. "I'm a—I'm a—"

"**Naja**! What are you?" said the Pigeon. "**Ich kann** see you are trying to invent something!"

"I—I'm a little girl," said Alice, rather doubtfully, as she remembered the number of changes she had gone through that day.

"A likely story indeed!" said the Pigeon in a tone of the deepest contempt. "**Ich habe gesehen** a good many little girls in **meiner Zeit, aber** never one **mit** such a neck as that! No, no! You are a serpent; **und** there's no use denying it. **Ich** suppose you will be telling me next that you never tasted an egg!"

"**Ich** have tasted eggs, certainly," said Alice, **die** was a **sehr** truthful child; "**aber** little girls eat eggs quite as much as serpents do, you know."

"**Ich** do not believe it," said the Pigeon; "**aber wenn sie** do, why then **sie** are a kind of serpent, that's all **ich kann** say."

This was such a new idea to Alice, that she was quite silent for a minute **oder** two, which gave the Pigeon the opportunity of adding, "You are looking for eggs, **ich weiß** that **gut** enough; **und** what does it matter to me whether you are a little girl **oder** a serpent?"

"It matters a good deal to me," said Alice hastily; "**aber** I'm not looking for eggs, as it happens; **und wenn ich** was, **ich würde** not want yours: **ich esse sie nicht gern** raw."

"Well, be off, then!" said the Pigeon **in** a sulky tone, as it settled down again in its nest. Alice crouched down among the trees as **gut** as she could, for her neck kept getting entangled among the branches, **und** every now **und** then she had to stop **und** untwist it. After a while she remembered that she still held the pieces of mushroom in her hands, **und** she set **ans Werk sehr** carefully, nibbling first at one **und** then at the other, **und** growing sometimes taller **und** sometimes shorter, until she had succeeded in bringing herself down to her usual height.

It was so long since she had been anything near the right size, that it felt quite strange at first; **aber** she got **gewöhnt daran** in a few minutes, **und** began talking to herself, as usual. "Come, there's half my plan done now! **Wie** puzzling all these changes are! I'm never sure what I'm going to be, from one minute to another! However, **ich** have got back to my right size: the next thing is, to get **in** that beautiful garden—how is that to be done, **ich** wonder?" As she said this, she came suddenly upon an open place, **mit** a little house in it about four feet high. "Whoever lives there," thought Alice, "it will never do to come upon **sie** this size: why, **ich würde** frighten **sie** out of their wits!" So she began nibbling at the righthand bit again, **und** did not venture to go near the house till she had brought herself down to nine inches high.

33

## weeve

### Chapter 4

| German | Pronunciation | English |
|---|---|---|
| ich sehe nicht | ix se:he nixt | I do not see |
| naja | na:ja | oh well |
| ach | ax | oh |
| wie haben | vi: ha:bən | as have |
| häufig | hoyhfik | frequently |
| ich möchte | ix møxtə | I would like to |
| gewöhnt daran | ge:vø:nt da:ran | used to it |
| ans Werk | ans veək | to the work |
| ich habe gesehen | ix ha:be ge:se:ən | I have seen |
| meiner Zeit | maiənər t͡sait | in my time |
| ich esse sie nicht | ix ese si: nixt | i don't eat them |
| gern | geən | gladly |
| in | in | in |
| ich würde | ix vyədə | I would |
| gut | gut | well |
| machen | ma:xən | do |
| ich kann | ix kan | I can |

# 6

## Pig and Pepper

> **Weeve Reading Tip:** Trust the process - the less you worry about your speed of acquisition the quicker the passive language acquisition will occur. Get lost in the story and let the language learning take care of itself.

For a minute **oder** two she stood looking at the house, **und** wondering what **zu tun** next, **als** suddenly a footman in livery came running out of the wood—(she considered him to be a footman **weil** he was in livery: otherwise, judging by his face only, **sie würde** have called him a fish)—and rapped loudly at the door **mit** his knuckles. It was opened by another footman in livery, **mit** a round face, **und** large eyes like a frog; **und** both footmen, Alice noticed, had powdered hair that curled all over their heads. She felt **sehr** curious **zu wissen** what it was all about, **und** crept a little **Weg** out of the wood to listen.

The Fish-Footman begann by producing from under his arm a great letter, nearly as large as himself, **und** this he handed over to the other, saying, in a solemn tone, "For the Duchess. An invitation from the Queen to play croquet." The Frog-Footman repeated, in the same solemn tone, only changing the order of the words a little, "From the Queen. An invitation for the Duchess to play croquet."

Then **sie** both bowed low, **und** their curls got entangled together.

Alice laughed so much at this, that she had to run back **in** the wood for fear of their hearing her; **und als** she next peeped out

35

the Fish-Footman was gone, **und** the other was sitting on the ground near the door, staring stupidly up **in** the sky.

Alice went timidly up to the door, **und** knocked.

"There's no sort of use in knocking," said the Footman, "**und** that for two reasons. First, **weil** I'm on the same side of the door as you are; secondly, **weil Sie machen** such a noise inside, no one could possibly hear you." **Und** certainly **gab es** a most extraordinary noise going on within—a constant howling **und** sneezing, **und** every now **und** then a great crash, **als ob** a dish **oder** kettle had been broken to pieces.

"Please, then," said Alice, "**wie** am **ich** to get in?"

"There might be some sense in your knocking," the Footman went on without attending to her, "**wenn wir** had the door between us. For instance, <u>**wenn Sie wären**</u> inside, you might knock, **und ich** could let you out, you know." He was looking up **in** the sky **die ganze** Zeit he was speaking, **und** this Alice thought decidedly uncivil. "**Aber** perhaps he can't help it," she said to herself; "his eyes are so **sehr** nearly at the top of his head. **Aber** at any rate he might answer questions.—How am **ich** to get in?"

she repeated, aloud.

"**Ich** shall sit here," the Footman remarked, "till tomorrow—"

At this moment the door of the house opened, **und** a large plate came skimming out, straight at the Footman's head: it just grazed his nose, **und** broke to pieces against one of the trees behind him.

"—or next day, maybe," the Footman continued in the same tone, exactly **als ob** nothing had happened.

"**Wie** am **ich** to get in?" asked Alice again, in a louder tone.

"Are you to get in at all?" said the Footman. "That's the first question, **wissen Sie**.

It was, no doubt: only Alice did not like to be told so. "It's really dreadful," she muttered to herself, "**wie** all the creatures argue. It's enough to drive one crazy!"

The Footman seemed to think this a good opportunity for repeating his remark, **mit** variations. "**Ich** shall sit here," he said, "on **und** off, for days **und** days."

"**Aber** what am **ich zu tun**?" said Alice.

"Anything <u>**Sie wollen**</u>," said the Footman, **und** began whistling.

"Oh, there's no use in talking to him," said Alice desperately: "he's perfectly idiotic!" **Und** she opened the door **und** went **in**.

The door led right in a large kitchen, which was full of smoke from one end to the other: the Duchess was sitting on a three-legged stool in the middle, nursing a baby; the cook was leaning over the fire, stirring a large cauldron which seemed to be full of soup.

"There's certainly too much pepper in that soup!" Alice said to herself, as **gut** as she could for sneezing.

**Es gab** certainly too much of it in the air. Even the Duchess sneezed occasionally; **und** as for the baby, it was sneezing **und** howling alternately without a moment's pause. The only things in the kitchen that did not sneeze, were the cook, **und** a large cat which was sitting on the hearth **und** grinning from ear to ear.

"Please would you tell me," said Alice, a little timidly, for she was not quite sure whether it was good manners for her to speak first, "why your cat grins like that?"

"It's a Cheshire cat," said the Duchess, "**und** that's why. Pig!"

She said the last word **mit** such sudden violence that Alice quite jumped; **aber sie sah** in another moment that it was addressed to the baby, **und** not to her, so she took courage, **und** went on again:—

"**Ich** did not know that Cheshire cats always grinned; in fact, **ich** did not know that cats could grin."

"**Sie** all can," said the Duchess; "**und** most of 'em do."

"**Ich kenne keine** that do," Alice said **sehr** politely, feeling quite pleased to have got **in** a conversation.

"**Sie wissen nicht** much," said the Duchess; "**und** that's a fact."

Alice did not at all like the tone of this remark, **und** thought it would be as **gut** to introduce some other subject of conversation. While she was trying to fix on one, the cook took the cauldron of soup off the fire, **und** at once set **sich an die Arbeit machen** throwing everything within her reach at the Duchess **und** the baby—the fire-irons came first; then followed a shower of saucepans, plates, **und** dishes. The Duchess took no notice of **ihnen** even **als sie** hit her; **und** the baby was howling so much already, that it was quite impossible to say whether the blows hurt it **oder** not.

"Oh, please mind what you are doing!" cried Alice, jumping up **und** down in an agony of terror. "Oh, there goes his precious nose!" as an unusually large saucepan flew close by it, **und sehr** nearly carried it off.

"**Wenn** everybody minded their own business," the Duchess said in a hoarse growl, "the world would go round a deal faster **als** it does."

"Which wouldn't be an advantage," said Alice, **die** felt **sehr** glad to get an opportunity of showing off a little of her knowledge. "Just think of what work it would make **mit** the day **und** night! **<u>Sie verstehen</u>**, the earth takes twenty-four hours to turn round on its axis—"

"Talking of axes," said the Duchess, "chop off her head!"

Alice glanced rather anxiously at the cook **um zu sehen, ob** she meant to take the hint; **aber** the cook was busily stirring the soup, **und** seemed not to be listening, so she went on again: "Twenty-four hours, **ich** think; **oder** is it twelve? I—"

"Oh, do not bother me," said the Duchess; "**Ich** never could abide figures!" **<u>Und damit</u>** she began nursing her child again, singing a sort of lullaby to it as she did so, **und** giving it a violent shake at the end of every line:

> *"Speak roughly to your little*
> *boy,*
> ***Und** beat him **wenn** he*
> *sneezes:*
> *He only does it to annoy,*
> ***Weil** he **weiß** it teases."*


CHORUS.

*(In which the cook **und** the baby joined):*

*"Wow! wow! wow!"*

While the Duchess sang the second verse of the song, she kept tossing the baby violently up **und** down, **und** the poor little thing howled so, that Alice could hardly hear the words:—

> *"**Ich** speak severely to my*
> *boy,*
> *ich beat him **wenn** he*
> *sneezes;*
> *For **<u>er kann</u>** thoroughly enjoy*
> *The pepper **wenn** he*
> *pleases!"*


CHORUS.

*"Wow! wow! wow!"*

"Here! **Sie können** nurse it a bit, **wenn Sie möchten**!" the Duchess said to Alice, flinging the baby at her as she spoke. "**Ich** must go **und** get ready to play croquet **mit** the Queen," **und** she hurried out of the room. The cook threw a frying-pan after her as she went out, **aber** it just missed her.

Alice caught the baby **mit** some difficulty, as it was a queer-shaped little creature, **und** held out its arms **und** legs in all directions, "just like a star-fish," thought Alice. The poor little thing was snorting like a steam-engine **als** she caught it, **und** kept doubling itself up **und** straightening itself out again, so that altogether, for the first minute **oder** two, it was as much as she could do to hold it.

As soon as **sie hatte herausbekommen** the proper **Weise** of nursing it, (which was to twist it up **in** a sort of knot, **und** then keep tight hold of its right ear **und** left foot, so as to prevent its undoing itself,) she carried it out **in** the open air. "**Wenn ich** do not take this child away **mit** me," thought Alice, "**sie** are sure to kill it in a day **oder** two: wouldn't it be murder to leave it behind?" She said the last words out loud, **und** the little thing grunted in reply (it had left off sneezing by this time). "Do not grunt," said Alice; "that's not at all a proper **Weise** of expressing yourself."

The baby grunted again, **und** Alice looked **sehr** anxiously **in** its face **um zu sehen** what was the matter **mit** it. There could be no doubt that it had a **sehr** turn-up nose, much more like a snout **als** a real nose; **außerdem** its eyes were getting extremely small for a baby: altogether Alice did not like the look of the thing at all. "**Aber** perhaps it was only sobbing," she thought, **und** looked **in** its eyes again, **um zu sehen**, **ob** there were any tears.

No, **es gab** no tears. "**Wenn** you are going to turn **in** a pig, my dear," said Alice, seriously, "**Ich** will have nothing more **zu tun mit** you. Mind now!" The poor little thing sobbed again (**oder** grunted, it was impossible to say which), **und sie** went on for some while in silence.

Alice was just beginning to think to herself, "Now, what am **ich zu tun mit** this creature **wenn ich** get it home?" **als** it grunted again, so violently, that she looked down **auf** its face in some alarm. This time there could be no mistake about it: it was neither more nor less **als** a pig, **und** she felt that it would be quite absurd for her to carry it further.

So she set the little creature down, **und** felt quite relieved **zu sehen** it trot away quietly **in** the wood. "**Wenn** it had grown up," she said to herself, "it would have made a dreadfully ugly child: **aber** it makes rather a handsome pig, **ich** think." **Und** she began thinking over other children **sie kannte**, **die** might do **sehr gut** as pigs, **und** was just saying to herself, "**wenn** one only knew

39

the right **Weg** to change them—" **als** she was a little startled by seeing the Cheshire Cat sitting on a bough of a tree a few yards off.

The Cat only grinned **als** it saw Alice. It looked good-natured, she thought: still it had **sehr** long claws **und** a great many teeth, so she felt that it ought to be treated **mit** respect.

"Cheshire Puss," she began, rather timidly, as she did not at all know whether it would like the name: however, it only grinned a little wider. "Come, it's pleased so far," thought Alice, **und** she went on. "Would you tell me, please, which **Weg ich** ought to go from here?"

"That depends a good deal on where you want to get to," said the Cat.

"**Ich** do not much care where—" said Alice.

"Then it doesn't matter which **Weg** you go," said the Cat.

"—so long as **ich** get somewhere," Alice added as an explanation.

"Oh, you are sure **zu** that," said the Cat, "**wenn** you only walk long enough."

Alice felt that this couldn't be denied, so she tried another question. "What sort of **<u>Leute</u>** live about here?"

"In that direction," the Cat said, waving its right paw round, "lives a Hatter: **und** in that direction," waving the other paw, "lives a March Hare. Visit either, **die Sie wollen**: **sie** are both mad."

"**Aber ich** do not want to go among mad **Leuten**," Alice remarked.

"Oh, you can't help that," said the Cat: "**wir** are all mad here. I'm mad. You are mad."

"**<u>Woher wissen Sie</u>**, **<u>dass</u>** I'm mad?" said Alice.

"You must be," said the Cat, **<u>sonst wären Sie</u>** not have come here."

Alice did not think that proved it at all; however, she went on "**Und woher wissen Sie** that you are mad?"

"**<u>Zuerst</u>/ Zunächst**," said the Cat, "a dog's not mad. You grant that?"

"**Ich** suppose so," said Alice.

"**<u>Nun</u>**, then," the Cat went on, "**sie sehen**,, a dog growls **wenn** it's angry, **und** wags its tail **wenn** it's pleased. Now **ich** growl

**wenn** I'm pleased, **und** wag my tail **wenn** I'm angry. Therefore I'm mad."

"**Ich** call it purring, not growling," said Alice.

"Call it what **Sie wollen**" said the Cat. "Do you play croquet **mit** the Queen to-day?"

"**Ich möchte** it **sehr** much," said Alice, "**aber ich** haven't been invited yet."

"<u>**Sie werden sehen**</u> me there," said the Cat, **und** vanished.

Alice was not much surprised at this, she was getting so **gewöhnt daran** queer things happening. While she was looking at the place where it had been, it suddenly appeared again.

"By-the-bye, what became of the baby?" said the Cat. "I'd nearly forgotten to ask."

"It turned **in** a pig," Alice quietly said, just **als ob** it had come back in a natural **Weg**.

"**Ich** thought it would," said the Cat, **und** vanished again.

Alice waited a little, half expecting **zu sehen** it again, **aber** it did not appear, **und** after a minute **oder** two she walked on in the direction in which the March Hare was said to live. "**Ich habe gesehen** hatters before," she said to herself; "the March Hare will be much the most interesting, **und** perhaps as this is May it won't be raving mad—at least not so mad as it was in March." As she said this, she looked up, <u>**und da war**</u> the Cat again, sitting on a branch of a tree.

"Did you say pig, **oder** fig?" said the Cat.

"**Ich** said pig," replied Alice; "**und ich** wish **Sie würden** not keep appearing **und** vanishing so suddenly: **Sie machen** one quite giddy."

"All right," said the Cat; **und** this time it vanished quite slowly, beginning **mit** the end of the tail, **und** ending **mit** the grin, which remained some time after the rest of it had gone.

"**Na ja! Ich** have **häufig** seen a cat without a grin," thought Alice; "**aber** a grin without a cat! It's the most curious thing **ich** ever saw in my life!"

She had not gone much farther before she came in sight of the house of the March Hare: she thought it must be the right house, **weil** the chimneys were shaped like ears **und** the roof was thatched **mit** fur. It was so large a house, that she did not like to go nearer till she had nibbled some more of the lefthand bit of mushroom, **und** raised herself to about two feet high: even then she walked up towards it rather timidly, saying to herself "Suppose it should be raving mad after all! **Ich** almost wish I'd gone **zu sehen** the Hatter instead!"

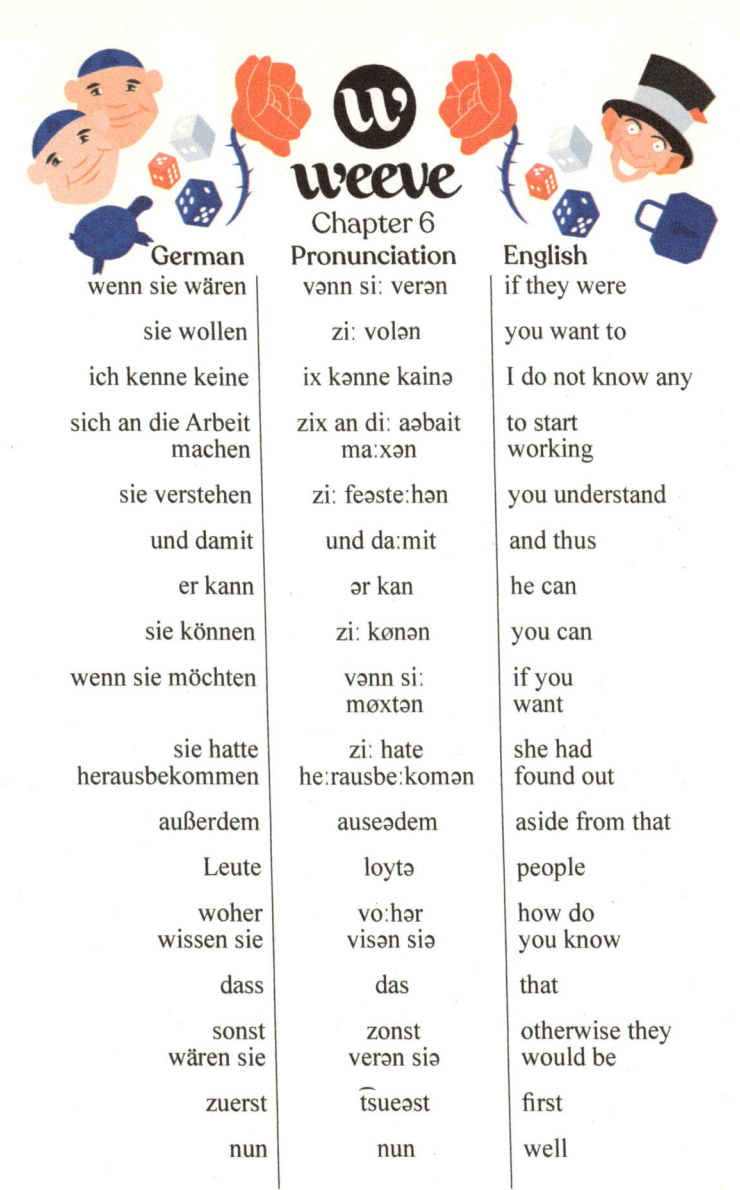

# weeve
## Chapter 6

| German | Pronunciation | English |
|---|---|---|
| wenn sie wären | vənn si: verən | if they were |
| sie wollen | zi: volən | you want to |
| ich kenne keine | ix kənne kainə | I do not know any |
| sich an die Arbeit machen | zix an di: aəbait ma:xən | to start working |
| sie verstehen | zi: feəste:hən | you understand |
| und damit | und da:mit | and thus |
| er kann | ər kan | he can |
| sie können | zi: kønən | you can |
| wenn sie möchten | vənn si: møxtən | if you want |
| sie hatte herausbekommen | zi: hate he:rausbe:komən | she had found out |
| außerdem | auseədem | aside from that |
| Leute | loytə | people |
| woher wissen sie | vo:hər visən siə | how do you know |
| dass | das | that |
| sonst wären sie | zonst verən siə | otherwise they would be |
| zuerst | t͡sueəst | first |
| nun | nun | well |

## weeve
### Chapter 6

| German | Pronunciation | English |
|---|---|---|
| sie werden sehen | zi: veədən se:hən | you will see |
| und da war | und da vaə | and there was |
| weil sie | vail siə | because they |
| wissen sie | visən siə | you know |
| es gab | es gap | there were |
| die | diə | the |
| um zu sehen | um t͡su se:hən | to see |

# 7
# A MAD TEA PARTY

**Weeve Reading Tip:** Returning to your weeve after a break can be difficult. Try flipping back to the last vocabulary table, refresh yourself with the words in the story and continue reading.

**Es gab** a table set out under a tree in front of the house, **und** the March Hare **und** the Hatter were having tea at it: a Dormouse was sitting between **ihnen**, fast asleep, **und** the other two **benutzten** it as a cushion, resting their elbows on it, **und** talking over its head. "**Sehr** uncomfortable for the Dormouse," thought Alice; "only, as it's asleep, **ich** suppose it doesn't mind."

The table was a large one, **aber** the three were all crowded together at one corner of it: "No room! No room!" **sie** cried out **als sie sahen** Alice coming. "There's plenty of room!" said Alice indignantly, **und** she sat down in a large arm-chair at one end of the table.

"Have some wine," the March Hare said in an encouraging tone.

Alice looked all round the table, **aber es gab** nothing on it **außer** tea. "**Ich sehe keinen** wine," she remarked.

"**Es gibt** none," said the March Hare.

"Then it was not **sehr** civil of you to offer it," said Alice angrily.

"It was not **sehr** civil of you to sit down without being invited," said the March Hare.

"**Ich** did not know it was your table," said Alice; "it's laid for a great many more **als** three."

"Your hair wants cutting," said the Hatter. He had been looking at Alice for some time **mit** great curiosity, **und** this was his first speech.

"<u>**Sie sollten**</u> learn not **zu machen** personal remarks," Alice said **mit** some severity; "it's **sehr** rude."

The Hatter opened his eyes **sehr** wide on hearing this; **aber** all he said was, "Why is a raven like a writing-desk?"

"Come, **wir** shall have some fun now!" thought Alice. "I'm glad **sie** have begun asking riddles.—I believe **ich kann** guess that," she added aloud.

"Do you mean that you think <u>**Sie könnten**</u> find out the answer to it?" said the March Hare.

"Exactly so," said Alice.

"Then **sollten Sie** say what you mean," the March Hare went on.

"**Ich** do," Alice hastily replied; "at least—at least **ich** mean what **ich** say—that's the same thing, **wissen Sie**."

"Not the same thing a bit!" said the Hatter. "You might just as **gut** say that '**Ich sehe** what **ich** eat' is the same thing as '**Ich** eat what **ich** see'!"

"You might just as **gut** say," added the March Hare, "that '**Ich mag** what **ich** get' is the same thing as '**Ich** get what **ich** like'!"

"You might just as **gut** say," added the Dormouse, **der** seemed to be talking in his sleep, "that '**Ich** breathe **wenn ich** sleep' is the same thing as '**Ich** sleep **wenn ich** breathe'!"

"It is the same thing **mit** you," said the Hatter, **und** here the conversation dropped, **und** the party sat silent for a minute, while Alice thought over all she could remember about ravens **und** writing-desks, which was not much.

The Hatter was the first to break the silence. "What day of the month is it?" he said, turning to Alice: he had taken his watch out of his pocket, **und** was looking at it uneasily, shaking it every now **und** then, **und** holding it to his ear.

Alice considered a little, **und** then said "The fourth."

"Two days wrong!" sighed the Hatter. "**Ich** told you butter wouldn't suit the works!" he added looking angrily at the March Hare.

"It was the best butter," the March Hare meekly replied.

"Yes, **aber** some crumbs must have got in **auch**," the Hatter grumbled: "**Sie sollten** not have put it in **mit** the bread-knife."

The March Hare took the watch **und** looked at it gloomily: then he dipped it **in** his cup of tea, **und** looked at it again: **aber** he could think of nothing better to say **als** his first remark, "It was the best butter, **wissen Sie**."

Alice had been looking over his shoulder **mit** some curiosity. "What a funny watch!" she remarked. "It tells the day of the month, **und** doesn't tell what o'clock it is!"

"Why should it?" muttered the Hatter. "Does your watch tell you what year it is?"

"Of course not," Alice replied **sehr** readily: "**aber** that's **weil** it stays the same year for such a long time together."

"Which is just the case **mit** mine," said the Hatter.

Alice felt dreadfully puzzled. The Hatter's remark seemed to have no sort of meaning in it, **und** yet it was certainly English. "**Ich** do not quite understand you," she said, as politely as she could.

"The Dormouse is asleep again," said the Hatter, **und** he poured a little hot tea upon its nose.

The Dormouse shook its head impatiently, **und** said, without opening its eyes, "Of course, of course; just what **ich** was going to remark myself."

"Have you guessed the riddle yet?" the Hatter said, turning to Alice again.

"No, **ich** give it up," Alice replied: "what's the answer?"

"**Ich** haven't the slightest idea," said the Hatter.

"Nor **ich**," said the March Hare.

Alice sighed wearily. "**Ich** think you might do something better **mit** the time," she said, "**als** waste it in asking riddles that have no answers."

"**Wenn Sie kennen würden** Time as **gut** as **ich** do," said the Hatter, "**würden Sie** not talk about wasting it. It's him."

"**Ich weiß nicht** what you mean," said Alice.

"Of course you do not!" the Hatter said, tossing his head contemptuously. "**Ich** dare say you never even spoke to Time!"

47

"Perhaps not," Alice cautiously replied: "**aber ich weiß, dass ich** have to beat time **wenn ich** learn music."

"Ah! that accounts for it," said the Hatter. "He won't stand beating. Now, **wenn** you only kept on good terms **mit** him, he'd do almost anything, was Sie wollen mit the clock. For instance, suppose it were nine o'clock in the morning, just time to begin lessons: you'd only have to whisper a hint to Time, **und** round goes the clock in a twinkling! Half-past one, time for dinner!"

("**Ich** only wish it was," the March Hare said to itself in a whisper.)

"That would be grand, certainly," said Alice thoughtfully: "**aber** then—I shouldn't be hungry for it, **wissen Sie**."

"Not at first, perhaps," said the Hatter: "**aber** you could keep it to half-past one as long as **Sie möchten**."

"Is that <u>**die Art**</u> you manage?" Alice asked.

The Hatter shook his head mournfully. "Not **ich**!" he replied. "**Wir** quarrelled last March—just before he went mad, you know—" (pointing **mit** his tea spoon at the March Hare,) "—it was at the great concert given by the Queen of Hearts, **und ich** had to sing

'Twinkle, twinkle, little bat! **Wie ich** wonder what you are at!'

**Kennen Sie** the song, perhaps?"

"**Ich** have heard something like it," said Alice.

"It goes on, <u>**wissen Sie**</u>"" the Hatter continued, "in this **Weise**:—

'Up above the world you fly, Like a tea-tray in the sky. Twinkle, twinkle—'"

Here the Dormouse shook itself, **und** began singing in its sleep "Twinkle, twinkle, twinkle, twinkle —" **und** went on so long that **sie** had to pinch it **um es zu stoppen**.

"**Na ja**, I'd hardly finished the first verse," said the Hatter, "**als** the Queen jumped up **und** bawled out, 'He's murdering **die Zeit**! Off **mit** his head!'"

"**Wie** dreadfully savage!" exclaimed Alice.

"**Und** ever since that," the Hatter went on in a mournful tone, "he won't do a thing **ich** ask! It's always six o'clock now."

A bright idea came **in** Alice's head. "Is that the reason so many tea-things are put out here?" she asked.

"Yes, that's it," said the Hatter **mit** a sigh: "it's always tea-time,

**und wir** have no time to wash the things between whiles."

"Then you keep moving round, **ich** suppose?" said Alice.

"Exactly so," said the Hatter: "as the things get used up."

"**Aber** what happens **wenn** you come to the beginning again?" Alice ventured to ask.

"Suppose **wir** change the subject," the March Hare interrupted, yawning. "I'm getting tired of this. **Ich** vote the young lady tells us a story."

"I'm afraid **ich kenne keine**," said Alice, rather alarmed at the proposal.

"Then the Dormouse shall!" **sie** both cried. "Wake up, Dormouse!" **Und sie** pinched it on both sides at once.

The Dormouse slowly opened his eyes. "**Ich** was not asleep," he said in a hoarse, feeble voice: "**Ich** heard every word you fellows were saying."

"Tell us a story!" said the March Hare.

"Yes, please do!" pleaded Alice.

"**Und** be quick about it," added the Hatter, "**oder** you will be asleep again before it's done."

", **es waren <u>einmal</u>** three little sisters," the Dormouse began in a great hurry; "**und** their names were Elsie, Lacie, **und** Tillie; **und sie** lived at the bottom of a well—"

"What did **sie** live on?" said Alice, **die** always took a great interest in questions of eating **und** drinking.

"**Sie** lived on treacle," said the Dormouse, after thinking a minute **oder** two.

"**Sie** couldn't have done that, **wissen Sie**," Alice gently remarked; "they'd have been ill."

"So **waren sie**," said the Dormouse; "**sehr** ill."

Alice tried to fancy to herself what such an extraordinary <u>**Lebensweise**</u> would be like, **aber** it puzzled her too much, so she went on: "**Aber** why did **sie** live at the bottom of a **Brunnen**?"

"Take some more tea," the March Hare said to Alice, **sehr** earnestly.

"**Ich** have had nothing yet," Alice replied in an offended tone, "so **ich** can't take more."

"You mean you can't take less," said the Hatter: "it's **sehr** easy to take more **als** nothing."

"Nobody asked your opinion," said Alice.

"Who **macht** personal remarks now?" the Hatter asked triumphantly.

Alice did not quite know what to say to this: so she helped herself to some tea **und** bread-and-butter, **und** then turned to the Dormouse, **und** repeated her question. "Why did **sie** live at the bottom of a **Brunnen**?"

The Dormouse again took a minute **oder** two to think about it, **und** then said, "It was a treacle-well."

"There's no such thing!" Alice was becoming sehr angry, **aber** the Hatter **und** the March Hare went "Sh! sh!" **und** the Dormouse sulkily remarked, "**Wenn** you can't be civil, you'd better finish the story for yourself."

"No, please go on!" Alice said **sehr** humbly; "**Ich** won't interrupt again. **Ich** dare say there may be one."

"One, indeed!" said the Dormouse indignantly. However, he consented to go on. "**Und** so these three little sisters—they were learning to draw, you know—"

"What did **sie** draw?" said Alice, quite forgetting her promise.

"Treacle," said the Dormouse, without considering at all this time.

"**Ich** want a clean cup," interrupted the Hatter: "let's all move one place on."

He moved on as he spoke, **und** the Dormouse followed him: the March Hare moved **in** the Dormouse's place, **und** Alice rather unwillingly took the place of the March Hare. The Hatter was the only one **der** got any advantage from the change: **und** Alice was a good deal worse off **als** before, as the March Hare had just upset the milk-jug **in** his plate.

Alice did not wish to offend the Dormouse again, so she began **sehr** cautiously: "**Aber ich** do not understand. Where did **sie** draw the treacle from?"

"**Sie könnten** draw water out of a water-well," said the Hatter; "so **ich würde** think you could draw treacle out of a treacle-well—eh, stupid?"

"**Aber sie waren** in the **Brunnen**," Alice said to the Dormouse, not choosing to notice this last remark.

"Of course **sie waren**," said the Dormouse; "—well in."

This answer so confused poor Alice, that she let the Dormouse go on for some time without interrupting it.

"<u>**Sie lernten**</u> to draw," the Dormouse went on, yawning **und** rubbing its eyes, for it was getting **sehr** sleepy; "**und sie** drew all manner of things—everything that begins **mit** an M—"

"Why **mit** an M?" said Alice.

"Why not?" said the March Hare.

Alice was silent.

The Dormouse had closed its eyes by this time, **und** was going off **in** a doze; **aber**, on being pinched by the Hatter, it woke up again **mit** a little shriek, **und** went on: "—that begins **mit** an M, such as mouse-traps, **und** the moon, **und** memory, **und** muchness—you know you say things are "much of a muchness" —did you ever see such a thing as a drawing of a muchness?"

"Really, now you ask me," said Alice, **sehr** much confused, "**Ich** do not think—"

"Then **Sie sollten** not talk," said the Hatter.

This piece of rudeness was more **als** Alice could bear: she got up in great disgust, **und** walked off; the Dormouse fell asleep instantly, **und** neither of the others took the least notice of her going, though she looked back once **oder** twice, half hoping that **sie würden** call after her: the last time **sie sah sie, sie waren** trying to put the Dormouse **in** the teapot.

"At any rate **ich** will never go there again!" said Alice as she picked her **Weg** through the wood. "It's the stupidest tea-party **ich** ever was at **in** all my life!"

Just as she said this, she noticed that one of the trees had a door leading right in it. "That's **sehr** curious!" she thought. "**Aber** everything's curious today. Ich think ich kann genauso gut go in at once." **Und** in she went.

Once more she found herself in the long hall, **und** close to the little glass table. "Now, **ich** will manage better this time," she said to herself, **und** began by taking the little golden key, **und** unlocking the door that led **in** the garden. Then she went **an die Arbeit** nibbling at the mushroom (she had kept a piece of it in her pocket) till she was about a foot high: then she walked down the little passage: **und** then —she found herself at last in the beautiful garden, among the bright flower-beds **und** the cool fountains.

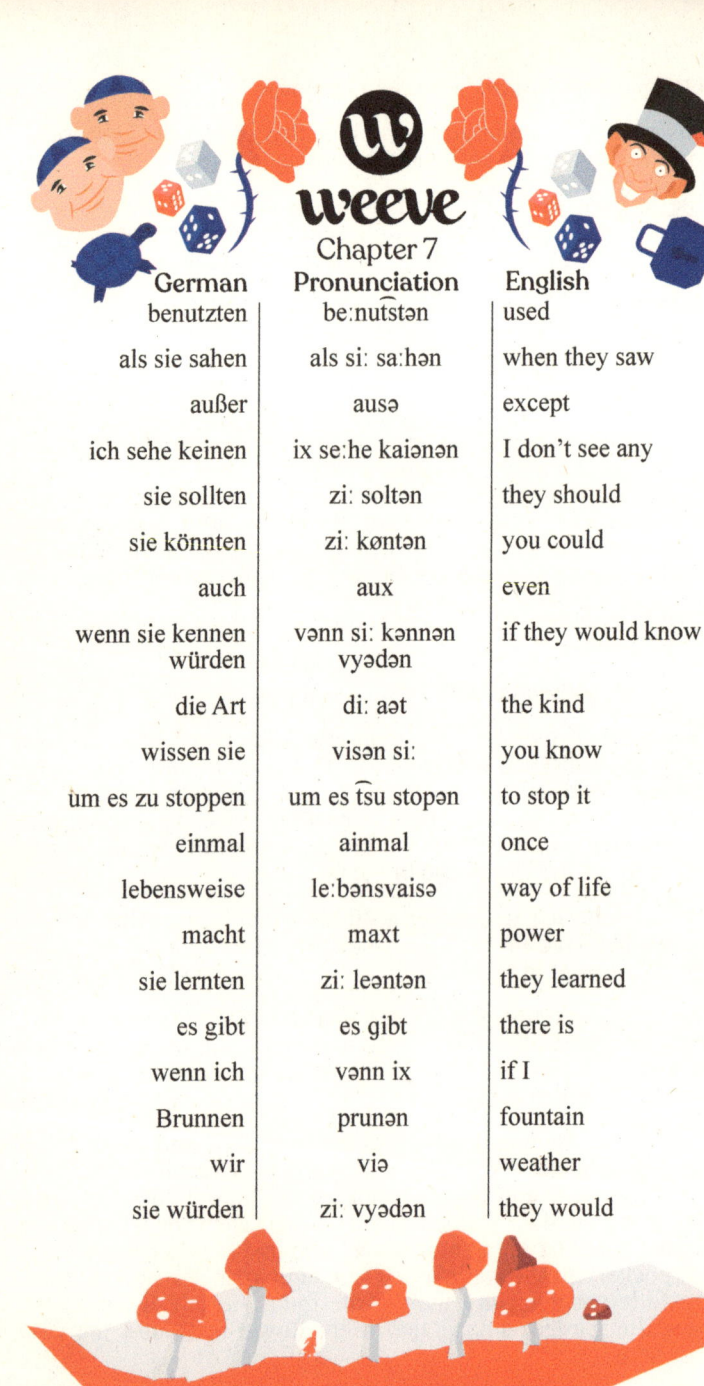

# weeve

## Chapter 7

| German | Pronunciation | English |
|---|---|---|
| benutzten | be:nutstən | used |
| als sie sahen | als si: sa:hən | when they saw |
| außer | ausə | except |
| ich sehe keinen | ix se:he kaiənən | I don't see any |
| sie sollten | zi: soltən | they should |
| sie könnten | zi: køntən | you could |
| auch | aux | even |
| wenn sie kennen würden | vənn si: kənnən vyədən | if they would know |
| die Art | di: aət | the kind |
| wissen sie | visən si: | you know |
| um es zu stoppen | um es tsu stopən | to stop it |
| einmal | ainmal | once |
| lebensweise | le:bənsvaisə | way of life |
| macht | maxt | power |
| sie lernten | zi: leəntən | they learned |
| es gibt | es gibt | there is |
| wenn ich | vənn ix | if I |
| Brunnen | prunən | fountain |
| wir | viə | weather |
| sie würden | zi: vyədən | they would |

# 8
# THE QUEEN'S CROQUET GROUND

**Weeve Reading Tip:** Read to the end of chapters. This way when you pick your book back up you can refresh your memory of the latest words that were introduced and you can continue on with your story.

A large rose-tree stood near the entrance of the garden: the roses growing on it were white, **aber es gab** three gardeners at it, busily painting **sie** red. Alice thought this a **sehr** curious thing, **und** she went nearer to watch **sie, und** just as she came up to **ihnen** she heard one of **ihnen** say, "Look out now, Five! Do not go splashing paint over me like that!"

"**Ich** couldn't help it," said Five, in a sulky tone; "Seven jogged my elbow."

On which Seven looked up **und** said, "That's right, Five! Always lay the blame on others!"

"You'd better not talk!" said Five. "**Ich** heard the Queen say only yesterday you deserved to be beheaded!"

"What for?" said the one **der** had spoken first.

"That's none of your business, Two!" said Seven.

"Yes, it is his business!" said Five, "**und ich** will tell him—it was for bringing the cook tulip-roots instead of onions."

Seven flung down his brush, **und** had just begun "**Nun**, of all the unjust things—" **als** his eye chanced to fall upon Alice, as she

53

stood watching **sie, und** he checked himself suddenly: the others looked round **auch, und** all of **ihnen** bowed low.

"Would you tell me," said Alice, a little timidly, "why you are painting those roses?"

Five **und** Seven said nothing, **aber** looked at Two. Two began in a low voice, "Why the fact is, **sehen Sie**, Miss, this here ought to have been a red rose-tree, **und wir** put a white one in by mistake; **und wenn** the Queen was to find it out, **wir würden** all have our heads cut off, **wissen Sie**. So **sehen Sie**,, Miss, **wir** are doing our best, afore she comes, to—" At this moment Five, **der** had been anxiously looking across the garden, called out "The Queen! The Queen!" **und** the three gardeners instantly threw themselves flat upon their faces. **Es gab** a sound of many footsteps, **und** Alice looked round, eager **zu sehen** the Queen.

First came ten soldiers carrying clubs; these were all shaped like the three gardeners, oblong **und** flat, **mit** their hands **und** feet at the corners: next the ten courtiers; these were ornamented all over **mit** diamonds, **und** walked two **und** two, as the soldiers did. After these came the royal children; **es waren** ten of **ihnen**, **und** the little dears came jumping merrily along hand in hand, in couples: **sie waren** all ornamented **mit** hearts. Next came the guests, mostly Kings **und** Queens, **und** among **ihnen** Alice recognised the White Rabbit: it was talking in a hurried nervous manner, smiling at everything that was said, **und** went by without noticing her. Then followed the Knave of Hearts, carrying the King's crown on a crimson velvet cushion; **und**, last of all this grand procession, came THE KING **UND** QUEEN OF HEARTS.

Alice was rather doubtful whether she ought not to lie down on her face like the three gardeners, **aber** she couldn't remember ever having heard of such a rule at processions; "**und** besides, what would be the use of a procession," thought she, "**wenn die Leute** had all to lie down upon their faces, so that **sie** couldn't see it?" So she stood still where she was, **und** waited.

**Als** the procession came opposite to Alice, **sie** all stopped **und** looked at her, **und** the Queen said severely "**Wer** is this?" She said it to the Knave of Hearts, **der** only bowed **und** smiled in reply.

"Idiot!" said the Queen, tossing her head impatiently; **und**, turning to Alice, she went on, "What's your name, child?"

"My name is Alice, so please your Majesty," said Alice **sehr** politely; **aber** she added, to herself, "Why, **sie** are only a pack of cards, after all. <u>**Ich brauche**</u> not be afraid of **ihnen**!"

"**Und wer** are these?" said the Queen, pointing to the three gardeners **die** were lying round the rose-tree; for, **sehen Sie**,, as

**sie waren** lying on their faces, **und** the pattern on their backs was the same as the rest of the pack, she couldn't tell whether **sie waren** gardeners, **oder** soldiers, **oder** courtiers, **oder** three of her own children.

"**Wie** should **ich wissen**?" said Alice, surprised at her own courage. "It's no business of mine."

The Queen turned crimson **vor** fury, **und**, after glaring at her for a moment like a wild beast, screamed "Off **mit** her head! Off—"

"Nonsense!" said Alice, **sehr** loudly **und** decidedly, **und** the Queen was silent.

The King laid his hand upon her arm, **und** timidly said "Consider, my dear: she is only a child!"

The Queen turned angrily away from him, **und** said to the Knave "Turn **sie** over!"

The Knave did so, **sehr** carefully, **mit** one foot.

"Get up!" said the Queen, in a shrill, loud voice, **und** the three gardeners instantly jumped up, **und** began bowing to the King, the Queen, the royal children, **und** everybody else.

"Leave off that!" screamed the Queen. "**Ihr macht** me giddy." **Und** then, turning to the rose-tree, she went on, "What have you been doing here?"

"May it please your Majesty," said Two, in a **sehr** humble tone, going down on one knee as he spoke, "**wir** were trying—"

"**Ich verstehe**!" said the Queen, **die** had meanwhile been examining the roses. "Off **mit** their heads!" **und** the procession moved on, three of the soldiers remaining behind to execute the unfortunate gardeners, **die** ran to Alice for protection.

"You sha not be beheaded!" said Alice, **und** she put **sie in** a large flower-pot that stood near. The three soldiers wandered about for a minute **oder** two, looking for **ihnen**, **und** then quietly marched off after the others.

"Are their heads off?" shouted the Queen.

"Their heads are gone, **wenn** it please your Majesty!" the soldiers shouted in reply.

"That's right!" shouted the Queen. "Can you play croquet?"

The soldiers were silent, **und** looked at Alice, as the question was evidently meant for her.

"Yes!" shouted Alice.

"Come on, then!" roared the Queen, **und** Alice joined the procession, wondering **sehr** much what would happen next.

"It's—it's a **sehr** fine day!" said a timid voice at her side. She was walking by the White Rabbit, **das** was peeping anxiously **in** her face.

"**Sehr**," said Alice: "—where's the Duchess?"

"Hush! Hush!" said the Rabbit in a low, hurried tone. He looked anxiously over his shoulder as he spoke, **und** then raised himself upon tiptoe, put his mouth close to her ear, **und** whispered "She's under sentence of execution."

"What for?" said Alice.

"Did you say 'What a pity!'?" the Rabbit asked.

"No, **ich** did not," said Alice: "**Ich** do not think it's at all a pity. **Ich** said 'What for?'"

"She boxed the Queen's ears—" the Rabbit began. Alice gave a little scream of laughter. "Oh, hush!" the Rabbit whispered in a frightened tone. "The Queen will hear you! **sehen Sie,**, she came rather late, **und** the Queen said—"

"Get to your places!" shouted the Queen in a voice of thunder, **und die Leute** began running about in all directions, tumbling up against each other; however, **sie** got settled down in a minute **oder** two, **und** the game began. Alice thought she had never seen such a curious croquet-ground in her life; it was all ridges **und** furrows; the balls were live hedgehogs, the mallets live flamingoes, **und** the soldiers had to double themselves up **und** to stand on their hands **und** feet, **um** the arches **zu machen**.

The chief difficulty Alice found at first was in managing her flamingo: she succeeded in getting its body tucked away, comfortably enough, under her arm, **mit** its legs hanging down, **aber** generally, just as she had got its neck nicely straightened out, **und** was going to give the hedgehog a blow **mit** its head, it would twist itself round **und** look up in her face, **mit** such a puzzled expression that she couldn't help bursting out laughing: **und als** she had got its head down, **und** was going to begin again, it was **sehr** provoking to find that the hedgehog had unrolled itself, **und** was in the act of crawling away: besides all this, **gab es** generally a ridge **oder** furrow **im Weg** wherever she wanted to send the hedgehog to, **und**, as the doubled-up soldiers were always getting up **und** walking off to other parts of the ground, Alice soon came to the conclusion that it was a **sehr** difficult game indeed.

The players all played at once without waiting for turns, quarrelling all the while, **und** fighting for the hedgehogs; **und** in a **sehr** short time the Queen was in a furious passion, **und** went stamping about, **und** shouting "Off **mit** his head!" **oder** "Off **mit** her head!" about once in a minute.

Alice began to feel **sehr** uneasy: to be sure, she had not as yet had any dispute **mit** the Queen, **<u>aber sie wusste</u>**, that it might happen any minute, "**und** then," thought she, "what would become of me? **Sie** are dreadfully fond of beheading **Leute** here; the great wonder is, that there's any one left alive!"

She was looking about for some **<u>Fluchtweg</u>**, **und** wondering whether she could get away without being seen, **als** she noticed a curious appearance in the air: it puzzled her **sehr** much at first, **aber**, after watching it a minute **oder** two, **<u>sie erkannte</u>** it to be a grin, **und** she said to herself "It's the Cheshire Cat: now **ich** shall have somebody to talk to."

"**Wie** are you getting on?" said the Cat, as soon as there was mouth enough for it to speak mit.

Alice waited till the eyes appeared, **und** then nodded. "It's no use speaking to it," she thought, "till its ears have come, **oder** at least one of **ihnen**." In another minute the whole head appeared, **und** then Alice put down her flamingo, **und** began an account of the game, feeling **sehr** glad she had someone to listen to her. The Cat seemed to think that there was enough of it now in sight, **und** no more of it appeared.

"**Ich** do not think **sie** play at all fairly," Alice began, in rather a complaining tone, "**und sie** all quarrel so dreadfully one can't hear oneself speak—and **sie** do not seem to have any rules in particular; at least, **<u>wenn es welche gibt</u>**, nobody attends to them—and you have no idea **wie** confusing it is all the things being alive; for instance, there's the arch **ich** have got to go through next walking about at the other end of the ground—and **<u>ich hätte sollen</u>** croqueted the Queen's hedgehog just now, only it ran away **als** it saw mine coming!"

"**<u>Wie gefällt Ihnen</u>** the Queen?" said the Cat in a low voice.

"Not at all," said Alice: "she's so extremely—" Just then she noticed that the Queen was close behind her, listening: so she went on, "—likely to win, that it's hardly worth while finishing the game."

The Queen smiled **und** passed on.

"**<u>Mit wem</u>** are you talking?" said the King, going up to Alice, **und** looking at the Cat's head **mit** great curiosity.

"It's a friend of mine—a Cheshire Cat," said Alice: "allow me to introduce it."

"Mir gefällt nicht the look of it at all," said the King: "however, it may kiss my hand **wenn** it **<u>will</u>**."

"I'd rather not," the Cat remarked.

"Do not be impertinent," said the King, "**und** do not look at me like that!" He got behind Alice as he spoke.

"A cat may look at a king," said Alice. "**Ich** have read that in some book, **aber ich** do not remember where."

"**Nun**, it must be removed," said the King **sehr** decidedly, **und** he called the Queen, **die** was passing at the moment, "My dear! **Ich** wish **<u>du würdest</u>** have this cat removed!"

The Queen had only one **Weg** of settling all difficulties, great **oder** small. "Off **mit** his head!" she said, without even looking round.

"**Ich** will fetch the executioner myself," said the King eagerly, **und** he hurried off.

Alice thought she might as **<u>genauso gut</u>** go back, **und** see **wie** the game was going on, as she heard the Queen's voice in the distance, screaming **vor** passion. She had already heard her sentence three of the players to be executed for having missed their turns, **und** she did not like the look of things at all, as the game was in such confusion that she never knew whether it was her turn **oder** not. So she went in search of her hedgehog.

The hedgehog was engaged in a fight **mit** another hedgehog, which seemed to Alice an excellent opportunity for croqueting one of **ihnen mit** the other: the only difficulty was, that her flamingo was gone across to the other side of the garden, where Alice could see it trying in a helpless sort of **Weise** to fly up **in** a tree.

**<u>Bis</u>** she had caught the flamingo **und** brought it back, the fight was over, **und** both the hedgehogs were out of sight: "**aber** it doesn't matter much," thought Alice, "as all the arches are gone from this side of the ground." So she tucked it away under her arm, that it might not escape again, **und** went back for a little more conversation **mit** her friend.

**Als** she got back to the Cheshire Cat, she was surprised to find quite a large crowd collected round it: **es gab** a dispute going on between the executioner, the King, **und** the Queen, **die** were all talking at once, while all the rest were quite silent, **und** looked **sehr** uncomfortable.

The moment Alice appeared, she was appealed to by all three to settle the question, **und sie** repeated their arguments to her, though, as **sie** all spoke at once, she found it **sehr** hard indeed **zu**

**verstehen** exactly what **sie** said.

The executioner's argument was, that you couldn't cut off a head unless **es gab** a body to cut it off from: that he had never had **zu tun** such a thing before, **und** he was not going to begin at diese Zeitpunkt of seinem life.

The King's argument was, that anything that had a head could be beheaded, **und** that **man sollte** not to talk nonsense.

The Queen's argument was, that **wenn** something was not done about it in less **als** no time she'd have everybody executed, all round. (It was this last remark that had made the whole party look so grave **und** anxious.)

Alice could think of nothing else to say **außer** "It belongs to the Duchess: you'd better ask her about it."

"She's in prison," the Queen said to the executioner: "fetch her here." **Und** the executioner went off like an arrow.

The Cat's head began fading away the moment he was gone, **und**, by the time he had come back **mit** the Duchess, it had entirely disappeared; so the King **und** the executioner ran wildly up **und** down looking for it, while the rest of the party went back to the game.

## weeve
### Chapter 7

| German | Pronunciation | English |
|---|---|---|
| ich brauche | ix prauxə | I need |
| vor | foə | before |
| ich verstehe | ix feəste:ə | I understand |
| im Weg | im vek | in the way |
| aber sie wusste | abər si: vustə | but she knew |
| Fluchtweg | fluxtvek | escape route |
| sie erkannte | zi: eəkantə | she recognized |
| wenn es welche gibt | vənn es velxe gibt | if there are any |
| ich hätte sollen | ix hete solən | I should have |
| wie gefällt ihnen | vi: ge:felt i:nən | how do you like |
| mit wem | mit vem | with whom |
| will | vil | want |
| du würdest | du vyədest | you would |
| genauso gut | ge:nauhso gut | as good as |
| bis | bis | until |
| man sollte | man soltə | one should |
| wer | və | who |
| nun | nun | well |
| Leute | loytə | people |

# 9

# THE MOCK TURTLE'S STORY

"Student comprehension scores were 50% higher for information presented in story form than for similar information presented in expository forms."- J. David Cooper, author of Literacy: Helping Children Construct Meaning

"You can't think **wie** glad **ich** am **zu sehen** you again, you dear old thing!"

said the Duchess, as she tucked her arm affectionately **in** Alice's, **und sie** walked off together.

Alice was **sehr** glad to find her in such a pleasant temper, **und** thought to herself that perhaps it was only the pepper that had made her so savage **als sie** met in the kitchen.

"**Wenn** I'm a Duchess," she said to herself, (not in a **sehr** hopeful tone though), "**Ich** won't have any pepper in my kitchen at all. Soup does **sehr gut** without—Maybe it's always pepper that makes **Leute** hot-tempered," she went on, **sehr** much pleased at having found out a new kind of rule, "**und** vinegar that makes **sie** sour—and camomile that makes **sie** bitter—and—and barley-sugar **und** such things that make children sweet-tempered. **Ich** only wish **Leute** knew that: then **sie wären** not be so stingy about it, you know—"

She had quite forgotten the Duchess by this time, **und** was a little startled **als** she heard her voice close to her ear. "You are thinking about something, my dear, **und** that makes you forget to talk. **Ich** can't tell you just now what the moral of that is, **aber ich** shall remember it in a bit."

"Perhaps it has not one," Alice ventured to remark.

"Tut, tut, child!" said the Duchess. "Everything's got a moral, **wenn** only **Sie könnten** find it." **Und** she squeezed herself up closer to Alice's side as she spoke.

Alice did not much like keeping so close to her: first, **weil** the Duchess was **sehr** ugly; **und** secondly, **weil** she was exactly the right height to rest her chin upon Alice's shoulder, **und** it was an uncomfortably sharp chin. However, she did not like to be rude, so she bore it as **gut** as she could.

"The game's going on rather better now," she said, by **Weg** of keeping up the conversation a little.

"'Tis so," said the Duchess: "**und** the moral of that is— 'Oh,'tis love,'tis love, that makes **die Welt** go round!'"

"Somebody said," Alice whispered, "that it's done by everybody minding their own business!"

"Ah, **ja**! It means much the same thing," said the Duchess, digging her sharp little chin **in** Alice's shoulder as she added, "**und** the moral of that is— 'Take care of the sense, **und** the sounds will take care of themselves.'"

"**Wie** fond she is of finding morals in things!" Alice thought to herself.

"**Ich** dare say you are wondering why **ich** do not put my arm round your waist," the Duchess said after a pause: "the reason is, that I'm doubtful about the temper of your flamingo. Shall **ich** try the experiment?"

"He might bite," Alice cautiously replied, not feeling at all anxious to have the experiment tried.

"**Sehr** true," said the Duchess: "flamingoes **und** mustard both bite. **Und** the moral of that is— 'Birds of a feather flock together.'"

"Only mustard isn't a bird," Alice remarked.

"Right, as usual," said the Duchess: "what a clear **Art** you have of putting things!"

"It's a mineral, **ich** think," said Alice.

"Of course it is," said the Duchess, **die** seemed ready to agree to everything that Alice said; "there's a large mustard-mine near here. **Und** the moral of that is— 'The more **es gibt** of mine, the less **es gibt** of yours.'"

"Oh, **ich weiß!**" exclaimed Alice, **die** had not attended to this last remark, "it's a vegetable. It doesn't look like one, **aber** it is."

"**Ich** quite agree mit you," said the Duchess; "**und** the moral of that is— 'Be what Sie seem to be'—or wenn you'd like it put more simply— 'Never imagine yourself not to be otherwise als what it might appear to others that what Sie waren oder might have been was not otherwise als what you had been would have appeared to sie to be otherwise.'"

"Ich think **ich würde** understand that better," Alice said **sehr** politely, "**wenn ich** had it written down: **aber ich** can't quite follow it as you say it."

"That's nothing to what **ich** could say **wenn ich** chose," the Duchess replied, in a pleased tone.

"Pray do not trouble yourself to say it any longer **als** that," said Alice.

"Oh, do not talk about trouble!" said the Duchess. "Ich schenke you a present of everything ich have said as yet."

"A cheap sort of present!" thought Alice. "I'm glad **sie** do not give birthday presents like that!" **Aber** she did not venture to say it out loud.

"Thinking again?" the Duchess asked, **mit** another dig of her sharp little chin.

"**Ich** have a right to think," said Alice sharply, for she was beginning to feel a little worried.

"Just about as much right," said the Duchess, "as pigs have to fly; **und** the m—"

**Aber** here, to Alice's great surprise, the Duchess's voice died away, even in the middle of her favourite word 'moral,' **und** the arm that was linked **in** hers began to tremble. Alice looked up, **und** there stood the Queen in front of **ihnen**, **mit** her arms folded, frowning like a thunderstorm.

"A fine day, your Majesty!" the Duchess began in a low, weak voice.

"Now, **ich** give you fair warning," shouted the Queen, stamping on the ground as she spoke; "either you **oder** your head must be off, **und** that in about half no time! Take your choice!"

The Duchess took her choice, **und** was gone in a moment.

"Let's go on **mit** the game," the Queen said to Alice; **und** Alice was too much frightened to say a word, **aber** slowly followed her back to the croquet-ground.

The other guests had taken advantage of the Queen's absence, **und** were resting in the shade: however, the moment **sie sahen** her, **sie** hurried back to the game, the Queen merely remarking that a moment's delay would cost **sie** their lives.

**Die ganze Zeit die sie <u>spielten</u>** the Queen never left off quarrelling **mit** the other players, **und** shouting "Off **mit** his head!" **oder** "Off **mit** her head!" Those whom she sentenced were taken **in** custody by the soldiers, **die** of course had to leave off being arches **zu tun** this, so that by the end of half an hour **oder** so **es gab** no arches left, **und** all the players, except the King, the Queen, **und** Alice, were in custody **und** under sentence of execution.

Then the Queen left off, quite out of breath, **und** said to Alice, "Have you seen the Mock Turtle yet?"

"No," said Alice. "**Ich** do not even know what a Mock Turtle is."

"It's the thing Mock Turtle Soup is made from," said the Queen.

"**Ich** never saw one, **oder** heard of one," said Alice.

"Come on, then," said the Queen, "**und** he shall tell you his **Geschichte**,"

As **sie** walked off together, Alice heard the King say in a low voice, to the company generally, "You are all pardoned." "Come, that's a good thing!" she said to herself, for she had felt quite unhappy at the number of executions the Queen had ordered.

**Sie sehr** soon came upon a Gryphon, lying fast asleep in the sun. (**Wenn Sie nicht wissen** what a Gryphon is, look at the picture.) "Up, lazy thing!" said the Queen, "**und** take this young lady **zu sehen** the Mock Turtle, **und** to hear his **Geschichte**. **Ich** must go back **und** see after some executions **ich** have ordered;" **und** she walked off, leaving Alice alone **mit** the Gryphon. Alice did not quite like the look of the creature, **aber** on the whole she thought it would be quite as safe to stay **mit** it as to go after that savage Queen: so she waited.

The Gryphon sat up **und** rubbed its eyes: then it watched the Queen till she was out of sight: then it chuckled. "What fun!" said the Gryphon, half to itself, half to Alice.

"What is the fun?" said Alice.

"Why, she," said the Gryphon. "It's all her fancy, that: **sie** never executes nobody, **wissen Sie**. Come on!"

"Everybody says 'come on!' here," thought Alice, as she went slowly after it: "**Ich** never was so ordered about in all my life, never!"

**Sie** had not gone far before **sie sahen** the Mock Turtle in the distance, sitting sad **und** lonely on a little ledge of rock, **und**, as **sie** came nearer, Alice could hear him sighing **als ob** his heart would break. She pitied him deeply. "What is his sorrow?" she asked the Gryphon, **und** the Gryphon answered, **sehr** nearly in the same words as before, "It's all his fancy, that: he has not got no sorrow, **wissen Sie**. Come on!"

So **sie** went up to the Mock Turtle, **die** looked at **sie mit** large eyes full of tears, **aber** said nothing.

"This here young lady," said the Gryphon, "she wants to **wissen** your **Geschichte**, she do."

"**Ich** will tell it her," said the Mock Turtle in a deep, hollow tone: "sit down, both of you, **und** do not speak a word till **ich** have finished."

So **sie** sat down, **und** nobody spoke for some minutes. Alice thought to herself, "**Ich weiß nicht, wie er kann** ever finish, **wenn** he doesn't begin." **Aber** she waited patiently.

"Once," said the Mock Turtle at last, **mit** a deep sigh, "**Ich** was a real Turtle."

These words were followed by a **sehr** long silence, broken only by an occasional exclamation of "Hjckrrh!" from the Gryphon, **und** the constant heavy sobbing of the Mock Turtle. Alice was **<u>schon fast</u>** getting up **und** saying, "Thank you, sir, for your interesting story," **aber** she couldn't help thinking there must be more to come, so she sat still **und** said nothing.

"**Als wir** were little," the Mock Turtle went on at last, more calmly, though still sobbing a little now **und** then, "**wir** went to school in the sea. The master was an old Turtle—we called him **<u>immer</u>** Tortoise—"

"Why did you call him Tortoise, **wenn** he was not one?" Alice asked.

"**Wir** called him Tortoise **weil** he taught us," said the Mock Turtle angrily: "really you are **sehr** dull!"

"You ought to be ashamed of yourself for asking such a simple question," added the Gryphon; **und** then **sie** both sat silent **und** looked at poor Alice, **die** felt ready to sink **in** the earth. At last the Gryphon said to the Mock Turtle, "Drive on, old fellow! Do not be all day about it!" **und** he went on in these words:

"Yes, **wir** went to school in the sea, though **Sie könnten** not believe it—"

65

"**Ich** never said **ich** did not!" interrupted Alice.

"You did," said the Mock Turtle.

"Hold your tongue!" added the Gryphon, before Alice could speak again. The Mock Turtle went on.

"**Wir** had the best of educations—in fact, **wir** went to school every day—"

"**Ich** have been to a day-school, too," said Alice; "<u>**Sie brauchen**</u> not be so proud as all that."

"**Mit** extras?" asked the Mock Turtle a little anxiously.

"Yes," said Alice, "**wir** learned French **und** music."

"**Und** washing?" said the Mock Turtle.

"Certainly not!" said Alice indignantly.

"Ah! then yours was not a really good school," said the Mock Turtle in a tone of great relief. "Now at ours **man** had at the end of the bill, 'French, music, **und** washing —extra.'"

"You couldn't have wanted it much," said Alice; "living at the bottom of the sea."

"**Ich** couldn't afford to learn it." said the Mock Turtle **mit** a sigh. "**Ich** only took the regular course."

"What was that?" inquired Alice.

"Reeling **und** Writhing, of course, <u>**damit zu beginnen**</u>," the Mock Turtle replied; "**und** then the different branches of Arithmetic—Ambition, Distraction, Uglification, **und** Derision."

"**Ich** never heard of 'Uglification,'" Alice ventured to say. "What is it?"

The Gryphon lifted up both its paws in surprise. "What! Never heard of uglifying!" it exclaimed. "**Wissen Sie** what to beautify is, **ich** suppose?"

"Yes," said Alice doubtfully: "it means—to—make—anything—prettier."

"**Nun**, then," the Gryphon went on, "**wenn Sie nicht wissen** what to uglify is, you are a simpleton."

Alice did not feel encouraged to ask any more questions about it, so she turned to the Mock Turtle, **und** said "What else had you to learn?"

"**Na ja, es gab** Mystery," the Mock Turtle replied, counting off the subjects on his flappers, "—Mystery, ancient **und** modern, **mit** Seaography: then Drawling—the Drawling-master was an old conger-eel, that **immer kam** once a week: he taught us Drawling, Stretching, **und** Fainting in Coils."

"What was that like?" said Alice.

"**Nun, ich** can't show it you myself," the Mock Turtle said: "I'm too stiff. **Und** the Gryphon never learnt it."

"Had not time," said the Gryphon: "**Ich** went to the Classics master, though. He was an old crab, he was."

"**Ich** never went to him," the Mock Turtle said **mit** a sigh: "he taught Laughing **und** Grief, **sie pflegten** to say."

"So he did, so he did," said the Gryphon, sighing in his turn; **und** both creatures hid their faces in their paws.

"**Und wie** many hours a day did you do lessons?" said Alice, in a hurry to change the subject.

"Ten hours the first day," said the Mock Turtle: "nine the next, **und** so on."

"What a curious plan!" exclaimed Alice.

"That's the reason **sie** are called lessons," the Gryphon remarked: "**weil sie** lessen from day to day."

This was quite a new idea to Alice, **und** she thought it over a little before **sie machte** her next remark. "Then the eleventh day must have been a holiday?"

"Of course it was," said the Mock Turtle.

"**Und wie haben** you manage on the twelfth?" Alice went on eagerly.

"That's enough about lessons," the Gryphon interrupted in a **sehr** decided tone: "tell her something about the games now."

# weeve
## Chapter 9

| German | Pronunciation | English |
|---|---|---|
| die Welt | diː velt | the world |
| spielten | ʃpiːltən | played |
| schon fast | ʃon fast | almost |
| immer | imə | always |
| sie brauchen | ziː prauhxən | they need |
| damit zu beginnen | daːmit t͡su beːginən | to start with |
| immer kam | imər kam | always came |
| sie pflegten | ziː p͡flektən | they used to |
| Geschichte | geːʃixtə | story |
| sie könnten | ziː køntən | you could |

# 10
# THE LOBSTER QUADRILLE

"We have two very different ways of going about getting better in another language, you can acquire language, you can learn a language and they're very different processes." – Stephen Krashen, expert in linguistics at University of Southern California

The Mock Turtle sighed deeply, **und** drew the back of one flapper across his eyes. He looked at Alice, **und** tried to speak, **aber** for a minute **oder** two sobs choked his voice. "Same as **als** he had a bone in his throat," said the Gryphon: **und** it <u>**begann**</u> shaking him **und** punching him in the back. At last the Mock Turtle recovered his voice, **und**, **mit** tears running down his cheeks, he went on again:—

"**Sie können** not have lived much under the sea—" ("**Ich** haven't," said Alice)— "**und** perhaps **Sie wurden** never even introduced to a lobster—" (Alice began to say "**Ich** once tasted—" **aber** checked herself hastily, **und** said "No, never") "—so **sie können** have no idea what a delightful thing a Lobster Quadrille is!"

"No, indeed," said Alice. "What sort of a dance is it?"

"Why," said the Gryphon, "you first form **in** a line along the sea-shore—"

"Two lines!" cried the Mock Turtle. "Seals, turtles, salmon, **und** so on; then, **wann** you have cleared all the jelly-fish out of the way—"

"That generally <u>**braucht**</u> some time," interrupted the Gryphon.

69

"—you advance twice—"

"Each **mit** a lobster as a partner!" cried the Gryphon.

"Of course," the Mock Turtle said: "advance twice, set to partners—"

"—change lobsters, **und** retire in same order," continued the Gryphon.

"Then, **wissen Sie**," the Mock Turtle went on, "you throw the—"

"The lobsters!" shouted the Gryphon, **mit** a bound **in** the air.

"—as far out to sea as you can—"

"Swim after **ihnen**!" screamed the Gryphon.

"Turn a somersault in the sea!" cried the Mock Turtle, capering wildly about.

"Change lobsters again!" yelled the Gryphon at the top of its voice.

"Back to land again, **und** that's all the first figure," said the Mock Turtle, suddenly dropping his voice; **und** the two creatures, **die** had been jumping about like mad things all this time, sat down again **sehr** sadly **und** quietly, **und** looked at Alice.

"It must be a **sehr** pretty dance," said Alice timidly.

"**Möchten Sie sehen**, a little of it?" said the Mock Turtle.

"**Sehr** much indeed," said Alice.

"Come, let's try the first figure!" said the Mock Turtle to the Gryphon. "**Wir können** do without lobsters, **wissen Sie**. Which shall sing?"

"Oh, you sing," said the Gryphon. "**Ich** have forgotten the words."

So **sie** began solemnly dancing round **und** round Alice, every now **und** then treading on her toes **wenn sie** passed too close, **und** waving their forepaws to mark **die Zeit**, while the Mock Turtle sang this, **sehr** slowly **und** sadly:—

"Will you walk a little faster?" said a whiting to a snail. "There's a porpoise close behind us, **und** he's treading on my tail. See **wie** eagerly the lobsters **und** the turtles all advance! **Sie** are waiting on the shingle—will you come **und** join the dance? Will you, won't you, will you, won't you, will you join the dance? Will you, won't you, will you, won't you, won't you join the dance?

"**Sie können** really have no notion **wie** delightful it will be **wenn**

**sie** take us up **und** throw us, **mit** the lobsters, out to sea!"

**Aber** the snail replied "Too far, too far!" **und** gave a look askance— Said he thanked the whiting kindly, <u>**aber er wollte**</u> not join the dance. Wouldn't, couldn't, wouldn't, couldn't, wouldn't join the dance. Wouldn't, couldn't, wouldn't, couldn't, couldn't join the dance.

"What matters it **wie** far **wir** go?" his scaly friend replied. "**Es gibt** another shore, **wissen Sie**, upon the other side. The further off from England the nearer is to France— Then turn not pale, beloved snail, **aber** come **und** join the dance. Will you, won't you, will you, won't you, will you join the dance? Will you, won't you, will you, won't you, won't you join the dance?"

"Thank you, it's a **sehr** interesting dance to watch," said Alice, feeling **sehr** glad that it was over at last: "**und ich** do so like that curious song about the whiting!"

"Oh, as to the whiting," said the Mock Turtle, "they—you have seen **sie**, of course?"

"Yes," said Alice, "**Ich** have **häufig** seen **sie** at dinn—" she checked herself hastily.

"<u>**Ich weiß nicht wo**</u> Dinn may be," said the Mock Turtle, "**aber falls** you have seen **sie** so **häufig**, of course **wissen Sie** what **sie** are like."

"**Ich** believe so," Alice replied thoughtfully. "**Sie** have their tails in their mouths—and **sie** are all over crumbs."

"You are wrong about the crumbs," said the Mock Turtle: "crumbs would all wash off in the sea. **Aber sie** have their tails in their mouths; **und** the reason is—" here the Mock Turtle yawned **und** shut his eyes.— "Tell her about the reason **und** all that," he said to the Gryphon.

"The reason is," said the Gryphon, "that **sie würden** go **mit** the lobsters to the dance. So **sie** got thrown out to sea. So **sie** had to fall a long **Weg**. So **sie** got their tails fast in their mouths. So **sie** couldn't get **sie** out again. That's all."

"Thank you," said Alice, "it's **sehr** interesting. **Ich** never knew so much about a whiting before."

"**Ich kann** tell you more **als** that, **wenn Sie möchten**" said the Gryphon. "Do you know why it's called a whiting?"

"**Ich** never thought about it," said Alice. "Why?"

"It does the boots **und** shoes," the Gryphon replied **sehr** solemnly.

Alice was thoroughly puzzled. "Does the boots **und** shoes!" she

71

repeated in a wondering tone.

"Why, what are your shoes done **mit**?" said the Gryphon. "**Ich** mean, what makes **sie** so shiny?"

Alice looked down at **sie**, **und** considered a little before she gave her answer. "**Sie** are done **mit** blacking, **ich** believe."

"Boots **und** shoes under the sea," the Gryphon went on in a deep voice, "are done **mit** a whiting. Now **wissen Sie**."

"**Und** what are they made of?" Alice asked in a tone of great curiosity.

"Soles **und** eels, of course," the Gryphon replied rather impatiently: "any shrimp could have told you that."

"**Wenn** I'd been the whiting," said Alice, whose thoughts were still running on the song, "I'd have said to the porpoise, 'Keep back, please: **wir** do not want you **mit** us!'"

"**Sie sind** obliged to have him **mit ihnen**," the Mock Turtle said: "no wise fish would go anywhere without a porpoise."

"Wouldn't it really?" said Alice in a tone of great surprise.

"Of course not," said the Mock Turtle: "why, **wenn** a fish came to me, **und** told me he was going a journey, **ich sollte** say '**Mit** what porpoise?'"

"Do not you mean 'purpose'?" said Alice.

"**Ich** mean what **ich** say," the Mock Turtle replied in an offended tone. **Und** the Gryphon added "Come, let's hear some of your adventures."

"**Ich** could tell you my adventures—beginning from this morning," said Alice a little timidly: "**aber** it's no use going back to yesterday, **weil ich** was a different person then."

"Explain all that," said the Mock Turtle.

"No, no! The adventures first," said the Gryphon in an impatient tone: "explanations take such a dreadful time."

So Alice began telling **ihnen** her adventures from **die Zeit**, **als** she first saw the White Rabbit. She was a little nervous about it just at first, the two creatures got so close to her, one on each side, **und** opened their eyes **und** mouths so **sehr** wide, **aber** she gained courage as she went on. Her listeners were perfectly quiet till she got to the part about her repeating "You are old, Father William," to the Caterpillar, **und** the words all coming different, **und** then the Mock Turtle drew a long breath, **und** said "That's **sehr** curious."

"It's all about as curious as it can be," said the Gryphon.

"It all came different!" the Mock Turtle repeated thoughtfully. "**Ich** should like to hear her try **und** repeat something now. Tell her to begin." He looked at the Gryphon as **ob** he thought it had some kind of authority over Alice.

"Stand up **und** repeat ''Tis the voice of the sluggard,''" said the Gryphon.

"**Wie** the creatures order one about, **und** make one repeat lessons!"

thought Alice; "**Ich** might as **gut** be at school at once." However, she got up, **und** began to repeat it, **aber** her head was so full of the Lobster Quadrille, that she hardly knew what she was saying, **und** the words came **sehr** queer indeed:—

> *"'Tis the voice of the Lobster;*
> *ich heard him declare,*
>
> *"You have baked me too brown, **ich** must sugar my hair."*
>
> *As a duck **mit** its eyelids, so he **mit** his nose*
>
> *Trims his belt **und** his buttons, **und** turns out his toes."*
>
> ***Wenn** the sands are all dry, he is gay as a lark,*
>
> ***Und** will talk in contemptuous tones of the Shark,*
>
> ***Aber**, wann the tide rises **und** sharks are around,*
>
> *His voice has a timid **und** tremulous sound.*

"That's different from what

was ich sagte als ich was a child," said the Gryphon.

"**Gut, ich** never heard it before," said the Mock Turtle; "**aber** it sounds uncommon nonsense."

Alice said nothing; she had sat down **mit** her face in her hands, wondering **wenn** anything would ever happen in a natural **Weg** again.

73

"**Ich möchte** have it explained," said the Mock Turtle.

"She can't explain it," said the Gryphon hastily. "Go on **mit** the next verse."

"**Aber** about his toes?" the Mock Turtle persisted. "**Wie** could he turn **sie** out **mit** his nose, **wissen Sie**?"

"It's the first position in dancing." Alice said; **aber** was dreadfully puzzled by the whole thing, **und** longed to change the subject.

"Go on **mit** the next verse," the Gryphon repeated impatiently: "it begins '**Ich** passed by his garden.'"

Alice did not dare to disobey, though she felt sure it would all come wrong, **und** she went on in a trembling voice:—

"**Ich** passed by his garden, **und** marked, **mit** one eye, **Wie** the Owl **und** the Panther were sharing a pie—"

The Panther took pie-crust, **und** gravy, **und** meat, While the Owl had the dish as its share of the treat. **Als** the pie was all finished, the Owl, as a boon, Was kindly permitted to pocket the spoon: While the Panther received knife **und** fork **mit** a growl, **Und** concluded the banquet—

"What is the use of repeating all that stuff," the Mock Turtle interrupted, "**wenn** you do not explain it as you go on? It's by far the most confusing thing **ich** ever heard!"

"Yes, **ich** think you'd better leave off," said the Gryphon: **und** Alice was only too glad **zu machen** so.

"Shall **wir** try another figure of the Lobster Quadrille?" the Gryphon went on. "**Oder möchten Sie** the Mock Turtle to sing you a song?"

"Oh, a song, please, **wenn** the Mock Turtle would be so kind," Alice replied, so eagerly that the Gryphon said, in a rather offended tone, "Hm! No accounting for tastes! Sing her 'Turtle Soup,' will you, old fellow?"

The Mock Turtle sighed deeply, **und** began, in a voice sometimes choked **mit** sobs, to sing this:—

> *"Beautiful Soup, so rich **und** green,*
>
> *Waiting in a hot tureen!*
>
> ***Wer** for such dainties wouldn't stoop?*
>
> *Soup of the evening, beautiful*

*Soup!*

*Soup of the evening, beautiful Soup!*

*Beau—ootiful Soo—oop!*

*Beau—ootiful Soo—oop!*

*Soo—oop of the e—e—evening, Beautiful, beautiful Soup!*

*"Beautiful Soup!* **Wer** *cares for fish,*

*Game,* **oder** *any other dish?*

**Wer** *wouldn't give all else for* **zwei** *pennyworth only of beautiful Soup?*

*Pennyworth only of beautiful Soup?*

*Beau—ootiful Soo—oop!*

*Beau—ootiful Soo—oop!*

*Soo—oop of the e—e—evening, Beautiful, beauti—FUL SOUP!"*

"Chorus again!" cried the Gryphon, **und** the Mock Turtle had just begun to repeat it, **als** a cry of "The trial's beginning!" was heard in the distance.

"Come on!" cried the Gryphon, **und**, **nahm** Alice by the hand, it hurried off, without waiting for the end of the song.

"What trial is it?" Alice panted as she ran; **aber** the Gryphon only answered "Come on!" **und** ran the faster, while more **und** more faintly came, carried on the breeze that followed **ihnen**, the melancholy words:—

*"Soo—oop of the e—e—evening, Beautiful, beautiful Soup!"*

## weeve
### Chapter 10

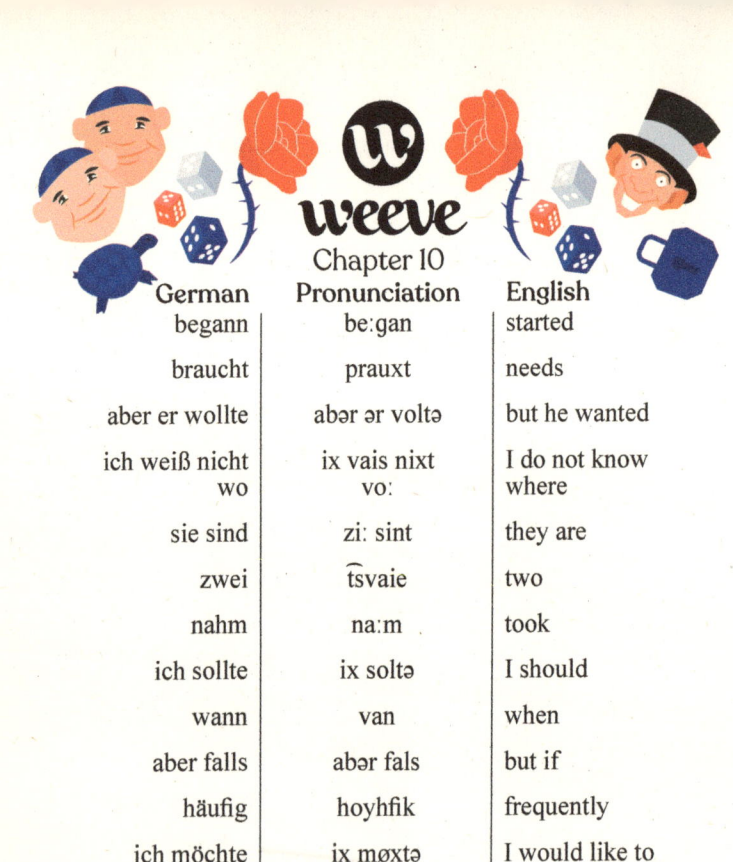

| German | Pronunciation | English |
|---|---|---|
| begann | beːgan | started |
| braucht | prauxt | needs |
| aber er wollte | abər ər voltə | but he wanted |
| ich weiß nicht wo | ix vais nixt voː | I do not know where |
| sie sind | ziː sint | they are |
| zwei | t͡svaie | two |
| nahm | naːm | took |
| ich sollte | ix soltə | I should |
| wann | van | when |
| aber falls | abər fals | but if |
| häufig | hoyhfik | frequently |
| ich möchte | ix møxtə | I would like to |

# 11

## WHO STOLE THE TARTS?

"We have two very different ways of going about getting better in another language, you can acquire language, you can learn a language and they're very different processes." – Stephen Krashen, expert in linguistics at University of Southern California

The King **und** Queen of Hearts were seated on their throne **als sie** arrived, **mit** a great crowd assembled about them—all sorts of little birds **und** beasts, as **gut** as the whole pack of cards: the Knave was standing before **ihnen**, in chains, **mit** a soldier on each side to guard him; **und** near the King was the White Rabbit, **mit** a trumpet in one hand, **und** a scroll of parchment in the other. In the **ganz** middle of the court was a table, **mit** a large dish of tarts upon it: **sie** looked so good, that it made Alice quite hungry to look at them— "**Ich** wish they'd get the trial done," she thought, "**und** hand round the refreshments!"

**Aber** there seemed to be no chance of this, so she began looking at everything about her, to pass away **die Zeit**.

Alice had never been in a court of justice before, **aber** she had read <u>**darüber**</u> in books, **und** she was quite pleased **zu** <u>**finden**</u> that **sie kannte** the name of nearly everything there. "That's the judge," she said to herself, "<u>**wegen**</u> his great wig."

The judge, <u>**übrigens**</u>, was the King; **und** as he wore his crown over the wig, (look at the frontispiece **wenn** you want **zu sehen**, **wie** he did it,) he did not look at all comfortable, **und** it was

77

certainly not becoming.

"**Und** that's the jury-box," thought Alice, "**und** those twelve creatures," (she was obliged to say "creatures," **wie Sie sehen**,, **weil** some of **ihnen** were animals, **und** some were birds,) "**Ich** suppose **sie** are the jurors." She said this last word **zwei oder** three **Mal** over to herself, being rather proud of it: for she thought, **und** rightly too, that **sehr** few little girls of her age knew the meaning of it at all. However, "jury-men" would have done just as **gut**.

The twelve jurors were all writing **sehr** busily on slates. "What are **sie** doing?" Alice whispered to the Gryphon. "**Sie** can't have anything to put down yet, before the trial's begun."

"**Sie** are putting down their names," the Gryphon whispered in reply, "for fear **sie werden** forget **sie** before the end of the trial."

"Stupid things!" Alice began in a loud, indignant voice, **aber** she stopped hastily, for the White Rabbit cried out, "Silence in the court!" **und** the King put on his spectacles **und** looked anxiously round, **um herauszufinden wer** was talking.

Alice could see, as **gut** as **ob** she were looking over their shoulders, that all the jurors were writing down "stupid things!" on their slates, **und** she could even make out that one of **ihnen** did not know **wie** to spell "stupid," **und** that he had to ask his neighbour to tell him. "A nice muddle their slates will be in before the trial's over!" thought Alice.

One of the jurors had a pencil that squeaked. This of course, Alice couldn't stand, **und** she went round the court **und** got behind him, **und sehr** soon found an opportunity **um** it <u>**wegzunehmen**</u> She did it so quickly that the poor little juror (it was Bill, the Lizard) couldn't make out at all what had become of it; so, after hunting all about for it, he was obliged to write **mit** one finger for the rest of the day; **und** this was of **sehr** little use, as it left no mark on the slate.

"Herald, read the accusation!" said the King.

On this the White Rabbit blew three blasts on the trumpet, **und** then unrolled the parchment scroll, **und** read as follows:—

"The Queen of Hearts, **sie machte** some tarts, All on a summer day: The Knave of Hearts, he stole those tarts, **Und** took **sie** quite away!"

"Consider your verdict," the King said to the jury.

"Not yet, not yet!" the Rabbit hastily interrupted. "There's a great deal to come before that!"

"Call the first witness," said the King; **und** the White Rabbit blew three blasts on the trumpet, **und** called out, "First witness!"

The first witness was the Hatter. He came in **mit** a teacup in one hand **und** a piece of bread-and-butter in the other. "**Ich** beg pardon, your Majesty," he began, "for bringing these in: **aber ich** had not quite finished my tea **als ich** was sent for."

"You ought to have finished," said the King. "**Wann** did you begin?"

The Hatter looked at the March Hare, **der** had followed him **in** the court, arm-in-arm **mit** the Dormouse. "Fourteenth of March, **ich** think it was," he said.

"Fifteenth," said the March Hare.

"Sixteenth," added the Dormouse.

"Write that down," the King said to the jury, **und** the jury eagerly wrote down all three dates on their slates, **und** then added **sie** up, **und** reduced the answer to shillings **und** pence.

"Take off your hat," the King said to the Hatter.

"It isn't mine," said the Hatter.

"Stolen!" the King exclaimed, turning to the jury, **die** instantly made a memorandum of the fact.

"**Ich** keep **sie** to sell," the Hatter added as an explanation; "**Ich** have none of my own. I'm a hatter."

Here the Queen put on her spectacles, **und** began staring at the Hatter, **der** turned pale **und** fidgeted.

"Give your evidence," said the King; "**und** do not be nervous, **oder ich** will have you executed on the spot."

This did not seem to encourage the witness at all: he kept shifting from one foot to the other, looking uneasily at the Queen, **und** in his confusion he bit a large piece out of his teacup instead of the bread-and-butter.

Just at this moment Alice felt a **sehr** curious sensation, which puzzled her a good deal until <u>**sie fand heraus**</u> what it was: she was beginning to grow larger again, **und** she thought at first **sie würde** get up **und** leave the court; **aber** on second thoughts she decided to remain **wo** she was as long as **es gab** room for her.

"**Ich** wish **du würdest** not squeeze so." said the Dormouse, **der** was sitting next to her. "**Ich kann** hardly breathe."

"**Ich** can't help it," said Alice **sehr** meekly: "I'm growing."

"You have no right to grow here," said the Dormouse.

"Do not talk nonsense," said Alice more boldly: "**Sie wissen** you

79

are growing too."

"Yes, **aber ich** grow at a reasonable pace," said the Dormouse: "not in that ridiculous fashion." **Und** he got up **sehr** sulkily **und** crossed over to the other side of the court.

All this time the Queen had never left off staring at the Hatter, **und**, just as the Dormouse crossed the court, she said to one of the officers of the court, "Bring me the list of the singers in the last concert!"

on which the wretched Hatter trembled so, that he shook both his shoes off.

"Give your evidence," the King repeated angrily, "**oder ich** will have you executed, whether you are nervous **oder** not."

"I'm a poor man, your Majesty," the Hatter began, in a trembling voice, "—and **ich** had not begun my tea—not above a week **oder** so—and what **mit** the bread-and-butter getting so thin—and the twinkling of the tea—"

"The twinkling of the what?" said the King.

"It began **mit** the tea," the Hatter replied.

"Of course twinkling begins **mit** a T!" said the King sharply. "Do you take me for a dunce? Go on!"

"I'm a poor man," the Hatter went on, "**und** most things twinkled after that—only the March Hare said—"

"**Ich** did not!" the March Hare interrupted in a great hurry.

"You did!" said the Hatter.

"**Ich** deny it!" said the March Hare.

"He denies it," said the King: "leave out that part."

"**Gut**, at any rate, the Dormouse said—" the Hatter went on, looking anxiously round **um zu sehen, ob er würde** deny it too: **aber** the Dormouse denied nothing, being fast asleep.

"After that," continued the Hatter, "**Ich** cut some more bread-and-butter—"

"**Aber** what did the Dormouse say?" one of the jury asked.

"That **ich** can't remember," said the Hatter.

"You must remember," remarked the King, "**oder ich** will have you executed."

The miserable Hatter dropped his teacup **und** bread-and-butter,

**und** went down on one knee. "I'm a poor man, your Majesty," he began.

"You are a **sehr** poor speaker," said the King.

Here one of the guinea-pigs cheered, **und** was immediately suppressed by the officers of the court. (As that is rather a hard word, **ich** will just explain to you **wie** it was done. **Sie** had a large canvas bag, which tied up at the mouth **mit** strings: **in** this **sie** slipped the guinea-pig, head first, **und** then sat upon it.)

"I'm glad **ich habe gesehen** that done," thought Alice. "**Ich** have so **häufig** read in the newspapers, at the end of trials, "**Es gab** some attempts at applause, which was immediately suppressed by the officers of the court," **und ich** never understood what it meant till now."

"**Wenn** that's all **was Sie wissen** about it, **Sie können** stand down," continued the King.

"**Ich** can't go no lower," said the Hatter: "I'm on the floor, as it is."

"Then **Sie können** sit down," the King replied.

Here the other guinea-pig cheered, **und** was suppressed.

"Come, that finished the guinea-pigs!" thought Alice. "Now **wir** shall get on better."

"I'd rather finish my tea," said the Hatter, **mit** an anxious look at the Queen, **die** was reading the list of singers.

"**Sie können** go," said the King, **und** the Hatter hurriedly left the court, without even waiting to put his shoes on.

"—and just take his head off outside," the Queen added to one of the officers: **aber** the Hatter was out of sight before the officer could get to the door.

"Call the next witness!" said the King.

The next witness was the Duchess's cook. She carried the pepper-box in her hand, **und** Alice guessed **wer** it was, even before she got **in** the court, by **der Art, wie die Menschen** near the door began sneezing all at once.

"Give your evidence," said the King.

"Sha'n't," said the cook.

The King looked anxiously at the White Rabbit, **das** said in a low voice, "Your Majesty must cross-examine this witness."

"**Gut, wenn ich** must, **ich** must," the King said, **mit** a melancholy air, **und**, after folding his arms **und** frowning at the cook till his eyes were nearly out of sight, he said in a deep voice, "What are tarts made of?"

"Pepper, mostly," said the cook.

"Treacle," said a sleepy voice behind her.

"Collar that Dormouse," the Queen shrieked out. "Behead that Dormouse! Turn that Dormouse out of court! Suppress him! Pinch him! Off **mit** his whiskers!"

For some minutes the whole court was in confusion, getting the Dormouse turned out, **und**, als sie had settled down again, the cook had disappeared.

"Never mind!" said the King, **mit** an air of great relief. "Call the next witness." **Und** he added in an undertone to the Queen, "Really, my dear, you must cross-examine the next witness. It quite makes my forehead ache!"

Alice watched the White Rabbit as he fumbled over the list, feeling **sehr** curious **um zu sehen** what the next witness would be like, "—for **sie** haven't got much evidence yet," she said to herself. Imagine her surprise, **als** the White Rabbit read out, at the top of his shrill little voice, the name "Alice!"

# weeve
## Chapter 11

| German | Pronunciation | English |
|---|---|---|
| darüber | daːrybə | about that |
| finden | findən | find |
| wegen | veːgən | because |
| übrigens | ypriːgəns | by the way |
| wegzunehmen | vekt͡suːneːmən | to take away |
| sie fand heraus | ziː fand heːraus | she found out |
| was sie wissen | vas siː visən | what you know |
| sie kannte | ziː kantə | she knew |
| mal | mal | times |
| ich habe gesehen | ix haːbe geːseːən | I have seen |
| sie können | ziː kønən | you can |
| und | unt | and |

# 12

## ALICE'S EVIDENCE

"Language acquisition does not require extensive use of conscious grammatical rules, and does not require tedious drill." – Stephen Krashen, expert in linguistics at University of Southern California

"Here!" cried Alice, quite forgetting in the flurry of the moment **wie** large she had grown in the last few minutes, **und** she jumped up in such a hurry that she tipped over the jury-box **mit** the edge of her skirt, upsetting all the jurymen on to the heads of the crowd below, **und** there **sie** lay sprawling about, reminding her **sehr** much of a globe of goldfish she had accidentally upset the week before.

"Oh, **ich** beg your pardon!" she exclaimed in a tone of great dismay, **und** began picking **sie** up again as quickly as she could, for the accident of the goldfish kept running in her head, **und** she had a vague sort of idea that **sie** must be collected at once **und** put back **in** the jury-box, **oder sie würden** die.

"The trial cannot proceed," said the King in a **sehr** grave voice, "until all the jurymen are back in their proper places— all," **er** repeated **mit** great emphasis, **sah** hard at Alice as **er** said so.

Alice looked at the jury-box, **und** saw that, in her haste, she had put the Lizard in head downwards, **und** the poor little thing was waving its tail about in a melancholy **Weg**, being quite unable to move. She soon got it out again, **und** put it right; "not that it signifies much," she said to herself; "**Ich sollte** think it would be quite as much use in the trial one **Weg** up as the other."

As soon as the jury had a little recovered from the shock of being upset, **und** their slates **und** pencils had been found **und** handed back to **ihnen**, **sie** set **begannen sehr** diligently to write out a **Geschichte** of the accident, all except the Lizard, **die** seemed too much overcome **zu machen** anything **aber** sit **mit** its mouth open, gazing up **in** the roof of the court.

"What **wissen Sie** about this business?" the King said to Alice.

"Nothing," said Alice.

"Nothing whatever?" persisted the King.

"Nothing whatever," said Alice.

"That's **sehr** important," the King said, turning to the jury. **Sie begannen** to write this down on their slates, **als** the White Rabbit interrupted: "Un important, your Majesty means, of course," **er** said in a **sehr** respectful tone, **aber** frowning **und making** faces at him as **er** spoke.

"Un important, of course, **ich** meant," the King hastily said, **und** went on to himself in an undertone,

"important—unimportant—unimportant—important—" as **ob er** were trying which word sounded best.

Some of the jury wrote it down "important," **und** some "unimportant." Alice could see this, as she was near enough to look over their slates; "**aber** it doesn't matter a bit," she thought to herself.

At this moment the King, **der** had been for some time busily writing in his note-book, cackled out "Silence!" **und** read out from his book, "Rule Forty-two. All persons more **als** a mile high to leave the court."

Everybody looked at Alice.

"I'm not a mile high," said Alice.

"You are," said the King.

"Nearly **zwei** miles high," added the Queen.

"**Gut**, **ich** sha not go, at any rate," said Alice: "besides, that's not a regular rule: you invented it just now."

"It's the oldest rule in the book," said the King.

"Then it ought to be Number One," said Alice.

The King turned pale, **und** shut his note-book hastily. "Consider your verdict," **er** said to the jury, in a low, trembling voice.

"There's more evidence to come yet, please your Majesty," said the White Rabbit, jumping up in a great hurry; "this paper has just been picked up."

"What's in it?" said the Queen.

"**Ich** haven't opened it yet," said the White Rabbit, "**aber** it seems to be a letter, written by the prisoner to—to somebody."

"It must have been that," said the King, "unless it was written to nobody, which isn't usual, **wissen Sie**."

"**Wen** is it directed to?" said one of the jurymen.

"It isn't directed at all," said the White Rabbit; "in fact, there's nothing written on the outside." **Er** unfolded the paper as **er** spoke, **und** added "It isn't a letter, after all: it's a set of verses."

"Are **sie** in the prisoner's handwriting?" asked another of the jurymen.

"No, **sie** are not," said the White Rabbit, "**und** that's the queerest thing about it." (The jury all looked puzzled.)

"**Er** must have imitated somebody else's hand," said the King. (The jury all brightened up again.)

"Please your Majesty," said the Knave, "**Ich** did not write it, **und sie** can't prove **ich** did: there's no name signed at the end."

"**Wenn** you did not sign it," said the King, "that only makes the matter worse. You must have meant some mischief, **oder** else you'd have signed your name like an honest man."

**Es gab** a general clapping of hands at this: it was the first really clever thing the King had said that day.

"That proves his guilt," said the Queen.

"It proves nothing of the sort!" said Alice. "Why, you do not even know what **sie** are about!"

"Read **sie**," said the King.

The White Rabbit put on his spectacles. "**Wo** shall **ich** begin, please your Majesty?" **er** asked.

"Begin at the beginning," the King said gravely, "**und** go on till you come to the end: then stop."

These were the verses the White Rabbit read:—

"**Sie** told me you had been to her, **Und** mentioned me to him: She gave me a good character, **Aber** said **ich** couldn't swim.

**Er** sent **ihnen** word **ich** had not gone (**Wir wissen** it to be true): **Wenn sie sollte** push the matter on, What would become of you?

**Ich** gave her one, **sie** gave him **zwei**, You gave us three **oder** more; **Sie** all returned from him to you, Though **sie waren** mine before.

**Wenn ich oder sie sollte** chance to be Involved in this affair, **Er** trusts to you to set **sie** free, Exactly as **wir** were.

My notion was that you had been (Before she had this fit) An obstacle that came between Him, **und** ourselves, **und** it.

Do not let him know **sie mochte sie** best, For this must ever be A secret, kept from all the rest, Between yourself **und** me."

"That's the most important piece of evidence **wir** have heard yet," said the King, rubbing his hands; "so now let the jury—"

"**Wenn** any one of **ihnen** can explain it," said Alice, (she had grown so large in the last few minutes that she was not a bit afraid of interrupting him,) "**Ich** will give him sixpence. **Ich** do not believe there's an atom of meaning in it."

The jury all wrote down on their slates, "She doesn't believe there's an atom of meaning in it," **aber** none of **ihnen** attempted to explain the paper.

"**Wenn** there's no meaning in it," said the King, "that saves **eine Welt** of trouble, **wissen Sie**, as **wir brauchen** not try **finden** any. **Und** yet **ich** do not know," **er** went on, spreading out the verses on his knee, **und sah** at **sie mit** one eye; "**Ich** seem **um zu sehen** some meaning in **sie**, after all. — said **ich** couldn't swim —" you can't swim, can you?" **er** added, turning to the Knave.

The Knave shook his head sadly. "**Sehe ich** like it **aus**? "**er** said. (Which **er** certainly did not, being made entirely of cardboard.)

"All right, so far," said the King, **und er** went on muttering over the verses to himself: "'**Wir wissen** it to be true —' that's the jury, of course— '**Ich** gave her one, **sie** gave him **zwei** —' why, that must be what **er** did **mit** the tarts, you know—"

"**Aber**, it goes on 'sie all returned from him to you,'" said Alice.

"Why, there **sie** are!" said the King triumphantly, pointing to the tarts on the table. "Nothing can be clearer **als** that. Then again— 'before she had this fit —' you never had fits, my dear, **ich** think?" **er** said to the Queen.

"Never!" said the Queen furiously, throwing an inkstand at the Lizard as she spoke. (The unfortunate little Bill had left off writing on his slate **mit** one finger, as **er fand heraus** it made no mark; **doch er** now hastily began again, the ink **zu benutzten**, that was trickling down his face, as long as it lasted.)

"Then the words do not fit you," said the King, **sah** round the court **mit** a smile. **Es gab** a dead silence.

"It's a pun!" the King added in an offended tone, **und** everybody laughed, "Let the jury consider their verdict," the King said, for about the twentieth time that day.

"No, no!" said the Queen. "Sentence first—verdict afterwards."

"Stuff **und** nonsense!" said Alice loudly. "The idea of having the sentence first!"

"Hold your tongue!" said the Queen, turning purple.

"**Ich** won't!" said Alice.

"Off **mit** her head!" the Queen shouted at the top of her voice. Nobody moved.

"**Wer** cares for you?" said Alice, (she had grown to her full size by this time.) "You are nothing **aber** a pack of cards!"

At this the whole pack rose up **in** the air, **und** came flying down upon her: she gave a little scream, half of fright **und** half of anger, **und** tried to beat **sie** off, **und** found herself lying on the bank, **mit** her head in the lap of her sister, **die** was gently brushing away some dead leaves that had fluttered down from the trees upon her face.

"Wake up, Alice dear!" said her sister; "Why, what a long sleep you have had!"

"Oh, **ich** have had such a curious dream!" said Alice, **und** she told her sister, as **gut** as she could remember **sie**, all these strange Adventures of hers that you have just been reading about; **und wann** she had finished, her sister kissed her, **und** said, "It was a curious dream, dear, certainly: **aber** now run in to your tea; it's getting late." So Alice got up **und** ran off, thinking **während** she ran, as **gut** she might, what a wonderful dream it had been.

**Aber** her sister sat still just as she left her, leaning her head on her hand, watching the setting sun, **und** thinking of little Alice **und** all her wonderful Adventures, till she too began dreaming after a fashion, **und** this was her dream:—

First, she dreamed of little Alice herself, **und** once again the tiny hands were clasped upon her knee, **und** the bright eager eyes **schaute** up **in** hers—she could hear the **genauen** tones of her voice, **und** see that queer little toss of her head to keep back the wandering hair that would always get **in** her eyes—and still as she listened, **oder** seemed to listen, the whole place around her became alive **mit** the strange creatures of her little sister's dream.

The long grass rustled at her feet as the White Rabbit hurried by—the frightened Mouse splashed <u>**seinen Weg**</u> through the neighbouring pool—she could hear the rattle of the teacups as the March Hare **und** his friends shared their never-ending meal, **und** the shrill voice of the Queen ordering off her unfortunate guests to execution—once more the pig-baby was sneezing on the Duchess's knee, **während** plates **und** dishes crashed around it—once more the shriek of the Gryphon, the squeaking of the Lizard's slate-pencil, **und** the choking of the suppressed guinea-pigs, filled the air, mixed up **mit** the distant sobs of the miserable Mock Turtle.

So she sat on, **mit** closed eyes, **und** half believed herself in Wonderland, though **sie wusste** she had **aber** to open **sie** again, **und** all would change to dull reality—the grass would be only rustling in the wind, **und** the pool rippling to the waving of the reeds—the rattling teacups would change to tinkling sheep-bells, **und** the Queen's shrill cries to the voice of the shepherd boy— and the sneeze of the baby, the shriek of the Gryphon, **und** all the other queer noises, would change (**sie wusste**) to the confused clamour of the busy farm-yard—while the lowing of the cattle in the distance would take the place of the Mock Turtle's heavy sobs.

Lastly, she pictured to herself **wie** this same little sister of hers would, in the after-time, be herself a grown woman; **und wie sie würde** keep, through all her riper years, the simple **und** loving heart of her childhood: **und wie sie würde** gather about her other little children, **und** make their eyes bright **und** eager **mit** many a strange tale, perhaps even **mit** the dream of Wonderland of long ago: **und wie** she would feel **mit** all their simple sorrows, **und** find a pleasure in all their simple joys, remembering her own child-life, **und** the happy summer days.

# weeve

## Chapter 12

| German | Pronunciation | English |
|---|---|---|
| begannen | beːganən | started very much |
| sehr | seːə | |
| und | und | and |
| wen | vən | whom |
| sie mochte sie | ziː moxtə siə | she liked them |
| eine Welt | aiənə velt | one world |
| doch er | dox ə | but he |
| während | veːrənt | while |
| schaute | ʃautə | looked |
| genauen | geːnauən | exact |
| seinen Weg | zaiənən vek | his way |

# BOOK II

# THROUGH THE LOOKING GLASS

# 1
# LOOKING GLASS HOUSE

Paul Nation, internationally recognized scholar in linguistics, proposes that we pick up most words after reading them in context 12 to 15 times. Sometimes we need only read a word 2 times, but sometimes it takes 30 times- it just depends.

One thing was certain, that the white kitten had had nothing **damit zu tun**:—it was the black kitten's fault entirely. For the white kitten had been having its face washed by the old cat for the last quarter of an hour (**und** bearing it pretty **gut**, considering); so **wie Sie sehen**, that it couldn't have had any hand in the mischief.

**Der Weg** Dinah washed her children's faces was this: first she held the poor thing down by its ear **mit** one paw, **und** then **mit** the other paw she rubbed its face all over, the wrong **Weg**, beginning at the nose: **und** just now, as **ich** said, she was hard at work on the white kitten, which was lying quite still **und** trying to purr—no doubt feeling that it was all meant for its good.

**Aber** the black kitten had been finished **mit** earlier in the afternoon, **und** so, **während** Alice was sitting curled up in a corner of the great arm-chair, half talking to herself **und** half asleep, the kitten had been having a grand game of romps **mit** the ball of worsted Alice had been trying to wind up, **und** had been rolling it up **und** down till it had all come undone again; **und** there it was, spread over the hearth-rug, all knots **und** tangles, **mit** the kitten running after its own tail in the middle.

"Oh, you wicked little thing!" cried Alice, catching up the kitten, **und** giving it a little kiss **zu machen** it understand that it was in disgrace. "Really, Dinah ought to have taught you better manners! You ought, Dinah, **du weißt** you ought!" she added, **sah** reproachfully at the old cat, **und** speaking **in** as cross a voice as she could manage—and then she scrambled back in the arm-chair, **nahm** the kitten **und** the worsted **mit** her, **und** began winding up the ball again. **Aber** she did not get on **sehr** fast, as she was talking **die ganze Zeit**, sometimes to the kitten, **und** sometimes to herself. Kitty sat **sehr** demurely on her knee, pretending to watch the progress of the winding, **und** now **und** then putting out one paw **und** gently touching the ball, as **ob** it would be glad to help, **wenn** it might.

"**Weißt du** what to-morrow is, Kitty?" Alice began. "You'd have guessed **wenn** you'd been up in the window **mit** me—only Dinah was **beorderte** to you tidy, so you couldn't. **Ich** was watching the boys getting in sticks for the bonfire—and it wants plenty of sticks, Kitty! Only it got so cold, **und** it snowed so, **sie** had to leave off. Never mind, Kitty, **wir** will go **und** see the bonfire to-morrow." Here Alice wound **zwei oder** three turns of the worsted round the kitten's neck, just **zu sehen**, **wie** it would look: this led to a scramble, in which the ball rolled down upon the floor, **und** yards **und** yards of it got unwound again.

"**Weißt du, ich** was so angry, Kitty," Alice went on as soon as **sie waren** comfortably settled again, "**als ich gesehen habe** all the mischief you had been doing, **ich** was **sehr** nearly opening the window, **und** putting you out **in** the snow! **Und** you'd have deserved it, you little mischievous darling! What have you got to say for yourself? Now do not interrupt me!" she went on, holding up one finger. "I'm going to tell you all your faults. Number one: you squeaked twice **während** Dinah was washing your face this morning. Now you can't deny it, Kitty: **ich** heard you! What's that you say?" (pretending that the kitten was speaking.) "Her paw went **in** your eye? **Gut**, that's your fault, for keeping your eyes open—if you'd shut **sie** tight up, it wouldn't have happened. Now do not make any more excuses, **aber** listen! Number **zwei**: you pulled Snowdrop away by the tail just as **ich** had put down the saucer of milk **vor** her! What, **du warst** thirsty, were you? **Woher weißt du dass** she was not thirsty too? Now for number three: you unwound every bit of the worsted während ich not geschaut habe!

"That's three faults, Kitty, **und** you haven't been punished for any of **ihnen** yet. **Weißt du** I'm saving up all your punishments for Wednesday week—Suppose **sie** had saved up all my punishments!" she went on, talking more to herself **als** the kitten. "What would **sie** do at the end of a year? **Ich würde** be sent to prison, **ich** suppose, **wann** the day came. Or—let me see— suppose each punishment was to be going without a dinner: then,

**wann** the miserable day came, **ich müsste** to go without fifty dinners at once! **Gut, ich würde** not mind that much! I'd far rather go without **sie als** eat **sie**!

"Do you hear the snow against the window-panes, Kitty? **Wie** nice **und** soft it sounds! Just as **ob** some one was kissing the window all over outside. **Ich** wonder **ob** the snow loves the trees **und** fields, that it kisses **sie** so gently? **Und** then it covers **sie** up snug, **weißt du, mit** a white quilt; **und** perhaps it says, 'Go to sleep, darlings, till the summer comes again.' **Und wenn sie** wake up in the summer, Kitty, **sie** dress themselves all in green, **und** dance about—whenever the wind blows—oh, that's **sehr** pretty!" cried Alice, dropping the ball of worsted to clap her hands. "**Und ich** do so wish it was true! I'm sure the woods look sleepy in the autumn, **wenn** the leaves are getting brown.

"Kitty, can you play chess? Now, do not smile, my dear, I'm asking it seriously. **Weil, wenn wir** were playing just now, you watched just as **ob** you understood it: **und wenn ich** said 'Check!' you purred! **Gut**, it was a nice check, Kitty, **und** really **ich** might have won, **wenn** it had not been for that nasty Knight, that came wiggling down among my pieces. Kitty, dear, let's pretend—" **Und** here **ich** wish **ich** could tell you half the things Alice used to say, beginning **mit** her favourite phrase "Let's pretend." She had had quite a long argument **mit** her sister only the day before— all **weil** Alice had begun **mit** "Let's pretend **wir** are kings **und** queens;" **und** her sister, **wer** liked being **sehr** exact, had argued that **sie** couldn't, **denn es gab** only **zwei** of **ihnen, und** Alice had been reduced at last to say, "**Gut, sie können** be one of **ihnen** then, **und ich** will be all the rest." **Und** once she had really frightened her old nurse by shouting suddenly in her ear, "Nurse! Do let's pretend that I'm a hungry hyaena, **und** you are a bone."

**Aber** this **nimmt** us away from Alice's speech to the kitten. "Let's pretend that you are the Red Queen, Kitty! **Weißt du, ich** think **wenn** you sat up **und** folded your arms, you'd look exactly like her. Now do try, there's a dear!" **Und** Alice got the Red Queen off the table, **und** set it up **vor** the kitten as a model for it to imitate: however, the thing did not succeed, principally, Alice said, **weil** the kitten wouldn't fold its arms properly. So, to punish it, she held it up to the **Spiegel**-glass, that it might see **wie** sulky it was— "**und wenn** you are not good directly," she added, "**Ich** will put you through **im Spiegel**-glass House. **Wie** would **dir gefallen** that?"

"Now, **wenn** you will only attend, Kitty, **und** not talk so much, **ich** will tell you all my ideas about **Spiegel**-glass House. First, there's the room **wo man kann** see through the glass—that's just the same as our drawing room, only the things go the other **Weg**. **Ich kann** see all of it **wenn ich** get upon a chair—all **aber** the bit behind the fireplace. Oh! **Ich** do so wish **ich** could see that

3

bit! **Ich möchte** so much **wissen** whether **sie** have a fire in the winter: you never can tell, **weißt du**, unless our fire smokes, **und** then smoke comes up in that room too—but that may be only pretence, **damit** it look as **ob sie** had a fire. **Gut** then, the books are something like our books, only the words go the wrong **Weg**; **ich weiß** that, **weil ich** have held up one of our books to the glass, **und** then **sie** hold up one in the other room.

"**Wie** would it **dir gefallen** to live in **Spiegel**-glass House, Kitty? **Ich** wonder **wenn** they'd give you milk in there? Perhaps **Spiegel**-glass milk isn't good to drink—But oh, Kitty! now **wir** come to the passage. **Sie können** just see a little peep of the passage in **Spiegel**-glass House, **wenn** you leave the door of our drawing-room wide open: **und** it's **sehr** like our passage as far as **man kann** see, only **weißt du** it may be quite different on beyond. Oh, Kitty! **wie** nice it would be **wenn wir** could only get through **im Spiegel**--glass House! I'm sure it's got, oh! such beautiful things in it! Let's pretend there's **einen Weg** of getting through **darin**, somehow, Kitty. Let's pretend the glass has got all soft like gauze, so that **wir können** get through. Why, it's turning **in** a sort of mist now, **ich** declare! It will be easy enough to get through—" She was up on the chimney-piece **während** she said this, though she hardly knew **wie** she had got there. **Und** certainly the glass was beginning to melt away, just like a bright silvery mist.

In another moment Alice was through the glass, **und** had jumped lightly down **in** the **Spiegel**-glass room. The **allererste** thing she did was **sehen** whether **es gab** a fire in the fireplace, **und** she was quite pleased **um herauszufinden** that **es gab** a real one, blazing away as brightly as the one she had left behind. "So **ich** shall be as warm here as **ich** was in the old room," thought Alice: "warmer, in fact, **weil** there will be no one here to scold me away from the fire. Oh, what fun it will be, **wenn sie sehen**, me through the glass in here, **und** can't get at me!"

Then she began **zu schauen** about, **und** noticed that what could be seen from the old room was quite common **und** uninteresting, **aber** that all the rest was as different as possible. For instance, the pictures on the wall next the fire seemed to be all alive, **und** the **sehr** clock on the chimney-piece (**wissen Sie, man kann** only see the back of it in the **Spiegel**-glass) had got the face of a little old man, **und** grinned at her.

"**Sie** do not keep this room so tidy as the other," Alice thought to herself, as she noticed several of the chessmen down in the hearth among the cinders: **aber** in another moment, **mit** a little "Oh!" of surprise, she was down on her hands **und** knees watching **sie**. The chessmen were walking about, **zwei und zwei**!

"Here are the Red King **und** the Red Queen," Alice said (in a whisper, for fear of frightening **sie**), "**und da sind** the White

King **und** the White Queen sitting on the edge of the shovel—and here are **zwei** castles walking arm in arm—I do not think **sie können** hear me," she went on, as she put her head closer down, "**und** I'm nearly sure **sie** can't see me. **Ich** feel somehow as **ob ich** were invisible—"

Here something began squeaking on the table behind Alice, **und** made her turn her head just in time **um zu sehen** one of the White Pawns roll over **und** begin kicking: she watched it **mit** great curiosity **um zu sehen** what would happen next.

"It is the voice of my child!" the White Queen cried out as she rushed past the King, so violently that she knocked him over among the cinders. "My precious Lily! My imperial kitten!" **und** she began scrambling wildly up the side of the fender.

"Imperial fiddlestick!" said the King, rubbing his nose, which had been hurt by the fall. **Er** had a right to be a little annoyed **mit** the Queen, for **er** was covered **mit** ashes from head to foot.

Alice was **sehr** anxious to be of use, **und**, as the poor little Lily was nearly screaming herself **in** a fit, she hastily picked up the Queen **und** set her on the table by the side of her noisy little daughter.

The Queen gasped, **und** sat down: the rapid journey through the air had quite **genommen** away her breath **und** for a minute **oder zwei** she could do nothing **aber** hug the little Lily in silence. As soon as she had recovered her breath a little, she called out to the White King, **der** was sitting sulkily among the ashes, "Mind the volcano!"

"What volcano?" said the King, **sah** up anxiously **in** the fire, as **wenn er** thought that was the most likely place **zu finden** one.

"Blew—me—up," panted the Queen, **die** was still a little out of breath. "Mind you come up—the regular way—do not get blown up!"

Alice watched the White King as **er** slowly struggled up from bar to bar, till at last she said, "Why, you will be hours **und** hours getting to the table, at that rate. I'd far better help you, had not **ich**?" **Aber** the King took no notice of the question: it was quite clear that **er** could neither hear her nor see her.

So Alice picked him up **sehr** gently, **und** lifted him across more slowly **als** she had lifted the Queen, that she might not take his breath away: **aber, bevor** she put him on the table, she thought she might as **gut** dust him a little, **er** was so covered **mit** ashes.

She said afterwards that she had never seen in all her life such a face as the King made, **als er fand** himself held in the air by an invisible hand, **und** being dusted: **er** was far too much astonished

5

to cry out, **aber** his eyes **und** his mouth went on getting larger **und** larger, **und** rounder **und** rounder, till her hand shook so **mit** laughing that she nearly let him drop upon the floor.

"Oh! please do not make such faces, my dear!" she cried out, quite forgetting that the King couldn't hear her. "**Du bringst** me laugh so that **ich kann** hardly hold you! **Und** do not keep your mouth so wide open! All the ashes will get **darin** —there, now **ich** think you are tidy enough!" she added, as she smoothed his hair, **und** set him upon the table near the Queen.

The King immediately fell flat on his back, **und** lay perfectly still: **und** Alice was a little alarmed at what she had done, **und** went round the room **zu sehen, ob** she could find any water to throw over him. However, she could find nothing **aber** a bottle of ink, **und als** she got back **damit sie fand er** had recovered, **und er und** the Queen were talking together in a frightened whisper—so low, that Alice could hardly hear what **sie** said.

The King was saying, "**Ich** assure, you my dear, **ich** turned cold to the **sehr** ends of my whiskers!"

To which the Queen replied, "You haven't got any whiskers."

"The horror of that moment," the King went on, "**Ich** shall never, never forget!"

"You will, though," the Queen said, "**wenn du machst kein** memorandum of it."

Alice looked on **mit** great interest as the King took an enormous memorandum-book out of his pocket, **und** began writing. A sudden thought struck her, **und sie nahm** hold of the end of the pencil, which came some **Weg** over his shoulder, **und** began writing for him.

The poor King looked puzzled **und** unhappy, **und** struggled **mit** the pencil for some time without saying anything; **aber** Alice was too strong for him, **und** at last **er** panted out, "My dear! **Ich** really must get a thinner pencil. **Ich** can't manage this one a bit; it writes all manner of things that **ich** do not intend—"

"What manner of things?" said the Queen, **sah** over the book (in which Alice had put "The White Knight is sliding down the poker. **Er** balances **sehr** badly") "That's not a memorandum of your feelings!"

**Es gab** a book lying near Alice on the table, **und während** she sat watching the White King (for she was still a little anxious about him, **und** had the ink all ready to throw over him, in case **er** fainted again), she turned over the leaves, **fand** some part that she could read, "—for it's all in some language **die ich nicht kenne,**" she said to herself.

It was like this.

.YKCOWREBBAJ

*sevot yhtils eht dna, gillirb
sawT' ebaw eht ni elbmig dna
eryg diD,sevogorob eht erew
ysmim llA.ebargtuo shtar
emom eht dnA*

She puzzled over this for some time, **aber** at last a bright thought struck her. "Why, it's a **Spiegel**-glass book, of course! **Und wenn ich** hold it up to a glass, the words will all go the right **Weg** again."

This was the poem that Alice read.

### **JABBERWOCKY.**

*'Twas brillig,* **und** *the slithy toves*

*Did gyre* **und** *gimble in the wabe;*

*All mimsy were the borogoves,*

**Und** *the mome raths outgrabe.*


*"Beware the Jabberwock, my son!*

*The jaws that bite, the claws that catch!*

*Beware the Jubjub bird,* **und** *shun*

*The frumious Bandersnatch!"*


**Er nahm** *his vorpal sword in hand:*

*Long time the manxome foe* **er** *sought—*

*So rested* **er** *by the Tumtum tree,*

**Und** *stood awhile in thought.*


**Und** *as in uffish thought* **er** *stood,*

*The Jabberwock,* **mit** *eyes of flame,*

*Came whiffling through the tulgey wood,*

**Und** *burbled as it came!*


*One,* **zwei!** *One,* **zwei!** **Und** *through* **und** *through*

*The vorpal blade went snicker-snack!*

**Er** *left it dead,* **und mit** *its head*

**Er ging** *galumphing back.*


*"***Und** *hast thou slain the Jabberwock?*

*Come to my arms, my beamish boy!*

*O frabjous day! Callooh! Callay!"*

**Er** *chortled in his joy.*


*'Twas brillig,* **und** *the slithy toves*

*Did gyre* **und** *gimble in the wabe;*

*All mimsy were the borogoves,*

**Und** *the mome raths outgrabe.*

"It seems **sehr** pretty," she said **als** she had finished it, "**aber** it's rather hard to understand!" (**wie Sie sehen**, she did not like to confess, even to herself, that she couldn't make it out at all.) "Somehow it seems to fill my head **mit** ideas—only **ich** do not exactly know what **sie** are! However, somebody killed something: that's clear, at any rate—"

"**Aber** oh!" thought Alice, suddenly jumping up, "**wenn ich mich nicht** haste **ich** shall have **gehen** back through the **Spiegel-**glass, **bevor ich habe gesehen**, what the rest of the house is like! Let's have a look at the garden first!" She was out of the room in a moment, **und** ran down stairs—or, at least, it was not exactly running, **aber** a new invention of hers for getting down stairs quickly **und** easily, as Alice said to herself. She just kept the tips of her fingers on the hand-rail, **und** floated gently down without even touching the stairs **mit** her feet; then she floated on through the hall, **und** would have **gegangen** straight out at the door in the same **Weg**, **wenn** she had not caught hold of the door-post. She was getting a little giddy **mit** so much floating in the air, **und** was rather glad **zu finden** herself walking again in the natural **Weg**.

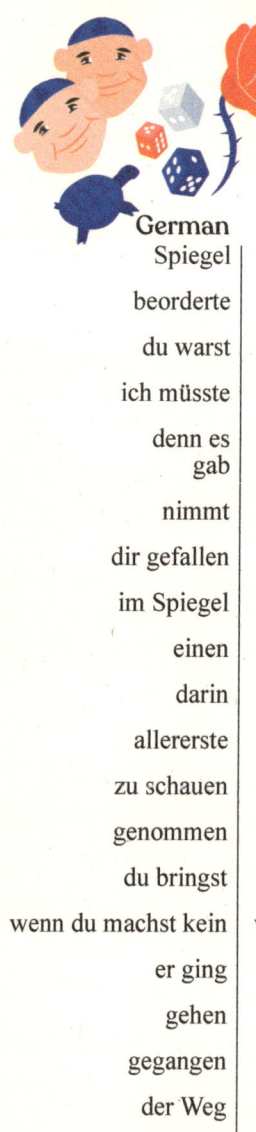

# weeve

## Chapter 2

| German | Pronunciation | English |
|---|---|---|
| Spiegel | ʃpi:gel | mirrors |
| beorderte | beoədeətə | ordered |
| du warst | du vaəst | you were |
| ich müsste | ix mystə | I would have to |
| denn es gab | dənn es gap | because there was |
| nimmt | nimt | takes |
| dir gefallen | dir ge:falən | you like |
| im Spiegel | im spi:gel | in the mirror |
| einen | aiənən | a |
| darin | da:rin | in this |
| allererste | ale:reəstə | very first |
| zu schauen | t͡su ʃauən | watch |
| genommen | ge:nomən | taken |
| du bringst | du priŋst | you bring |
| wenn du machst kein | vənn du makst kain | if you don't do any |
| er ging | ər giŋk | he went |
| gehen | ge:hən | walk |
| gegangen | ge:gaŋən | went |
| der Weg | dər vek | the way |
| die ganze Zeit | di: gant͡se t͡sait | the whole time |

# weeve
## Chapter 2

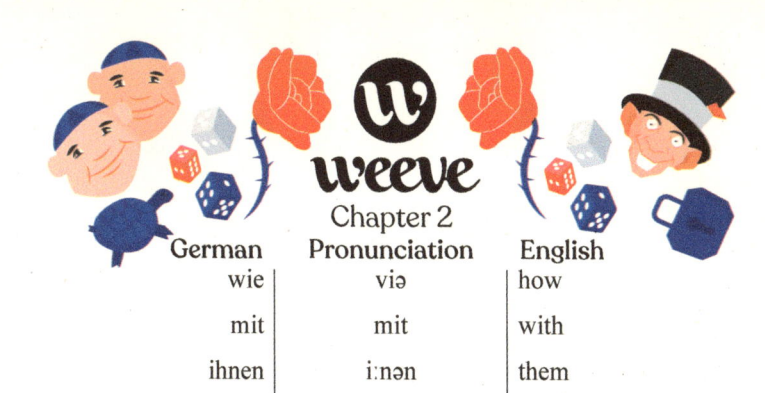

| German | Pronunciation | English |
|--------|---------------|---------|
| wie    | viə           | how     |
| mit    | mit           | with    |
| ihnen  | iːnən         | them    |

# 2

# THE GARDEN OF LIVE FLOWERS

"Vocabulary is no different than any other system or part of language, we acquired it the same way, by understanding messages, by reading them or by listening to them." – Jeff McQuillan, senior researcher at Center for Educational Development, Inc.

"**Ich würde** see the garden far better," said Alice to herself, "**wenn ich** could get to the top of that hill: **und** here's a path that leads straight to it—at least, no, it doesn't do that—" (after going a few yards along the path, **und** turning several sharp corners), "**aber ich** suppose it will at last. **Aber wie** curiously it twists! It's more like a corkscrew **als** a path! **Gut**, this turn <u>**geht**</u> to the hill, **ich** suppose—no, it doesn't! This **geht** straight back to the house! **Gut** then, **ich** will try it the other **Weg**."

**Und** so she did: wandering up **und** down, **und** trying turn after turn, **aber** always coming back to the house, do what **sie würde**. Indeed, once, **als** she turned a corner rather more quickly **als** usual, she ran against it **bevor** she could stop herself.

"It's no use talking about it," Alice said, **sie sah** up at the house **und** pretending it was arguing **mit** her. "I'm not going in again yet. **Ich weiß, ich müsste** get through the **Spiegel**-glass again—back **ins** old room—and there'd be an end of all my adventures!"

So, resolutely turning her back upon the house, she set out once more down the path, determined to keep straight on till she got to the hill. For a few minutes all went on **gut**, **und** she was just

12

saying, "**Ich** really shall do it this time—" **als** the path gave a sudden twist **und** shook itself (as she described it afterwards), **und** the next moment **sie fand** herself actually walking in at the door.

"Oh, it's too bad!" she cried. "**Ich** never saw such a house for getting **im Weg**! Never!"

However, **es gab** the hill full in sight, so **es gab** nothing to be done **aber** start again. This time she came upon a large flower-bed, **mit** a border of daisies, **und** a willow-tree growing in the middle.

"O Tiger-lily," said Alice, addressing herself to one that was waving gracefully about in the wind, "**Ich** wish you could talk!"

"**Wir können** talk," said the Tiger-lily: "**wenn** there's anybody worth talking to."

Alice was so astonished that she couldn't speak for a minute: it quite seemed **zu nehmen** her breath away. At length, as the Tiger-lily only went on waving about, she spoke again, in a timid voice—almost in a whisper. "**Und** can all the flowers talk?"

"As **gut** as **Sie können**," said the Tiger-lily. "**Und** a great deal louder."

"It isn't manners for us to begin, **wissen Sie**," said the Rose, "**und ich** really was wondering **wann** you'd speak! Said **ich** to myself, 'Her face has got some sense in it, though it's not a clever one!' Still, you are the right colour, **und** that **geht** a long **Weg**."

"**Ich** do not care about the colour," the Tiger-lily remarked. "**Wenn** only her petals curled up a little more, she'd be all right."

Alice did not like being criticised, so she began asking questions. "Are not you sometimes frightened at being planted out here, **mit** nobody **zu kümmern** of you?"

"There's the tree in the middle," said the Rose: "what else is it good for?"

"**Aber** what could it do, **wenn** any danger came?" Alice asked.

"It says 'Bough-wough!'" cried a Daisy: "that's why its branches are called boughs!"

"**Wussten Sie** that **nicht**?" cried another Daisy, **und** here **sie** all began shouting together, till the air seemed quite full of little shrill voices. "Silence, every one of you!" cried the Tiger-lily, waving itself passionately from side to side, **und** trembling **mit** excitement. "**Sie wissen, dass ich** can't get at them!" it panted, bending its quivering head towards Alice, "**oder sie würden** not dare **zu tun** it!"

13

"Never mind!" Alice said in a soothing tone, **und** stooping down to the daisies, **die** were just beginning again, she whispered, "**Wenn** you do not hold your tongues, **ich** will pick you!"

**Es gab** silence in a moment, **und** several of the pink daisies turned white.

"That's right!" said the Tiger-lily. "The daisies are worst of all. **Wenn** one speaks, **sie** all begin together, **und** it's enough **zu machen** one wither to hear **die Art**, <u>**wie sie singen**</u>!"

"**Wie** is it **ihr könnt** all talk so nicely?" Alice said, hoping to get it **in** a better temper by a compliment. "**Ich** have been in many gardens **schon**, **aber** none of the flowers could talk."

"Put your hand down, **und** feel the ground," said the Tiger-lily. "Then <u>**Sie warden wisen**</u> why."

Alice did so. "It's **sehr** hard," she said, "**aber ich sehe nicht**, what that has **damit zu tun**."

"In most gardens," the Tiger-lily said, "the beds <u>**werden gemacht**</u> too soft—so that the flowers are always asleep."

This sounded a **sehr** good reason, **und** Alice was quite pleased **zu wissen** it. "**Ich** never thought of that **vorher**!" she said.

"It's my opinion that you never think at all," the Rose said in a rather severe tone.

"**Ich** never saw anybody that looked stupider," a Violet said, so suddenly, that Alice quite jumped; for it had not spoken **zuvor**.

"Hold your tongue!" cried the Tiger-lily. "As **ob** you ever saw anybody! You keep your head under the leaves, **und** snore away there, till **sie wissen** no more what's <u>**los**</u> in **der Welt**, **als wenn Sie wären** a bud!"

"Are there any more **Menschen** in the garden besides me?" Alice said, not choosing to notice the Rose's last remark.

"There's one other flower in the garden that can move about like you," said the Rose. "**Ich** wonder **wie** you do it—" ("You are always wondering," said the Tiger-lily), "**aber** she's more bushy **als** you are."

"Is she like me?" Alice asked eagerly, for the thought crossed her mind, "There's another little girl in the garden, somewhere!"

"**Gut**, she has the same awkward shape as you," the Rose said, "**aber** she's redder—and her petals are shorter, **ich** think."

"Her petals are done up close, almost like a dahlia," the Tiger-lily interrupted: "not tumbled about anyhow, like yours."

"**Aber** that's not your fault," the Rose added kindly: "you are beginning to fade, you know—and then one can't help one's petals getting a little untidy."

Alice did not like this idea at all: so, to change the subject, she asked "Does she ever come out here?"

"**Ich** daresay **Sie werden sehen** her soon," said the Rose. "She's one of the thorny kind."

"**Wo** does she wear the thorns?" Alice asked **mit** some curiosity.

"Why all round her head, of course," the Rose replied. "**Ich** was wondering you had not got some too. **Ich** thought it was the regular rule."

"She's coming!" cried the Larkspur. "**Ich** hear her footstep, thump, thump, thump, along the gravel-walk!"

Alice looked round eagerly, **und** found that it was the Red Queen. "She's grown a good deal!" was her first remark. She had indeed: **als** Alice first found her in the ashes, she had been only three inches high—and here she was, half a head taller **als** Alice herself!

"It's the fresh air that does it," said the Rose: "wonderfully fine air it is, out here."

"**Ich** think **ich werde gehen und** meet her," said Alice, for, though the flowers were interesting enough, she felt that it would be far grander to have a talk **mit** a real Queen.

"You can't possibly do that," said the Rose: "**Ich würde** advise you to walk the other **Weg**."

This sounded nonsense to Alice, so she said nothing, **aber** set off at once towards the Red Queen. To her surprise, she lost sight of her in a moment, **und** found herself walking in at the front-door again.

A little provoked, she drew back, **und** after **sie suchte** everywhere for the queen (whom she spied out at last, a long **Weg** off), she thought **sie würde** try the plan, this time, of walking in the opposite direction.

It succeeded beautifully. She had not been walking a minute **bevor sie fand** herself face to face **mit** the Red Queen, **und** full in sight of the hill she had been so long aiming at.

"**Wo** do you come from?" said the Red Queen. "**Und wo** are you going? Look up, speak nicely, **und** do not twiddle your fingers **die ganze Zeit**."

Alice attended to all these directions, **und** explained, as **gut** as she could, that she had lost her way.

"**Ich weiß nicht** what you mean by **Ihrem Weg**," said the Queen: "all the **Wege** about here belong to me—but why did you come out here at all?" she added in a kinder tone. "Curtsey **während** you are thinking what to say, it saves time."

Alice wondered a little at this, **aber** she was too much in awe of the Queen to disbelieve it. "**Ich** will try it **wenn ich gehe** home," she thought to herself, "the next time I'm a little late for dinner."

"It's time for you to answer now," the Queen said, **sie sah** at her watch: "open your mouth a little wider **wenn** you speak, **und** always say 'your Majesty.'"

"**Ich** only wanted to **sehen** what the garden was like, your Majesty—"

"That's right," said the Queen, patting her on the head, which Alice did not like at all, "though, **wenn** you say 'garden,'—I have seen gardens, compared **mit** which this would be a wilderness."

Alice did not dare to argue the point, **aber** went on: "—and **ich** thought I'd try **und** find **meinen Weg** to the top of that hill—"

"**Wann** you say 'hill,'" the Queen interrupted, "**Ich** could show you hills, in comparison **mit** which you'd call that a valley."

"No, **ich sollte** not," said Alice, surprised **in** contradicting her at last: "a hill can't be a valley, **wissen sie**. That would be nonsense—"

The Red Queen shook her head, "**Sie können** call it 'nonsense' **wenn Sie möchten**," she said, "**aber ich** have heard nonsense, compared **mit** which that would be as sensible as a dictionary!"

Alice curtseyed again, as she was afraid from the Queen's tone that she was a little offended: **und sie** walked on in silence till **sie** got to the top of the little hill.

For some minutes Alice stood without speaking, **sie sah** out in all directions over the country—and a most curious country it was. **Es gab** a number of tiny little brooks running straight across it from side to side, **und** the ground **dazwischen** was divided up **in** squares by a number of little green hedges, that reached from brook to brook.

"**Ich** declare it's marked out just like a large chessboard!" Alice said at last. "There ought to be some men moving about somewhere—and so **es gibt!**" She added in a tone of delight, **und** her heart began to beat quick **mit** excitement as **sie redete** on. "It's a great huge game of chess that's being played—all over the world—if this is **die Welt** at all, **wissen Sie**. Oh, what fun it is! **Wie ich** wish **ich** was one of **ihnen**! **Ich** would not mind **zu**

16

**sein** a Pawn, **wenn** only **ich** might join—though of course **ich möchte** to be a Queen, best."

She glanced rather shyly at the real Queen as she said this, **aber** her companion only smiled pleasantly, **und** said, "That's easily managed. **Sie können** be the White Queen's Pawn, **wenn Sie möchten**, as Lily's too young to play; **und** you are in the Second Square to begin **mit**: **wenn** you get to the Eighth Square you will be a Queen—" Just at this moment, somehow **oder** other, **sie** began to run.

Alice never could quite make out, in thinking it over afterwards, **wie** it was that **sie** began: all she remembers is, that **sie** were running hand in hand, **und** the Queen went so fast that it was all she could do to keep up **mit** her: **und** still the Queen kept crying "Faster! Faster!" **aber** Alice felt she couldn't go faster, though she had not breath left to say so.

The most curious part of the thing was, that the trees **und** the other things round **sie** never changed their places at all: **egal wie** fast **sie liefen**, **sie** never seemed to pass anything. "**Ich** wonder **ob** all the things move along **mit uns**?" thought poor puzzled Alice. **Und** the Queen seemed to guess her thoughts, for she cried, "Faster! Do not try to talk!"

Not that Alice had any idea of doing that. She felt as **ob sie könnte** never talk again, she was getting so much out of breath: **und** still the Queen cried "Faster! Faster!" **und** dragged her along. "Are **wir** nearly there?" Alice managed to pant out at last.

"Nearly there!" the Queen repeated. "Why, **wir** passed it ten minutes ago! Faster!" **Und sie** ran on for **eine Weile** in silence, **mit** the wind whistling in Alice's ears, **und** almost blowing her hair off her head, she fancied.

"Now! Now!" cried the Queen. "Faster! Faster!" **Und sie liefen** so fast that at last **sie** seemed to skim through the air, hardly touching the ground **mit** their feet, till suddenly, just as Alice was getting quite exhausted, **sie** stopped, **und sie fand** herself sitting on the ground, breathless **und** giddy.

The Queen propped her up against a tree, **und** said kindly, "**Sie können** rest a little now."

Alice looked round her in great surprise. "Why, **ich** do believe **wir** have been under this tree the whole time! Everything's just as it was!"

"Of course it is," said the Queen, "what would you have it?"

"**Gut**, in our country," said Alice, still panting a little, "you'd generally get to somewhere else—if you ran **sehr** fast for a long time, as **wir** have been doing."

17

"A slow sort of country!" said the Queen. "Now, here, **sehen Siee**,, it **braucht** all the running **man kann** do, to keep in the same place. **Wenn man will** to get somewhere else, you must run at least twice as fast as that!"

"I'd rather not try, please!" said Alice. "I'm quite content to stay here—only **ich** am so hot **und** thirsty!"

"**Ich weiß** what you'd like!" the Queen said good-naturedly, **sie nahm** a little box out of her pocket. "Have a biscuit?"

Alice thought it wouldn't be civil to say "No," though it was not at all what **sie wollte**. So **sie nahm** it, **und** ate it as **gut** as she could: **und** it was **sehr** dry; **und** she thought she had never been so nearly choked in all her life.

"**Während** you are refreshing yourself," said the Queen, "**Ich** will just take the measurements." **Und sie nahm** a ribbon out of her pocket, marked in inches, **und** began measuring the ground, **und** sticking little pegs in here **und** there.

"At the end of **zwei** yards," she said, putting in a peg to mark the distance, "**Ich** shall give you your directions—have another biscuit?"

"No, thank you," said Alice: "one's quite enough!"

"Thirst quenched, **ich** hope?" said the Queen.

Alice did not know what to say to this, **aber** luckily the Queen did not wait for an answer, **aber** went on. "At the end of three yards **ich** shall repeat them—for fear of your forgetting **sie**. At the end of four, **ich** shall say good-bye. **Und** at the end of five, **ich** shall go!"

She had got all the pegs put in by this time, **und** Alice looked on **mit** great interest as she returned to the tree, **und** then began slowly walking down the row.

At the **zwei**-yard peg she faced round, **und** said, "A pawn **geht zwei** squares in its first move, **wissen Sie**. So **sie gehen sehr** quickly through the Third Square—by railway, **ich würde** think—and **Sie werden finden** yourself in the Fourth Square in no time. **Gut**, that square belongs to Tweedledum **und** Tweedledee—the Fifth is mostly water—the Sixth belongs to Humpty Dumpty—But **machen Sie** no remark?"

"I—I did not know **ich** had to **machen** one—just then," Alice faltered out.

"**Sie hätten sollen** said, 'It's extremely kind of you to tell me all this'—however, **wir** will suppose it said—the Seventh Square is all forest—however, one of the Knights will show you the way—and in the Eighth Square **wir** shall be Queens together, **und** it's all feasting **und** fun!" Alice got up **und** curtseyed, **und** sat down again.

At the next peg the Queen turned again, **und** this time she said, "Speak in French **wenn** you can't think of the English for a thing—turn out your toes as you walk—and remember **wer** you are!" She did not wait for Alice to curtsey this time, **aber** walked on quickly to the next peg, **wo** she turned for a moment to say "good-bye," **und** then hurried on to the last.

**Wie** it happened, Alice never knew, **aber** exactly as she came to the last peg, she was **Weg**. Whether she vanished **in** the air, **oder** whether she ran quickly **in** the wood ("**und sie kann** run **sehr** fast!" thought Alice), **Es gab** no **Weg** of guessing, **aber** she was **Weg, und** Alice began to remember that she was a Pawn, **und** that it would soon be time for her to move.

## weeve
### Chapter 2

| German | Pronunciation | English |
|---|---|---|
| geht | ge:t | goes |
| ins | ins | into the |
| zu nehmen | t͡su ne:mən | gain weight |
| zu kümmern | t͡su kymeən | take care of |
| wussten sie | vustən siə | did you know |
| wie sie singen | vi: si: siŋən | how they sing |
| sie warden wisen | zi: vaədən vi:sən | they will know |
| werden gemacht | veədən ge:maxt | will be done |
| los | los | come on |
| ich werde gehen und | ix veəde ge:hən unt | I will go and |
| sie suchte | zi: suxtə | she was looking for |
| ihrem Weg | i:rem vek | their way |
| Wege | vegə | ways |
| wenn ich gehe | vənn ix ge:ə | when I go |
| dazwischen | dat͡svi:ʃən | between |
| sie redete | zi: re:detə | she talked |
| sein | zain | be |
| egal wie | egal viə | no matter how |
| sie liefen | zi: li:fən | they ran |
| mit uns | mit uns | with us |

# weeve
## Chapter 2

| German | Pronunciation | English |
|---|---|---|
| ob sie könnte | ob si: køntə | if she could |
| eine Weile | aiəne vailə | a while |
| sehen siee | ze:hən si:ə | see you |
| sie hätten sollen | zi: hetən solən | they should have |
| sie sah | zi: sa: | she saw |
| sie werden sehen | zi: veədən se:hən | you will see |
| wenn sie möchten | vənn si: møxtən | if you want |
| die Art | di: aət | the kind |
| im Weg | im vek | in the way |

# 3
# LOOKING GLASS INSECTS

> "Language acquisition does not happen by learning grammar rules or memorising vocabulary lists." – Stephen Krashen, expert in linguistics at University of Southern California

Of course the first thing **zu tun** was **zu machen** a grand survey of the country she was going to travel through. "It's something **sehr** like learning geography," thought Alice, as she stood on tiptoe in hopes of being able **zu sehen** a little further. "Principal rivers—there are none. Principal mountains—I'm on the only one, **aber ich** do not think it's got any name. Principal towns—why, what are <u>**jene**</u> creatures, making honey down there? **Sie** can't be bees—nobody ever saw bees a mile off, you know—" **und** for some time she stood silent, watching one of **ihnen** that was bustling about among the flowers, poking its proboscis **in sie**, "just as **ob** it was a regular bee," thought Alice.

<u>**Jedoch**</u>, this was anything **aber** a regular bee: in fact it was an elephant—as Alice soon found out, though the idea quite took her breath away at first. "**Und** what enormous flowers **sie** must be!" was her next idea. "Something like cottages **mit** the roofs takenoff, **und** stalks put to them—and what quantities of honey **sie** must make! **Ich** think **ich werde gehen** down and—no, **ich** won't just yet," **sie redete** on, checking herself just as she was beginning to run down the hill, **und** trying **zu finden** some excuse for turning shy so suddenly. "It will never do **zu gehen** down among **ihnen** without a good long branch to brush **sie**

22

away—and what fun it will be **wenn sie** ask me **wie** my walk pleases **mir**. **Ich** shall say— 'Oh, **er** pleases **mir gut** enough—'" (here came the favourite little toss of the head), "'only it was so dusty **und** hot, **und** the elephants did tease so!'"

"**Ich** think **ich werde gehen** down the other **Weg**," she said after a pause: "**und** perhaps **ich kann** visit the elephants later on. Besides, **ich** do so want to get **in** the Third Square!"

So **mit** this excuse she ran down the hill **und** jumped over the first of the six little brooks.

\* \* \* \* \* \* \*

\* \* \* \* \* \*

\* \* \* \* \* \* \*

"Tickets, please!" said the Guard, putting his head in at the window. In a moment everybody was holding out a ticket: **sie waren** about the same size as **die Menschen, und** quite seemed to fill the carriage.

"Now then! Show your ticket, child!" the Guard went on, **er sah** angrily at Alice. **Und** a great many voices all said together ("like the chorus of a song," thought Alice), "Do not keep him waiting, child! Why, **seine Zeit** is worth a thousand pounds a minute!"

"I'm afraid **ich** haven't got one," Alice said in a frightened tone: "**es gab** no ticket-office **wo ich** came from." **Und** again the chorus of voices went on. "**Es gab** no room for one **wo** she came from. The land **es gibt** worth a thousand pounds an inch!"

"Do not make excuses," said the Guard: "**Sie hätten sollen** bought one from the engine-driver." **Und** once more the chorus of voices went on **mit** "The man that drives the engine. Why, the smoke alone is worth a thousand pounds a puff!"

Alice thought to herself, "Then there's no use in speaking." The voices did not join in this time, as she had not spoken, **aber** to her great surprise, **sie** all thought in chorus (**ich** hope you understand what **zu denken** in chorus means—for **ich** must confess that **ich** do not), "Better say nothing at all. Language is worth a thousand pounds a word!"

"**Ich** shall dream about a thousand pounds tonight, **ich weiß, ich** shall!" thought Alice.

All this time the Guard **sah** at her, first through a telescope, then through a microscope, **und** then through an opera-glass. At last **er** said, "You are travelling the wrong **Weg**," **und** shut up the window **und** went away.

"So young a child," said the gentleman sitting opposite to her (**er** was dressed in white paper), "ought **zu wissen** which **Weg** she's going, even **wenn** she doesn't know her own name!"

A Goat, that was sitting next to the gentleman in white, shut his eyes **und** said in a loud voice, "She ought **zu wissen, ihren Weg** to the ticket-office, even **wenn** she doesn't know her alphabet!"

**Es gab** a Beetle sitting next to the Goat (it was a **sehr** queer carriage-full of passengers altogether), **und**, as the rule seemed to be that **sie sollten** all speak in turn, **er redete** on **mit** "She will haveto **gehen** back from here as luggage!"

Alice couldn't see **wer** was sitting beyond the Beetle, **aber** a hoarse voice spoke next. "Change engines—" it said, **und** was obliged to leave off.

"It sounds like a horse," Alice thought to herself. **Und** an extremely small voice, close to her ear, said, "**Sie könnten** make a joke on that—something about 'horse' **und** 'hoarse,' **wissen sie**."

Then a **sehr** gentle voice in the distance said, "She must be labelled 'Lass, **mit** care,' you know—"

**Und** after that other voices went on ("What a number of **Menschen es gibt** in the carriage!" thought Alice), saying, "She must go by post, as she's got a head on her—" "She must be sent as a message by the telegraph—" "She must draw the train herself the rest of the way—" **und** so on.

**Aber** the gentleman dressed in white paper leaned forwards **und** whispered in her ear, "Never mind what **sie** all say, my dear, **aber** take a return-ticket every time the train stops."

"Indeed **ich** sha not!" Alice said rather impatiently. "**Ich** do not belong to this railway journey at all—I was in a wood just now—and **ich** wish **ich** could get back there."

"**Sie könnten** make a joke on that," said the little voice close to her ear: "something about 'you would, **wenn** you could,' **wissen Sie**."

"Do not tease so," said Alice, **sie sah** about in vain **um zu sehen, wo** the voice came from; "**wenn** you are so anxious to have a joke made, <u>**warum** machen sie nicht</u> one yourself?"

The little voice sighed deeply: it was **sehr** unhappy, evidently, **und** Alice would have said something pitying to comfort it, "**Wenn** it would only sigh like other **Menschen**!" <u>**sie dachte**</u>. **Aber** this was such a wonderfully small sigh, that **sie hätte** not heard it at all, **wenn** it had not come quite close to her ear. The consequence of this was that it tickled her ear **sehr** much, **und** quite took off her thoughts from the unhappiness of the poor little creature.

"**Ich weiß** you are a friend," the little voice went on; "a dear friend, **und** an old friend. **Und** you won't hurt me, though **ich** am an insect."

"What kind of insect?" Alice inquired a little anxiously. What she really wanted **zu wissen** was, whether it could sting **oder** not, **aber sie dachte**, this wouldn't be quite a civil question to ask.

"What, then you do not—" the little voice began, **als** it was drowned by a shrill scream from the engine, **und** everybody jumped up in alarm, Alice among the rest.

The Horse, **das** had put his head out of the window, quietly drew it in **und** said, "It's only a brook **wir** have to jump over." Everybody seemed satisfied **damit**, though Alice felt a little nervous at the idea of trains jumping at all. "**Jedoch**, it will take **uns in** the Fourth Square, that's some comfort!" she said to herself. In another moment she felt the carriage rise straight up **in** the air, **und** in her fright she caught at the thing nearest to her hand, which happened to be the Goat's beard.

\* \* \* \* \* \* \*

\* \* \* \* \* \*

\* \* \* \* \* \* \*

**Aber** the beard seemed to melt away as she touched it, **und sie fand** herself sitting quietly under a tree—while the Gnat (for that was the insect she had been talking to) was balancing itself on a twig just over her head, **und** fanning her **mit** its wings.

It certainly was a **sehr** large Gnat: "about the size of a chicken," Alice thought. Still, she couldn't feel nervous **damit**, after **sie** had been talking together so long.

"—then **Sie mögen nicht** all insects?" the Gnat went on, as quietly as **ob** nothing had happened.

"**Ich mag sie, wenn sie können** talk," Alice said. "None of **ihnen** ever talk, **wo ich** come from."

"What sort of insects do you rejoice in, **wo** you come from?" the Gnat inquired.

"**Ich** do not rejoice in insects at all," Alice explained, "**weil** I'm rather afraid of them—at least the large kinds. **Aber ich kann** tell you the names of some of **ihnen**."

"Of course **sie** answer to their names?" the Gnat remarked carelessly.

"**Ich** never knew **sie zu tun** it."

"What's the use of their having names," the Gnat said, "**wenn sie** won't answer to **ihnen**?"

"No use to **ihnen**," said Alice; "**aber** it's useful to **den Leuten die** name **sie**, **ich** suppose. **Wenn** not, **warum** do things have names at all?"

"**Ich** can't say," the Gnat replied. "Further on, in the wood down there, **sie** have got no names—however, go on **mit** your list of insects: you are wasting time."

"**Gut**, there's the Horse-fly," Alice began, counting off the names on her fingers.

"All right," said the Gnat: "half **Weg** up that bush, **Sie werden sehen** a Rocking-horse-fly, **wenn Sie schauen**. It's made entirely of wood, **und** gets about by swinging itself from branch to branch."

"What does it live on?" Alice asked, **mit** great curiosity.

"Sap **und** sawdust," said the Gnat. "Go on **mit** the list."

Alice looked up at the Rocking-horse-fly **mit** great interest, **und entschied sich**, that it must have been just repainted, it looked so bright **und** sticky; **und** then **sie redete** on.

"**Und** there's the Dragon-fly."

"Look on the branch above your head," said the Gnat, "**und** there **Sie werden finden** a snap-dragon-fly. Its body is made of plum-pudding, its wings of holly-leaves, **und** its head is a raisin burning in brandy."

"**Und** what does it live on?"

"Frumenty **und** mince pie," the Gnat replied; "**und** it makes its nest in a Christmas box."

"**Und** then there's the Butterfly," Alice went on, after **sie hatte genommen** a good look at the insect **mit** its head on fire, **und** had thought to herself, "**Ich** wonder **ob** that's the reason insects are so fond of flying **in** candles—because **sie wollen** to turn **in** Snap-dragon-flies!"

"Crawling at your feet," said the Gnat (Alice drew her feet back in some alarm), "**Sie können** observe a Bread-and-Butterfly. Its wings are thin slices of Bread-and-butter, its body is a crust, **und** its head is a lump of sugar."

"**Und** what does it live on?"

"Weak tea **mit** cream **in** it."

A new difficulty came in Alice's head. "Supposing it couldn't find any?" she suggested.

"Then it would die, of course."

"**Aber** that must happen <u>**sehr oft**</u>," Alice remarked thoughtfully.

"It always happens," said the Gnat.

After this, Alice was silent for a minute **oder zwei**, pondering. The Gnat amused itself meanwhile by humming round **und** round her head: at last it settled again **und** remarked, "**Ich** suppose **Sie wollen nicht** to lose your name?"

"No, indeed," Alice said, a little anxiously.

"**Und** yet **ich weiß nicht**," the Gnat went on in a careless tone: "only think **wie** convenient it would be **wenn** you could manage **zu gehen** home without it! For instance, **wenn** the governess wanted to call you to your lessons, **sie würde** call out 'come here—,' **und** there **sie würde** have to leave off, **weil** there wouldn't be any name for her to call, **und** of course <u>**Sie müssten**</u> not **gehen, wissen Sie**."

"That would never do, I'm sure," said Alice: "the governess would never think of excusing me lessons for that. **Wenn** she couldn't remember my name, she'd call me 'Miss!' as the servants do."

"Well, **wenn** she said 'Miss,' **und** did not say anything more," the Gnat remarked, "of course you'd miss your lessons. That's a joke. **Ich** wish **Sie hatte gemacht** it."

"**Warum** do you wish **ich habe gemacht** it?" Alice asked. "It's a **sehr** bad one."

**Aber** the Gnat only sighed deeply, **während zwei** large tears came rolling down its cheeks.

"**Sie sollten** not make jokes," Alice said, "**wenn** it makes you so unhappy."

Then came another of **jenen** melancholy little sighs, **und** this time the poor Gnat really seemed to have sighed itself away, for, **als** Alice looked up, **es gab** nothing whatever to be seen on the twig, **und**, as she was getting quite chilly **mit** sitting still so long, she got up **und** walked on.

She **sehr** soon came to an open field, **mit** a wood on the other side of it: it looked much darker **als** the last wood, **und** Alice felt a little timid about going <u>**dadrin**</u>. **Jedoch**, on second thoughts, **sie entschied zu gehen** on: "for **ich** certainly won't go back," **sie dachte** to herself, **und** this was the only **Weg** to the Eighth Square.

"This must be the wood," she said thoughtfully to herself, "**wo** things have no names. **Ich** wonder what will become of my name **wenn ich gehe** in? **Ich möchte nicht** to lose it at all— because they'd have to give me another, **und** it would be almost certain to be an ugly one. **Aber** then the fun would be trying **zu finden** the creature that had got my old name! That's just like the advertisements, **wissen Sie, wenn Leute** lose dogs— 'answers to the name of "Dash:" had on a brass collar'—just fancy calling everything you met 'Alice,' till one of **ihnen** answered! Only **sie würden** not answer at all, **wenn sie wären** wise."

She was rambling on in this **Weise, als** she reached the wood: it looked **sehr** cool **und** shady. "Well, at any rate it's a great comfort," she said as she stepped under the trees, "after being so hot, to get **in** the—into what?" **sie redete** on, rather surprised at not beingable **zu denken** of the word. "**Ich** mean to get under the—under the—under this, **wissen Sie!**" putting her hand on the trunk of the tree. "What does it call itself, **ich** wonder? **Ich** do believe it's got no name—why, to be sure it has not!"

She stood silent for a minute, **zu denken**: then she suddenly began again. "Then it really has happened, after all! **Und** now, **wer** am **ich**? **Ich** will remember, **wenn ich kann**! I'm determined **zu tun** it!" **Aber** beingdetermined did not help much, **und** all she could say, after a great deal of puzzling, was, "L, **ich weiß** it begins **mit** L!"

Just then a Fawn came wandering by: it looked at Alice **mit** its large gentle eyes, **aber** did not seem at all frightened. "Here then! Here then!" Alice said, as she held out her hand **und** tried to stroke it; **aber** it only started back a little, **und** then stood <u>un sah</u> at her again.

"What do you call yourself?" the Fawn said at last. Such a soft sweet voice it had!

"**Ich** wish **ich wusste!**" thought poor Alice. She answered, rather sadly, "Nothing, just now."

"Think again," it said: "that won't do."

Alice thought, **aber** nothing came of it. "Please, would you tell me what you call yourself?" she said timidly. "<u>**Meiner Ansicht nach**</u> that might help a little."

"**Ich** will tell you, **wenn** you will move a little further on," the Fawn said. "**Ich** can't remember here."

So **sie** walked on together though the wood, Alice **mit** her arms clasped lovingly round the soft neck of the Fawn, till **sie** came out **in** another open field, **und** here the Fawn gave a sudden bound **in** the air, **und** shook itself free from Alice's arms. "I'm a Fawn!" it cried out in a voice of delight, "**und**, dear me! you are a human child!" A sudden look of alarm came **in** its beautiful brown eyes, **und** in another moment it had darted away at full speed.

Alice stood **und sah** after it, almost ready to cry **mit** vexation at having lost her dear little fellow-traveller so suddenly. "**Jedoch, ich weiß** my name now." she said, "that's some comfort. Alice—Alice—I won't forget it again. **Und** now, which of these finger-posts ought **ich** to follow, **ich** wonder?"

It was not a **sehr** difficult question to answer, as **es gab** only one road through the wood, **und** the **zwei** finger-posts both pointed along it. "**Ich** will settle it," Alice said to herself, "**wann** the road divides **und sie** point different **Wege**."

**Aber** this did not seem likely to happen. **Sie ging** on **und** on, a long **Weg**, **aber** wherever the road divided **es gab** sure to be **zwei** finger-posts pointing the same **Weg**, one marked "TO TWEEDLEDUM'S HOUSE" **und** the other "TO THE HOUSE OF TWEEDLEDEE."

"**Ich** do believe," said Alice at last, "that **sie** live in the same house! **Ich** wonder **ich** never thought of that before—But **ich** can't stay there long. **Ich** will just call **und** say '**wie** d'you do?' **und** ask **ihnen den Weg** out of the wood. **Wenn ich** could only get to the Eighth Square **bevor** it gets dark!" So she wandered on, talking to herself as **sie ging**, till, on turning a sharp corner, she came upon **zwei** fat little men, so suddenly that she couldn't help starting back, **aber** in another moment she recovered herself, feeling sure that **sie** must be.

# weeve
## Chapter 3

| German | Pronunciation | English |
|---|---|---|
| jene | jənə | those |
| jedoch | je:dox | however |
| mir | miə | me |
| zu denken | t͡su dənkən | to think |
| warum | va:rum | why |
| sie dachte | zi: daxtə | she thought |
| und entschied sich | und ənt͡ʃi:d six | and decided |
| sehr oft | ze:r oft | very often |
| sie müssten | zi: mystən | they would have to |
| dadrin | datrin | in there |
| un sah | un sa: | un saw |
| meiner Ansicht nach | maiənər ansixt nax | in my opinion |
| ihren Weg | i:rən vek | your way |
| sie wollen | zi: volən | you want to |
| wenn sie wären | vənn si: verən | if they were |
| sie sollten | zi: soltən | they should |
| sie waren | zi: va:rən | they were |

# 4

# TWEEDLEDUM & TWEEDLEDEE

"Acquisition, I've described as a subconscious process and subconscious really means two things. First of all, it means while you're acquiring you don't really know you're acquiring. Second, once you're finished acquiring you're not really aware that anything has happened." – Stephen Krashen, expert in linguistics at University of Southern California

**Sie** were standing under a tree, each **mit** an arm round the other's neck, **und** Alice knew which was which in a moment, **weil** one of **ihnen** had "DUM" embroidered on his collar, **und** the other "DEE." "**Ich** suppose **sie** have each got 'TWEEDLE' round at the back of the collar," she said to herself.

**Sie** stood so still that she quite forgot **sie waren** alive, **und** she was just lookinground **zu sehen, ob** the word 'TWEEDLE' was written at the back of each collar, **als** she was startled by a voice coming from the one marked "DUM."

"<u>**Wenn sie denken,wir**</u>, wir are wax-works," **er** said, "you ought to pay, **wissen Sie**. Wax-works were not made to be looked at for nothing, nohow!"

"Contrariwise," added the one marked "DEE," "**wenn sie denken**, **wir** are alive, you ought to speak."

"I'm sure I'm **sehr** sorry," was all Alice could say; for the words of the old song kept ringing through her head like the ticking of a clock, **und** she could hardly help saying **sie** out loud:—

"Tweedledum **und** Tweedledee Agreed **zu haben** a battle; For Tweedledum said Tweedledee Had spoiled his nice new rattle.

Just then flew down a monstrous crow, As black as a tar-barrel; Which frightened both the heroes so, **Sie** quite forgot their quarrel."

"**Ich weiß** what you **denken** about," said Tweedledum: "**aber** it isn't so, nohow."

"Contrariwise," continued Tweedledee, "**wenn** it was so, it might be; **und wenn** it were so, it would be; **aber** as it isn't, it ai not. That's logic."

"**Ich dachte**," Alice said **sehr** politely, "which is the best **Weg** out of this wood: it's getting so dark. Would you tell me, please?"

**Aber** the little men only looked at each other **und** grinned.

**Sie sahen** so exactly like a couple of great schoolboys, that Alice couldn't help pointing her finger at Tweedledum, **und** saying "First Boy!"

"Nohow!" Tweedledum cried out briskly, **und** shut his mouth up again **mit** a snap.

"Next Boy!" said Alice, passing on to Tweedledee, though she felt quite certain **er würde** only shout out "Contrariwise!" **und** so **er** did.

"You have been wrong!" cried Tweedledum. "The first thing in a visit is to say '**Wie** d'ye do?' **und** shake hands!" **Und** here the **zwei** brothers gave each other a hug, **und** then **sie** held out the **zwei** hands that were free, to shake hands **mit** her.

Alice did not like shaking hands **mit** either of **ihnen** first, for fear of hurting the other one's feelings; so, as the best **Weg** out of the difficulty, **sie** took hold of both hands at once: the next moment **sie** weredancing round in a ring. This seemed quite natural (she remembered afterwards), **und** she was not even surprised to hear music playing: it seemed to come from the tree under which **sie** were dancing, **und** it was done (as **gut** as she could make it out) by the branches rubbing one across the other, like fiddles **und** fiddle-sticks.

"**Aber** it certainly was funny," (Alice said afterwards, **als** she was telling her sister the **Geschichte** of all this,) "**zu finden** myself singing 'Here **wir gehen** round the mulberry bush.' **Ich weiß nicht**, **wann ich** began it, **aber** somehow **ich** felt as **ob** I'd been singing it a long long time!"

The other **zwei** dancers were fat, **und sehr** soon out of breath. "Four **mal** round is enough for one dance," Tweedledum panted out, **und sie** left off dancing as suddenly as **sie hatten** begun: the music stopped at the same moment.

Then **sie** let go of Alice's hands, **und** stood **und sahen** at her for a minute: **es gab** a rather awkward pause, as Alice did not know **wie** to begin a conversation **mit Menschen** she had just been dancing **mit**. "It would never do to say 'Wie d'ye do?' now," she said to herself: "**wir** seem **zu haben** got beyond that, somehow!"

"**Ich** hope you are not much tired?" she said at last.

"Nohow. **Und** thank you **sehr** much for asking," said Tweedledum.

"So much obliged!" added Tweedledee. "**Gefällt** poetry **Ihnen**?"

"Ye-es, pretty well—some poetry," Alice said doubtfully. "Would you tell me which road leads out of the wood?"

"What shall **ich** repeat to her?" said Tweedledee, **er sah** round at Tweedledum **mit** great solemn eyes, **und** did not notice Alice's question.

"'The Walrus **und** the Carpenter' is the longest," Tweedledum replied, giving his brother an affectionate hug.

Tweedledee began instantly:

"The sun was shining—"

Here Alice ventured to interrupt him. "**Wenn** it's **sehr** long," she said, as politely as she could, "would you please tell me first which road—"

Tweedledee smiled gently, **und** began again:

"The sun was shining on the sea, Shining **mit** all his might: **Er** did his **sehr** best **zu machen** The billows smooth **und** bright— **Und** this was odd, **weil** it was The middle of the night.

The moon was shining sulkily, **Weil sie dachte**, the sun Had got no business to be there After the day was done— 'It's **sehr** rude of him,' she said, 'To come **und** spoil the fun!'

The sea was wet as wet could be, The sands were dry as dry. **Man könnte** see a cloud, **weil** No cloud was in the sky: No birds were flying over head— **Es gab** no birds to fly.

The Walrus **und** the Carpenter Were walking close at hand; **Sie** wept like anything **zu sehen** Such quantities of sand: '**Wenn** this were only cleared away,' **Sie** said, 'it would be grand!'

'**Wenn** seven maids **mit** seven mops Swept it for half a year, Do you suppose,' the Walrus said, 'That **sie konnten** get it clear?'

'**Ich** doubt it,' said the Carpenter, **Und** shed a bitter tear.

'O Oysters, come **und** walk **mit uns**!'

The Walrus did beseech. 'A pleasant walk, a pleasant talk, Along the briny beach: **Wir** cannot do **mit** more **als** four, To give a hand to each.'

The eldest Oyster looked at him. **Aber** never a word **er** said: The eldest Oyster winked his eye, **Und** shook his heavy head— Meaning to say **er** did not choose To leave the oyster-bed.

**Aber** four young oysters hurried up, All eager for the treat: Their coats were brushed, their faces washed, Their shoes were clean **und** neat— **Und** this was odd, **weil, wissen Sie, Sie hatten** not any feet.

Four other Oysters followed **ihnen, Und** yet another four; **Und** thick **und** fast **sie** came at last, **Und** more, **und** more, **und** more— All hopping through the frothy waves, **Und** scrambling to the shore.

The Walrus **und** the Carpenter Walked on a mile **oder** so, **Und** then **sie** rested on a rock Conveniently low: **Und** all the little Oysters stood **Und** waited in a row.

'**Die Zeit** has come,' the Walrus said, 'To talk of many things: Of shoes—and ships—and sealing-wax— Of cabbages—and kings— **Und warum** the sea is boiling hot— **Und** whether pigs have wings.'

'**Aber** wait a bit,' the Oysters cried, '**Bevor wir** have our chat; For some of **uns** are out of breath, **Und** all of **uns** are fat!'

'No hurry!' said the Carpenter. **Sie** thanked him much for that.

'A loaf of bread,' the Walrus said, 'Is what **wir** chiefly need: Pepper **und** vinegar besides Are **sehr** good indeed— Now **wenn** you are ready Oysters dear, **Wir können** begin to feed.'

'**Aber** not on **uns**!' the Oysters cried, Turning a little blue, 'After such kindness, that would be A dismal thing **zu tun**!'

'The night is fine,' the Walrus said 'Do you admire the view?

'It was so kind of you to come! **Und** you are **sehr** nice!'

The Carpenter said nothing **aber** 'Cut **uns** another slice: **ich** wish **Sie wären** not quite so deaf— **ich** have had to ask you twice!'

'It seems a shame,' the Walrus said, 'To play **sie** such a trick, After **wir** have brought **sie** out so far, **Und** made **sie** trot so quick!'

The Carpenter said nothing **aber** 'The butter's spread too thick!'

'**Ich** weep for you,' the Walrus said. '**Ich** deeply sympathize.' **Mit** sobs **und** tears **er** sorted out **Jene** of the largest size. Holding his pocket handkerchief **vor** his streaming eyes.

'O Oysters,' said the Carpenter. 'You have had a pleasant run!

Shall **wir** be trotting home again?'

**Aber** answer came there none— **Und** that was scarcely odd, **weil** They'd eaten every one." "**Ich mag** the Walrus best," said Alice: "<u>**weil man sieht**</u>, **dass er** was a little sorry for the poor oysters."

"**Er** ate more **als** the Carpenter, though," said Tweedledee. "**Sie sehen, dass er** held his handkerchief in front, so that the Carpenter couldn't count **wie** many **er nahm**: contrariwise."

"That was mean!" Alice said indignantly. "Then **ich mag** the Carpenter best—if **er** did not eat so many as the Walrus."

"**Doch er** ate as many as <u>**er konnte**</u> get," said Tweedledum.

This was a puzzler. After a pause, Alice began, "Well! **Sie waren** both **sehr** unpleasant characters—" Here she checked herself in some alarm, at hearing something that sounded to her like the puffing of a large steam-engine in the wood near **ihnen**, though she feared it was more likely to be a wild beast. "Are there any lions **oder** tigers about here?" she asked timidly.

"It's only the Red King snoring," said Tweedledee.

"Come **und** look at him!" the brothers cried, **und sie** each took one of Alice's hands, **und** led her up to **wo** the King was sleeping.

"Isn't **er** a lovely sight?" said Tweedledum.

Alice couldn't say honestly that **er** was. **Er hatte** a tall red nightcap on, **mit** a tassel, **und er** was lying crumpled up **in** a sort of untidy heap, **und** snoring loud— "fit to snore his head off!" as Tweedledum remarked.

"I'm afraid **er** will catch cold **mit** lying on the damp grass," said Alice, **die** was a **sehr** thoughtful little girl.

"He's dreaming now," said Tweedledee: "**und** what **denken Sie** he's dreaming about?"

Alice said "Nobody can guess that."

"Why, about you!" Tweedledee exclaimed, clapping his hands triumphantly. "**Und wenn er** left off dreaming about you, **wo** do you suppose you'd be?"

"**Wo ich** am now, of course," said Alice.

"Not you!" Tweedledee retorted contemptuously. "You'd be nowhere. Why, you are only a sort of thing in his dream!"

"**Wenn** that there King was to wake," added Tweedledum, "you'd go out—bang!—just like a candle!"

"**Ich würde** not!" Alice exclaimed indignantly. "Besides, **wenn**

I'm only a sort of thing in his dream, what are you, **ich möchte wissen?**"

"Ditto" said Tweedledum.

"Ditto, ditto" cried Tweedledee.

**Er** shouted this so loud that Alice couldn't help saying, "Hush! You will be waking him, I'm afraid, **wenn ihr macht** so much noise."

"**Gut**, it no use your talking about waking him," said Tweedledum, "**wenn** you are only one of the things in his dream. **Sie wissen sehr gut** you are not real."

"**Ich** am real!" said Alice **und** began to cry.

"You won't make yourself a bit realler by crying," Tweedledee remarked: "there's nothing to cry about."

"**Wenn ich** was not real," Alice said—half-laughing through her tears, it all seemed so ridiculous— "**Ich könnte** not cry."

"**Ich** hope you do not suppose **jene** are real tears?" Tweedledum interrupted in a tone of great contempt.

"**Ich weiß, ihr** are talking nonsense," Alice thought to herself: "**und** it's foolish to cry about it." So she brushed away her tears, **und** went on as cheerfully as **sie konnte**. "At any rate I'd better be getting out of the wood, for really it's coming on **sehr** dark. **Denkt ihr** it's going to rain?"

Tweedledum spread a large umbrella over himself **und** his brother, **und** looked up **in** it. "No, **ich denke nicht** it is," **er** said: "at least—not under here. Nohow."

"**Aber** it may rain outside?"

"It may—if it chooses," said Tweedledee: "**wir** have no objection. Contrariwise."

"Selfish things!" thought Alice, **und** she was just going to say "Good-night" **und** leave **sie, als** Tweedledum sprang out from under the umbrella **und** seized her by the wrist.

"**Sehen Sie**, that?" **er** said, in a voice choking **mit** passion, **und** his eyes grew large **und** yellow all in a moment, as **er** pointed **mit** a trembling finger at a small white thing lying under the tree.

"It's only a rattle," Alice said, after a careful examination of the little white thing. "Not a rattle-snake, **wissen Sie**," she added hastily, **sie dachte** that **er** was frightened: "only an old rattle—quite old **und** broken."

"**Ich wusste** it was!" cried Tweedledum, beginning to stamp about wildly **und** tear his hair. "It's spoilt, of course!" Here **er schaute** at Tweedledee, **der** immediately sat down on the ground, **und** tried to hide himself under the umbrella.

Alice laid her hand upon his arm, **und** said in a soothing tone, "**Sie brauchen** not be so angry about an old rattle."

"**Aber** it isn't old!" Tweedledum cried, in a greater fury **als** ever. "It's new, **ich** tell you—I bought it yesterday—my nice new RATTLE!" **und** his voice rose to a perfect scream.

All this time Tweedledee was trying his best to fold up the umbrella, **mit** himself in it: which was such an extraordinary thing **zu machen**, that it quite took off Alice's attention from the angry brother. **Aber er konnte** not quite succeed, **und** it ended in his rolling over, bundled up in the umbrella, **mit** only his head out: **und** there **er** lay, opening **und** shutting his mouth **und** his large eyes— "**es sah** more like a fish **als** anything else," Alice thought.

"Of course you agree **zu haben** a battle?" Tweedledum said in a calmer tone.

"**Ich** suppose so," the other sulkily replied, as **er** crawled out of the umbrella: "only <u>**sie müssen**</u> help **uns** to dress up, **wissen Sie**."

So the **zwei** brothers went off hand-in-hand **in** the wood, **und** returned in a minute **mit** their arms full of things—such as bolsters, blankets, hearth-rugs, table-cloths, dish-covers **und** coal-scuttles. "**Ich** hope you are a good hand at pinning **und** tying strings?" Tweedledum remarked. "Every one of these things has got to go on, somehow **oder** other."

Alice said afterwards **sie hatte** never seen such a fuss made about anything in all her life—the <u>**Weise wie die beiden**</u> bustled about—and the quantity of things **sie** put on—and the trouble **sie** gave her in tying strings **und** fastening buttons— "Really **sie** will be more like bundles of old clothes **als** anything else, **wenn sie** are ready!" she said to herself, as she arranged a bolster round the neck of Tweedledee, "to keep his head from beingcut off," as **er** said.

"**Wissen Sie**," **er** added **sehr** gravely, "it's one of the most serious things that can possibly happen to one in a battle—to get one's head cut off."

Alice laughed aloud: **aber** she managed to turn it **in** a cough, for fear of hurting his feelings.

"**Sehe ich** pale **aus**?" said Tweedledum, coming up **zu haben** his helmet tied on. (**Er** called it a helmet, though it certainly looked much more like a saucepan.)

"Well—yes—a little," Alice replied gently.

"I'm **sehr** brave generally," **er redete** on in a low voice: "only to-day **ich** happen **zu haben** a headache."

"**Und ich** have got a toothache!" said Tweedledee, **der** had overheard the remark. "I'm far worse off **als** you!"

"Then you'd better not fight to-day," said Alice, **sie dachte** it was a good opportunity **zu schließen** peace.

"**Wir müssen** have a bit of a fight, **aber ich** do not care about going on long," said Tweedledum. "**Wie viel Uhr ist es**?"

Tweedledee looked at his watch, **und** said "Half-past four."

"Let's fight till six, **und** then have dinner," said Tweedledum.

"**Sehr gut**," the other said, rather sadly: "**und sie kann** watch us—only you'd better not come **sehr** close," **er** added: "**Ich** generally hit everything **ich kann** see—when **ich** get really excited."

"**Und ich** hit everything within reach," cried Tweedledum, "whether **ich kann** see it **oder** not!"

Alice laughed. "**Ihr müsst** hit the trees pretty **häufig, ich würde** think," she said.

Tweedledum looked round him **mit** a satisfied smile. "**Ich** do not suppose," **er** said, "there will be a tree left standing, for ever so far round, **wenn wir** have finished!"

"**Und** all about a rattle!" said Alice, still hoping to make them a little ashamed of fighting for such a trifle.

"**Ich** would not have minded it so much," said Tweedledum, "**wenn** it had not been a new one."

"**Ich** wish the monstrous crow would come!" thought Alice.

"There's only one sword, **wissen Sie**," Tweedledum said to his brother: "**doch können Sie** have the umbrella—it's quite as sharp. Only **wir müssen** begin quick. It's getting as dark as it can."

"**Und** darker," said Tweedledee.

It was getting dark so suddenly that Alice thought there must be a thunderstorm coming on. "What a thick black cloud that is!" she said. "**Und wie** fast it comes! **Warum, ich** do believe it's got wings!"

"It's the crow!" Tweedledum cried out in a shrill voice of alarm: **und** the **zwei** brothers took to their heels **und** were out of sight in a moment.

Alice ran a little **Weg in** the wood, **und** stopped under a large tree. "It can never get at me here," **sie dachte**: "it's far too large to squeeze itself in among the trees. **Aber ich** wish it wouldn't flap its wings so—it makes quite a hurricane in the wood—here's somebody's shawl beingblown away!"

## weeve
### Chapter 4

| German | Pronunciation | English |
|---|---|---|
| wenn sie denken, wir | vənn si: dənkən, viə | if you think we |
| sie hatten | zi: hatən | they had |
| weil man sieht | vail man si:t | because you see |
| er konnte | ər kontə | he could |
| denkt ihr | dənkt i:ə | you think |
| ich denke nicht | ix dənke nixt | I do not think so |
| sie müssen | zi: mysən | you need to |
| weise wie die beiden | vaiese vi: di: baiedən | wise like the two |
| zu schließen | t͡su ʃli:sən | close |
| wie viel uhr ist es | vi: fi:l u:r ist es | what time is it |
| ihr müsst | i:r myst | you must |
| wenn wir | vənnviə | if we |
| doch können sie | dox kkønən siə | but you can |
| vor | foə | before |
| ich | ix | I |
| als | als | as |
| sehr | ze:ə | very |
| aber | abə | but |

40

# 5
## WOOL AND WATER

> In a 2019 study by Jeff McQuillan comparing students who read a story versus students who read a story and were given instruction about what the words meant, those who simply read the story learned 63% more words in that time.

She caught the shawl as she spoke, **und** looked about for the owner: in another moment the White Queen came running wildly through the wood, **mit** both arms stretched out wide, as **ob** she were flying, **und** Alice **sehr** civilly went to meet her **mit** the shawl.

"I'm **sehr** glad **ich** happened to be **im Weg**," Alice said, as <u>sie half</u> her to put on her shawl again.

The White Queen only looked at her in a helpless frightened sort of way, **und** kept repeating something in a whisper to herself that sounded like "bread-and-butter, bread-and-butter," **und** Alice felt that **wenn es** to be any conversation at all, <u>sie muss</u> manage it herself. So she began rather timidly: "Am **ich** addressing the White Queen?"

"**Gut**, yes, **wenn** you call that a-dressing," The Queen said. "It isn't my notion of the thing, at all."

Alice thought it would never do <u>zu streiten</u> at the **sehr** beginning of their conversation, so she smiled **und** said, "**Wenn** your Majesty will only tell me the right <u>Methode</u> to begin, **ich** will do it as **gut** as **ich kann**."

41

"**Aber ich will es nicht** done at all!" groaned the poor Queen. "**Ich** have been a-dressing myself for the last **zwei** hours."

It would have been all the better, as it seemed to Alice, **wenn sie hätte** got some one else to dress her, she was so dreadfully untidy. "Every single thing's crooked," Alice thought to herself, "**und** she's all over pins!—may **ich** put your shawl straight for you?" she added aloud.

"**Ich weiß nicht** what's the matter **damit**!" the Queen said, in a melancholy voice. "It's out of temper, **meiner Ansicht nach. Ich** have pinned it here, **und ich** have pinned it there, **aber** there's no pleasing it!"

"It can't go straight, **wissen Sie, wenn** you pin it all on one side," Alice said, as she gently put it right for her; "**und**, dear me, what a state your hair is in!"

"The brush has got entangled in it!" the Queen said **mit** a sigh. "**Und ich** lost the comb yesterday."

Alice carefully released the brush, **und** did her best to get the hair **in** order. "Come, **sie sehen** rather better now **aus**!" she said, after altering most of the pins. "**Aber** really **Sie sollten** have a lady's maid!"

"I'm sure **ich werde nehmen** you **mit** pleasure!" the Queen said. "Twopence a week, **und** jam every other day."

Alice couldn't help laughing, as she said, "**Ich möchte nicht dass** you hire me—and **ich** do not care for jam."

"It's **sehr** good jam," said the Queen.

"**Gut, ich will** none to-day, at any rate."

"**Sie könnten** not have it **wenn** you did want it," the Queen said. "The rule is, jam to-morrow **und** jam yesterday—but never jam to-day."

"It must come sometimes to 'jam to-day,'" Alice objected.

"No, it can't," said the Queen. "It's jam every other day: to-day isn't any other day, **wissen Sie**."

"**Ich** do not understand you," said Alice. "It's dreadfully confusing!"

"That's the effect of living backwards," the Queen said kindly: "it always makes one a little giddy at first—"

"Living backwards!" Alice repeated in great astonishment. "**Ich** never heard of such a thing!"

"—but there's one great advantage in it, that one's memory

works both **Richtungen**."

"I'm sure mine only works one **Richtung**," Alice remarked. "**Ich** can't remember things **bevor sie** happen."

"It's a poor sort of memory that only works backwards," the Queen remarked.

"What sort of things do you remember best?" Alice ventured to ask.

"Oh, things that happened the week after next," the Queen replied in a careless tone. "For instance, now," **sie redete** on, sticking a large piece of plaster on her finger as she spoke, "there's the King's Messenger. He's in prison now, beingpunished: **und** the trial doesn't even begin till next Wednesday: **und** of course the crime comes last of all."

"Suppose **er** never commits the crime?" said Alice.

"That would be all the better, wouldn't it?" the Queen said, as she bound the plaster round her finger **mit** a bit of ribbon.

Alice felt **es gab** no denying that. "Of course it would be all the better," she said: "**aber** it wouldn't be all the better his beingpunished."

"You are wrong there, at any rate," said the Queen: "were you ever punished?"

"Only for faults," said Alice.

"**Und Sie waren** all the better for it, **ich weiß**!" the Queen said triumphantly.

"Yes, **aber** then **ich hatte** done the things **ich** was punished for," said Alice: "that makes all the difference."

"**Aber wenn sie hätte** not done **sie**," the Queen said, "that would have been better still; better, **und** better, **und** better!" Her voice went higher **mit** each "better," till it got quite to a squeak at last.

Alice was just beginning to say "There's a mistake somewhere—," **als** the Queen began screaming so loud that **sie musste** leave the sentence unfinished. "Oh, oh, oh!" shouted the Queen, shaking her hand about as **ob sie wollte** to shake it off. "My finger's bleeding! Oh, oh, oh, oh!"

Her screams were so exactly like the whistle of a steam-engine, that Alice had to hold both her hands over her ears.

"What is the matter?" she said, as soon as **es gab** a chance of **zu machen** heard. "Have you pricked your finger?"

"**Ich** haven't pricked it yet," the Queen said, "**aber ich** soon

43

shall—oh, oh, oh!"

"**Wann** do you expect **zu tun** it?" Alice asked, feeling **sehr** much inclined to laugh.

"**Wenn ich** fasten my shawl again," the poor Queen groaned out: "the brooch will come undone directly. Oh, oh!" As she said the words the brooch flew open, **und** the Queen clutched wildly at it, **und** tried to clasp it again.

"Take care!" cried Alice. "You are holding it all crooked!" **Und** she caught at the brooch; **aber** it was too late: the pin had slipped, **und** the Queen had pricked her finger.

"That accounts for the bleeding, **sehen Sie,,**" she said to Alice **mit** a smile. "Now you understand **wie** things happen here."

"**Aber warum** do not you scream now?" Alice asked, holding her hands ready to put over her ears again.

"**Warum, ich** have done all the screaming already," said the Queen. "What would be the good of having it all over again?"

By this time it was getting light. "The crow must have flown away, **meiner Ansicht nach**," said Alice: "I'm so glad it's **Weg**. **Ich dachte** it was the night coming on."

"**Ich** wish **ich könnte** manage to be glad!" the Queen said. "Only **ich** never can remember the rule. **Sie müssen** be **sehr** happy, living in this wood, **und** beingglad whenever **Sie wollen**!"

"Only it is so **sehr** lonely here!" Alice said in a melancholy voice; **und** at the thought of her loneliness **zwei** large tears came rolling down her cheeks.

"Oh, do not go on like that!" cried the poor Queen, wringing her hands in despair. "Consider what a great girl you are. Consider what a long **Weg** you have come to-day. Consider what o'clock it is. Consider anything, only do not cry!"

Alice couldn't help laughing at this, even in the midst of her tears. "Can you keep from crying by considering things?" she asked.

"That's the wayit's done," the Queen said **mit** great decision: "nobody can do **zwei** things at once, **wissen Sie**. Let's consider your age to begin with—how old are you?"

"I'm seven **und** a half exactly."

"**sie brauchen** not say 'exactually,'" the Queen remarked: "**Ich kann** believe it without that. Now **ich** will give you something to believe. I'm just one hundred **und** one, five months **und** a day."

"**Ich** can't believe that!" said Alice.

"Can't you?" the Queen said in a pitying tone. "Try again: draw a long breath, **und** shut your eyes."

Alice laughed. "There's no use trying," she said: "one can't believe impossible things."

"**Ich** daresay you haven't had much practice," said the Queen. "**Als ich** was your age, **ich** always did it for half-an-hour a day. Why, sometimes **ich** have believed as many as six impossible things **vor** breakfast. There **geht** the shawl again!"

The brooch had come undone as she spoke, **und** a sudden gust of wind blew the Queen's shawl across a little brook. The Queen spread out her arms again, **und** went flying after it, **und** this time she succeeded in catching it for herself. "**Ich** have got it!" she cried in a triumphant tone. "Now you shall see me pin it on again, all by myself!"

"Then **ich** hope your finger is better now?" Alice said **sehr** politely, as she crossed the little brook after the Queen.

\* \* \* \* \* \* \*

\* \* \* \* \* \*

\* \* \* \* \* \* \*

"Oh, much better!" cried the Queen, her voice rising to a squeak as **sie redete** on. "Much be-etter! Be-etter! Be-e-e-etter! Be-e-ehh!" The last word ended in a long bleat, so like a sheep that Alice quite started.

**Sie sah** at the Queen, **die** seemed **zu haben** suddenly wrapped herself up in wool. Alice rubbed her eyes, **und** looked again. **Sie konnte** not make out what had happened at all. Was she in a shop? **Und** was that really—was it really a sheep that was sitting on the other side of the counter? Rub as **sie konnte, sie konnte** make nothing more of it: she was in a little dark shop, leaning **mit** her elbows on the counter, **und** opposite to her was an old Sheep, sitting in an arm-chair knitting, **und** every now **und** then leaving off **um zu sehen** at her through a great pair of spectacles.

"What is it <u>**ihr wollt**</u> to buy?" the Sheep said at last, **sie sah** up for a moment from her knitting.

"**Ich** do not quite know yet," Alice said, **sehr** gently. "**Ich sollte** like **zu sehen** all round me first, **wenn das geht**."

"**Sie können** look in front of you, **und** on both sides, **wenn Sie möchten**," said the Sheep: "**aber** you can't look all round you—unless you have got eyes at the back of your head."

45

**Aber** these, as it happened, Alice had not got: so she contented herself **mit** turning round, **sie sah** at the shelves as she came to **ihnen**.

The shop seemed to be full of all manner of curious things—but the oddest part of it all was, that whenever **sie sah** hard at any shelf, **um zu** make out exactly what it had on it, that particular shelf was always quite empty: though the others round it were crowded as full as **sie konnten** hold.

"Things flow about so here!" she said at last in a plaintive tone, after **sie hatte** spent a minute **oder** so in vainly pursuing a large bright thing, that looked sometimes like a doll **und** sometimes like a work-box, **und** was always in the shelf next above the one she **sah** at. "**Und** this one is the most provoking of all—but **ich** will tell you what—" she added, as a sudden thought struck her, "**Ich** will follow it up to the **sehr** top shelf of all. It will puzzle it **zu gehen** through the ceiling, **ich** expect!"

**Aber** even this plan failed: the "thing" went through the ceiling as quietly as possible, as **ob** it were quite **daran gewöhnt**.

"Are you a child **oder** a teetotum?" the Sheep said, as **sie nahm** up another pair of needles. "**Sie warden machen** me giddy soon, **wenn Sie gehen** on turning round like that." She was now working **mit** fourteen pairs at once, **und** Alice couldn't help looking at her in great astonishment.

"**Wie** can she knit **mit** so many?" the puzzled child thought to herself. "She gets more **und** more like a porcupine every minute!"

"Can you row?" the Sheep asked, handing her a pair of knitting-needles as she spoke.

"Yes, a little—but not on land—and not **mit** needles—" Alice was beginning to say, **als** suddenly the needles turned into oars in her hands, **und sie fand heraus, sie waren** in a little boat, gliding along **zwischen** banks: so **es gab** nothing for it **außer zu tun** her best.

"Feather!" cried the Sheep, as **sie nahm** up another pair of needles.

This did not sound like a remark that needed any answer, so Alice said nothing, **aber** pulled away. **Es gab** something **sehr** queer about the water, **sie dachte**, as every now **und** then the oars got fast in it, **und** would hardly come out again.

"Feather! Feather!" the Sheep cried again, **als sie nahm** more needles. "You will be catching a crab directly."

"A dear little crab!" thought Alice. "**Ich möchte** that."

"Did not you hear me say 'Feather'?" the Sheep cried angrily, **als**

**sie nahm** up quite a bunch of needles.

"Indeed **ich** did," said Alice: "you have said it **sehr** often—and **sehr** loud. Please, **wo** are the crabs?"

"In the water, of course!" said the Sheep, sticking some of the needles **in** her hair, as her hands were full. "Feather, **ich** say!"

"**Warum** do you say 'feather' so **häufig**?" Alice asked at last, rather vexed. "I'm not a bird!"

"You are," said the Sheep: "you are a little goose."

This offended Alice a little, so **es gab** no more conversation for a minute **oder zwei, während** the boat glided gently on, sometimes among beds of weeds (which made the oars stick fast in the water, worse then ever), **und** sometimes under trees, **aber** always **mit** the same tall river-banks frowning over their heads.

"Oh, please! **Es gibt** some scented rushes!" Alice cried in a sudden transport of delight. "There really are—and such beauties!"

"**Sie brauchen** not say 'please' to me about "em," the Sheep said, without looking up from her knitting: "**Ich** did not put "em there, **und** I'm not going **zu nehmen** "em away."

"No, **aber ich** meant—please, may **wir** wait **und** pick some?" Alice pleaded. "**Wenn** you do not mind stopping the boat for a minute."

"**Wie** am **ich** to stop it?" said the Sheep. "**Wenn** you leave off rowing, it will stop of itself."

So the boat was left to drift down the stream as it would, till it glided gently in among the waving rushes. **Und** then the little sleeves were carefully rolled up, **und** the little arms were plunged in elbow-deep to get the rushes a good long **Weg** down **bevor** breaking **sie** off—and for a **Weile** Alice forgot all about the Sheep **und** the knitting, as she bent over the side of the boat, **mit** just the ends of her tangled hair dipping **in** the water—while **mit** bright eager eyes she caught at one bunch after another of the darling scented rushes.

"**Ich** only hope the boat won't tipple over!" she said to herself. "Oh, what a lovely one! Only **ich könnte** not quite reach it." "**Und** it certainly did seem a little provoking ("almost as **ob** it happened on purpose," **sie dachte**) that, though she managed to pick plenty of beautiful rushes as the boat glided by, **Es gab** always a more lovely one that **sie konnte** not reach.

"The prettiest are always further!" she said at last, **mit** a sigh at the obstinacy of the rushes in growing so far off, as, **mit** flushed cheeks **und** dripping hair **und** hands, she scrambled back **in ihrem Platz**, **und** began to arrange her new-found treasures.

47

What mattered it to her just then that the rushes had begun to fade, **und** to lose all their scent **und** beauty, from the **sehr** moment that she picked **sie**? Even real scented rushes, **wissen Sie**, last only a **sehr** little while—and these, being dream-rushes, melted away almost like snow, as **sie** lay in heaps at her feet—but Alice hardly noticed this, **es gab** so many other curious things **zu denken** about.

**Sie waren nicht gegangen** much farther **bevor** the blade of one of the oars got fast in the water **und** wouldn't come out again (so Alice explained it afterwards), **und** the consequence was that the handle of it caught her under the chin, **und**, in spite of a series of little shrieks of "Oh, oh, oh!" from poor Alice, it swept her straight off the seat, **und** down among the heap of rushes.

**Jedoch**, she was not hurt, **und** was soon up again: the Sheep went on **mit** her knitting all the while, just as **ob** nothing had happened. "That was a nice crab you caught!" she remarked, as Alice got back **in ihrem Platz**, **sehr** much relieved **zu finden** herself still in the boat.

"Was it? **Ich** did not see it," Said Alice, peeping cautiously over the side of the boat **in** the dark water. "**Ich** wish it had not let go—I should so like **zu sehen** a little crab **zu nehmen** home **mit me!**" **Aber** the Sheep only laughed scornfully, **und** went on **mit** her knitting.

"Are there many crabs here?" said Alice.

"Crabs, **und** all sorts of things," said the Sheep: "plenty of choice, only **Sie müssen sich entscheide**. Now, what **wollen Sie** to buy?"

"To buy!" Alice echoed in a tone that was half astonished **und** half frightened—for the oars, **und** the boat, **und** the river, had vanished all in a moment, **und** she was back again in the little dark shop.

"**Ich möchte** to buy an egg, please," she said timidly. "**Wie viel kostet sie?**"

"Fivepence farthing for one—Twopence for **zwei**," the Sheep replied.

"Then **zwei** are cheaper **als** one?" Alice said in a surprised tone, **und nahm** out her purse.

"Only **Sie müssen** eat **sie** both, **wenn** you buy **zwei**," said the Sheep.

"Then **ich** will have one, please," said Alice, as she put the money down on the counter. For **sie dachte** to herself, "**Sie könnten** not be at all nice, **wissen Sie**."

The Sheep took the money, **und** put it away in a box: then she said "**Ich** never put things **in** people's hands—that would never do—you must get it for yourself." **Und** so saying, **sie ging** off to the other end of the shop, **und** set the egg upright on a shelf.

"**Ich** wonder **warum** it wouldn't do?" thought Alice, as she groped **ihren Weg** among the tables **und** chairs, for the shop was **sehr** dark towards the end. "The egg seems to get further away the more **ich** walk towards it. Let me see, is this a chair?Why, it's got branches, **ich** declare! **Wie sehr** odd **zu finden** trees growing here! **Und** actually here's a little brook!Well, this is the **sehr** queerest shop **ich** ever saw!"

\* \* \* \* \* \* \*

\* \* \* \* \* \*

\* \* \* \* \* \* \*

So **sie ging** on, wondering more **und** more at every step, as everything turned into a tree the moment she came up to it, **und** she quite expected the egg **zu tun** the same.

# weeve
## Chapter 5

| German | Pronunciation | English |
|---|---|---|
| sie half | zi: half | she helped |
| sie muss | zi: mus | she must |
| zu streiten | t͡su straietən | to argue |
| Methode | metodə | method |
| Richtungen | rixtuŋən | directions |
| Richtung | rixtuŋk | direction |
| sie musste | zi: mustə | she had to |
| ihr wollt | i:r volt | you want |
| in ihrem Platz | in i:rem plat͡s | in your place |
| sie müssen sich entscheide | zi: mysən six ənt͡ʃaidə | you have to decide |
| wie viel kostet sie | vi: fi:l kostet siə | how much does it cost |
| dass | das | that |
| sie brauchen | zi: prauhxən | they need |
| oder | odə | or |
| gut | gut | well |
| ich kann | ix kan | I can |

# 6
## HUMPTY DUMPTY

A study entitled The Inefficiency of Vocabulary Instruction showed that language learners pick up words incrementally, that is bit by bit as we are reading. We also pick them up incidentally, that is when you read a book it isn't to learn new vocabulary, learning vocabulary is just one of the consequences of reading.

**Jedoch**, the egg only got larger **und** larger, **und** more **und** more human: **wenn sie war** come within a few yards of it, **sie sah** that it had eyes **und** a nose **und** mouth; **und wenn sie war** come close to it, **sie sah** clearly that it was HUMPTY DUMPTY himself. "It can't be anybody else!" she said to herself. "I'm as certain of it, as **ob** his name were written all over his face."

It might have been written a hundred **Mal**, easily, on that enormous face. Humpty Dumpty was sitting **mit** his legs crossed, like a Turk, on the top of a high wall—such a narrow one that Alice quite wondered **wie er konnte** keep his balance—and, as his eyes were steadily fixed in the opposite direction, **und er** did not take the least notice of her, **sie dachte**, **er muss** be a stuffed figure after all.

"**Und wie** exactly like an egg **er** is!" she said aloud, standing **mit** her hands ready to catch him, for she was every moment expecting him to fall.

"It's **sehr** provoking," Humpty Dumpty said after a long silence, **sah** away from Alice as **er** spoke, "to be called an egg—Very!"

51

"**Ich** said **Sie sehen** like an egg, Sir," Alice gently explained. "**Und** some eggs are **sehr** pretty, **wissen Sie**" she added, hoping to turn her remark **in** a sort of a compliment.

"Some **Menschen**," said Humpty Dumpty, **sah** away from her as usual, "have no more sense **als** a baby!"

Alice did not know what to say to this: it was not at all like conversation, **sie dachte**, as **er** never said anything to her; in fact, his last remark was evidently addressed to a tree—so she stood **und** softly repeated to herself:—

"Humpty Dumpty sat on a wall: Humpty Dumpty had a great fall. All the King's horses **und** all the King's men Couldn't put Humpty Dumpty in **seinen Platz** again."

"That last line is much too long for the poetry," she added, almost out loud, forgetting that Humpty Dumpty would hear her.

"Do not stand there chattering to yourself like that," Humpty Dumpty said, **sah** at her for the first time, "**aber** tell me your name **und** your business."

"My name is Alice, but—"

"It's a stupid enough name!" Humpty Dumpty interrupted impatiently. "What does it mean?"

"Must a name mean something?" Alice asked doubtfully.

"Of course it must," Humpty Dumpty said **mit** a short laugh: "my name means the shape **ich** am—and a good handsome shape it is, too. **Mit** a name like yours, **sie könnte** be any shape, almost."

"**Warum** do you sit out here all alone?" said Alice, not wishing to begin an argument.

"**Warum**, **weil** there's nobody **mit** me!" cried Humpty Dumpty. "**Denken Sie dass ich** did not know the answer to that? Ask another."

"**Denken Sie** not you'd be safer down on the ground?" Alice went on, not **mit** any idea to **machen** another riddle, **aber** simply in her good-natured anxiety for the queer creature. "That wall is so **sehr** narrow!"

"What tremendously easy riddles you ask!" Humpty Dumpty growled out. "Of course **ich denke nicht** so! **Warum**, **wenn ich** ever did fall off—which there's no chance of—but **wenn ich** did—" Here **er** pursed his lips **und** looked so solemn **und** grand that Alice could hardly help laughing. "**Wenn ich** did fall," **er redete** on, "The King has promised me—with his **sehr** own mouth—to—to—"

"To send all his horses **und** all his men," Alice interrupted, rather unwisely.

"Now **ich** declare that's too bad!" Humpty Dumpty cried, breaking **in** a sudden passion. "You have been listening at doors—and behind trees—and down chimneys—or **Sie hätten können** not known it!"

"**Ich** haven't, indeed!" Alice said **sehr** gently. "It's in a book."

"Ah, **gut**! **Man darf** write such things in a book," Humpty Dumpty said in a calmer tone. "That's what you call a **Geschichte** of England, that is. Now, take a good look at me! I'm one that has spoken to a King, **ich** am: mayhap you will never see such another: **und** to show you I'm not proud, **sie können** shake hands **mit** me!" **Und er** grinned almost from ear to ear, as **er** leant forwards (**und** as nearly as possible fell off the wall in doing so) **und** offered Alice his hand. She watched him a little anxiously as **sie nahm** it. "**Wenn er** smiled much more, the ends of his mouth might meet behind," **sie dachte**: "**und** then **ich weiß nicht** what would happen to his head! I'm afraid it would come off!"

"Yes, all his horses **und** all his men," Humpty Dumpty went on. "They'd pick me up again in a minute, **sie würden**! **Jedoch**, this conversation **geht** a little too fast: let's go back to the last remark **aber** one."

"I'm afraid **ich** can't quite remember it," Alice said **sehr** politely.

"In that case **wir** start fresh," said Humpty Dumpty, "**und** it's my turn to choose a subject—" ("**Er** talks about it just as **ob** it was **ein Spiel**!" thought Alice.) "So here's a question for you. **Wie** old did you say **Sie sind**?"

Alice made a short calculation, **und** said "Seven years **und** six months."

"Wrong!" Humpty Dumpty exclaimed triumphantly. "You never said a word like it!"

"**Ich** though you meant '**Wie** old are you?'" Alice explained.

"**Wenn** I'd meant that, I'd have said it," said Humpty Dumpty.

Alice did not want to begin another argument, so she said nothing.

"Seven years **und** six months!" Humpty Dumpty repeated thoughtfully. "An uncomfortable sort of age. Now **wenn** you'd asked my advice, I'd have said 'Leave off at seven'—but it's too late now."

"**Ich** never ask advice about growing," Alice said indignantly.

"Too proud?" the other inquired.

Alice felt even more indignant at this suggestion. "**Ich** mean," she said, "that one can't help growing older."

"One can't, perhaps," said Humpty Dumpty, "**aber zwei** can. **Mit** proper assistance, **sie hätten können** left off at seven."

"What a beautiful belt you have got on!" Alice suddenly remarked.

(**Sie hatten** had quite enough of the subject of age, **sie dachte**: **und wenn sie** really **abwechseln** in choosing subjects, it was her turn now.) "At least," she corrected herself on second thoughts, "a beautiful cravat, **ich hätte sollen** said—no, a belt, **ich** mean—I beg your pardon!" she added in dismay, for Humpty Dumpty looked thoroughly offended, **und** she began to wish **sie hatte** not chosen that subject. "**Wenn ich** only knew," **sie dachte** to herself, "which was neck **und** which was waist!"

Evidently Humpty Dumpty was **sehr** angry, though **er** said nothing for a minute **oder zwei**. **Als er** did speak again, it was in a deep growl.

"It is a—most—provoking—thing," **er** said at last, "**wenn** a person doesn't know a cravat from a belt!"

"**Ich weiß** it's **sehr** ignorant of me," Alice said, in so humble a tone that Humpty Dumpty relented.

"It's a cravat, child, **und** a beautiful one, as you say. It's a present from the White King **und** Queen. There now!"

"Is it really?" said Alice, quite pleased to **finden** that **sie hatte** chosen a good subject, after all.

"**Sie** gave it me," Humpty Dumpty continued thoughtfully, as **er** crossed one knee over the other **und** clasped his hands round it, "**sie** gave it me—for an un-birthday present."

"**Ich** beg your pardon?" Alice said **mit** a puzzled **Luft**.

"I'm not offended," said Humpty Dumpty.

"**Ich** mean, what is an un-birthday present?"

"A present given **wann** it isn't your birthday, of course."

Alice considered a little. "**Ich mag** birthday presents best," she said at last.

"**Du weisst es nicht** what you are talking about!" cried Humpty Dumpty. "**Wie** many **Tage** are there in a year?"

"Three hundred **und** sixty-five," said Alice.

"**Und wie** many birthdays have you?"

"One."

"**Und wenn sie nehmen** one from three hundred **und** sixty-five, what remains?"

"Three hundred **und** sixty-four, of course."

Humpty Dumpty looked doubtful. "I'd rather see that done on paper," **er** said.

Alice couldn't help smiling as **sie nahm** out her memorandum-book, **und** worked the sum for him:

365 1 ____ 364 ___ Humpty Dumpty took the book, **und** looked at it carefully. "That seems to be done right—" **er** began.

"You are holding it upside down!" Alice interrupted.

"To be sure **ich** was!" Humpty Dumpty said gaily, as she turned it round for him. "**Ich dachte** it looked a little queer. As **ich** was saying, that seems to be done right—though **ich** haven't time to **sehen** it over thoroughly just now—and that shows that **es gibt** three hundred **und** sixty-four **Tage wenn man könnte** get un-birthday presents—"

"Certainly," said Alice.

"**Und** only one for birthday presents, **wissen Sie**. There's glory for you!"

"**Ich weiß nicht** what you mean by 'glory,'" Alice said.

Humpty Dumpty smiled contemptuously. "Of course you do not—till **ich** tell you. **Ich** meant 'there's a nice knock-down argument for you!'"

"**Aber** 'glory' doesn't mean 'a nice knock-down argument,'" Alice objected.

"**Wenn ich benutze** a word," Humpty Dumpty said in rather a scornful tone, "it means just what **ich** choose it to mean—neither more nor less."

"The question is," said Alice, "whether **Sie können** make words mean so many different things."

"The question is," said Humpty Dumpty, "which is to be master—that's all."

Alice was too much puzzled to say anything, so after a minute Humpty Dumpty began again. "**Sie** have a temper, some of them—particularly verbs, **sie** are the proudest—adjectives **man kann** do anything **mit ihnen**, **aber** not verbs—however, **ich kann** manage the whole lot of **ihnen**! Impenetrability! That's what **ich** say!"

"Would you tell me, please," said Alice "what that means?"

"Now you talk like a reasonable child," said Humpty Dumpty, **er sah sehr** much pleased **aus**. "**Ich** meant by 'impenetrability' that **wir** have had enough of that subject, **und** it would be just as **gut, wenn** you'd mention what you mean **zu tun** next, as **ich** suppose you do not mean to stop here all the rest **<u>Ihres Lebens</u>**."

"That's a great deal **zu machen** one word mean," Alice said in a thoughtful tone.

"**Wenn ich machen** a word do a lot of work like that," said Humpty Dumpty, "**Ich** always pay it extra."

"Oh!" said Alice. She was too much puzzled **zu machen** any other remark.

"Ah, **Sie sollten** see "em come round me of a Saturday night," Humpty Dumpty went on, wagging his head gravely from side to side: "for to get their wages, **wissen Sie**."

(Alice did not venture to ask **mit** what **er** paid **sie**; **und** so, **<u>sehen Sie</u>, ich** can't tell you.)

"You seem **sehr** clever at explaining words, Sir," said Alice. "Would you kindly tell me the meaning of the poem called 'Jabberwocky'?"

"Let's hear it," said Humpty Dumpty. "**Ich kann** explain all the poems that were ever invented—and a good many that haven't been invented just yet."

This sounded **sehr** hopeful, so Alice repeated the first verse:

'Twas brillig, **und** the slithy toves Did gyre **und** gimble in the wabe; All mimsy were the borogoves, **Und** the mome raths outgrabe.

"That's enough to begin **mit**," Humpty Dumpty interrupted: "**es gibt** plenty of hard words there. 'Brillig' means four o'clock in the afternoon—the time **wenn** you begin broiling things for dinner."

"That will do **sehr gut**," said Alice: "**und** 'slithy'?"

"**Gut**, 'slithy' means 'lithe **und** slimy.' 'Lithe' is the same as 'active.' **Sehen Sie**, it's like a portmanteau—there are **zwei** meanings packed up **in** one word."

"**Ich verstehe** it now," Alice remarked thoughtfully: "**und** what are 'toves'?"

"**Gut**, 'toves' are something like badgers—they are something like lizards—and **sie** are something like corkscrews."

"**Sie müssen** be **sehr** curious **<u>aussehende</u>** creatures."

"**Sie** are that," said Humpty Dumpty: "**auch sie machen** their nests under sun-dials—also **sie** live on cheese."

"**Und** what's the 'gyre' **und** to 'gimble'?"

"To 'gyre' is **zu gehen** round **und** round like a gyroscope. To 'gimble' is **zu machen** holes like a gimlet."

"**Und** 'the wabe' is the grass-plot round a sun-dial, **ich** suppose?" said Alice, surprised at her own ingenuity.

"Of course it is. It's called 'wabe,' **wissen Sie**, **weil** it **geht** a long **<u>Weg davor</u>**, **und** a long **Weg** behind it—"

"**Und** a long **Weg** beyond it on each side," Alice added.

"Exactly so. **Gut**, then, 'mimsy' is 'flimsy **und** miserable' (there's another portmanteau for you). **Und** a 'borogove' is a thin shabby-looking bird **mit** its feathers sticking out all round—something like a live mop."

"**Und** then 'mome raths'?" said Alice. "I'm afraid I'm giving you a great deal of trouble."

"**Gut**, a 'rath' is a sort of green pig: **aber** 'mome' I'm not certain about. **Meiner Ansicht nach** it's short for 'from home'—meaning that they'd lost **ihren Weg**, **wissen Sie**."

"**Und** what does 'outgrabe' mean?"

"**Gut**, 'outgrabing' is something **zwischen** bellowing **und** whistling, **mit** a kind of sneeze in the middle: **jedoch**, you will hear it done, maybe—down in the wood yonder—and **wenn** you have once heard it you will be quite content. Who's been repeating all that hard stuff to you?"

"**<u>Ich lese</u>** it in a book," said Alice. "**Aber ich hatte** some poetry repeated to me, much easier **als** that, by—Tweedledee, **meiner Ansicht nach** it was."

"As to poetry, **wissen Sie**," said Humpty Dumpty, stretching out one of his great hands, "**Ich kann** repeat poetry as **gut** as other folk, **wenn** it comes to that—"

"Oh, it need not come to that!" Alice hastily said, hoping to keep him from beginning.

"The piece I'm going to repeat," **er redete** on without noticing her remark, "was written entirely for your amusement."

Alice felt that in that case she really ought to listen to it, so she sat down, **und** said "Thank you" rather sadly.

"In winter, **wenn** the fields are white, **ich** sing this song for your delight—

only **ich** do not sing it," **er** added, as an explanation.

"**Ich verstehe** you do not," said Alice.

"**Wenn Sie können** see whether I'm singing **oder** not, you have sharper eyes **als** most." Humpty Dumpty remarked severely. Alice was silent.

"In spring, **wenn** woods are getting green, **ich** will try **und** tell you what **ich** mean."

"Thank you **sehr** much," said Alice.

"In summer, **wenn** the **Tage** are long, Perhaps you will understand the song:

In autumn, **wenn** the leaves are brown, Take pen **und** ink, **und** write it down."

"**Ich** will, **wenn ich kann** remember it so long," said Alice.

"**Sie brauchen** not go on making remarks like that," Humpty Dumpty said: "**sie** are not sensible, **und sie** put me out."

"**Ich** sent a message to the fish: **ich** told **ihnen** 'This is what **ich** wish.'

The little fishes of the sea, **Sie** sent an answer back to me.

The little fishes' answer was '**Wir** cannot do it, Sir, because— '"

"I'm afraid **ich** do not quite understand," said Alice.

"It gets easier further on," Humpty Dumpty replied.

"**Ich** sent to **ihnen** again to say 'It will be better to obey.'

The fishes answered **mit** a grin, '**Warum**, what a temper you are in!'

**Ich** told **ihnen** once, **ich** told **ihnen** twice: **Sie würden** not listen to advice.

**Ich nahm** a kettle large **und** new, Fit for the deed **die ich tun musste**.

My heart went hop, my heart went thump; **ich** filled the kettle at the pump.

Then some one came to me **und** said, 'The little fishes are in bed.'

**Ich** said to him, **ich** said it plain, 'Then **sie müssen** wake **sie** up again.'

**Ich** said it **sehr** loud **und** clear; **ich ging und** shouted in his ear."

Humpty Dumpty raised his voice almost to a scream as **er** repeated this verse, **und** Alice thought **mit** a shudder, "**Ich würde** not have been the messenger for anything!"

"**Doch er** was **sehr** stiff **und** proud; **Er** said '**Sie brauchen** not shout so loud!'

**Und er** was **sehr** proud **und** stiff; **Er** said 'I'd go **und** wake **sie**, if—'

**ich nahm** a corkscrew from the shelf: **ich ging** to wake **sie** up myself.

<u>**Und wenn ich gefunden habe**</u> the door was locked, **ich** pulled **und** pushed **und** kicked **und** knocked.

<u>**Und wenn ich gefunden habe**</u> the door was shut, **ich** tried to turn the handle, but—"

**Es gab** a long pause.

"Is that all?" Alice timidly asked.

"That's all," said Humpty Dumpty. "Good-bye."

This was rather sudden, Alice thought: **aber**, after such a **sehr** strong hint that she ought to be going, she felt that it would hardly be civil to stay. So she got up, **und** held out her hand. "Good-bye, till **wir** meet again!" she said as cheerfully as **sie konnte**.

"**Ich werde** not know you again **wenn wir** did meet," Humpty Dumpty replied in a discontented tone, giving her one of his fingers to shake; "you are so exactly like other **Menschen**."

"The face is what one **geht** by, generally," Alice remarked in a thoughtful tone.

"That's just what **ich** complain of," said Humpty Dumpty. "Your face is the same as everybody has—the **zwei** eyes, so—" (marking their <u>**Plätze**</u> in **der Luft mit** this thumb) "nose in the middle, mouth under. It's always the same. Now **wenn Sie hätten** the **zwei** eyes on the same side of the nose, for instance—or the mouth at the top—that would be some help."

"It wouldn't look nice," Alice objected. **Aber** Humpty Dumpty only shut his eyes **und** said "Wait till you have tried."

Alice waited a minute **zu sehen, ob er würde** speak again, **aber** as **er** never opened his eyes **oder** took any further notice of her, she said "Good-bye!" once more, **und**, getting no answer to this, she quietly walked away: **aber sie konnte** not help saying to herself as **sie ging**, "Of all the unsatisfactory—" (she repeated this aloud, as it was a great comfort **zu haben** such a long word to say) "of all the unsatisfactory **Leute die ich** ever met—" She never finished the sentence, for at this moment a heavy crash shook the forest from end to end.

# weeve
## Chapter 6

| German | Pronunciation | English |
|---|---|---|
| man darf | man daəf | one may |
| ein Spiel | ain spi:l | a game |
| abwechseln | apvekseln | alternate |
| Luft | luft | air |
| du weisst es nicht | du vaist es nixt | you do not know |
| Tage | tagə | days |
| wenn ich benutze | vənn ix be:nut͡sə | when i use |
| ihres Lebens | i:res le:bəns | of your life |
| sehen sie | se:hən siə | can you see it |
| aussehende | ause:həndə | looking |
| weg davor | veg da:foə | away from it |
| ich lese | ix lesə | I read |
| und wenn ich gefunden habe | und vənn ix ge:fundən habə | and when I've found |
| Plätze | plet͡sə | places |
| ich hätte sollen | ix hete solən | I should have |
| ich verstehe | ix feəste:ə | I understand |
| in | in | in |
| machen | ma:xən | do |
| sie sind | zi: sint | they are |

61

# 7

# THE LION AND THE UNICORN

> A study by Chun et al. (2012) showed that when a group of students were asked to memorize a list of words from a list they forgot 44% after 5 weeks. When compared to a group which read a text containing the same words they only forgot 17%.

The next moment soldiers came running through the wood, at first in twos **und** threes, then ten **oder** twenty together, **und** at last in such crowds that **sie** seemed to fill the whole forest. Alice got behind a tree, for fear of being run over, **und** watched **sie** go by.

**Sie dachte** that in <u>**ihrem ganzen Leben**</u>, **dass sie hatte** never seen soldiers so uncertain on their feet: **sie sind** always tripped over something **oder** other, **und** whenever one went down, several more always fell over him, so that the ground was soon covered **mit** little heaps of men.

Then came the horses. Having four feet, these managed rather better **als** the foot-soldiers: **aber** even **sie** stumbled now **und** then; **und** it seemed to be a regular rule that, whenever a horse stumbled the rider fell off instantly. The confusion got worse every moment, **und** Alice was **sehr** glad to get out of the wood **in** an open <u>**Ort**</u>, **wo sie fand** the White King seated on the ground, busily writing in his memorandum-book.

"**Ich** have sent **sie** all!" the King cried in a tone of delight, on seeing Alice. "Did you happen to meet any soldiers, my dear, as you came through the wood?"

"Yes, **ich** did," said Alice: "several thousand, **ich sollte** think."

"Four thousand **zwei** hundred **und** seven, that's the exact <u>**Zahl**</u>," the King said, referring to his book. "**Ich konnte** not send all the horses, **wissen Sie, weil zwei** of **ihnen** are wanted **im Spiel. Und ich** haven't sent the **zwei** Messengers, either. **Sie sind** to the town **gegangen**. Just look along the road, **und** tell me **ob Sie können** see either of **ihnen**."

"**Ich sehe** nobody on the road," said Alice.

"**Ich** only wish **ich hatte** such eyes," the King remarked in a fretful tone. "To be able **zu sehen** Nobody! **Und** at that distance, too! It's as much as **ich kann** do **zu sehen** real **Menschen**, by this light!"

All this was lost on Alice, **die** still **sah** intently along the road, shading her eyes **mit** one hand. "**Ich sehe** somebody now!" she exclaimed at last. "**Aber** he's coming **sehr** slowly—and what curious attitudes **er geht in**!" (For the messenger kept skipping up **und** down, **und** wriggling like an eel, as **er** came along, **mit** his great hands spread out like fans on each side.)

"Not at all," said the King. "He's an Anglo-Saxon Messenger— and <u>**diese**</u> attitudes are Anglo-Saxon attitudes. **Er** only does **sie, wenn** he's happy. His name is Haigha." (**Er** pronounced it so as to rhyme **mit** "mayor.")

"**Ich** love my love **mit** an H," Alice couldn't help beginning, "**weil er** is Happy. **Ich** hate him **mit** an H, **weil er** is Hideous. **Ich** fed him with—with—with Ham-sandwiches **und** Hay. His name is Haigha, **und er** lives—"

"<u>**Er wohnt**</u> on the Hill," the King remarked simply, without the least idea that **er** was joining in **dem Spiel, während** Alice was still hesitating for the name of a town beginning **mit** H. "The other Messenger's called Hatta. **Ich muss** have **zwei**, you know—to come **und** go. One to come, **und** one **zu gehen**."

"**Ich** beg your pardon?" said Alice.

"It isn't respectable to beg," said the King.

"**Ich** only meant that **ich** did not understand," said Alice. "**Warum** one to come **und** one **gehen**?"

"Did not **ich** tell you?" the King repeated impatiently. "**Ich muss** have two—to fetch **und** carry. One to fetch, **und** one to carry."

At this moment the Messenger arrived: **er** was far too much out of breath to say a word, **und** could only wave his hands about, **und** make the most fearful faces at the poor King.

"This young lady loves you **mit** an H," the King said, introducing

63

Alice in the hope of turning off the Messenger's attention from himself—but it was no use—the Anglo-Saxon attitudes only got more extraordinary every moment, **während** the great eyes rolled wildly from side to side.

"You alarm me!" said the King. "**Ich** feel faint—Give me a ham sandwich!"

On which the Messenger, to Alice's great amusement, opened a bag that hung round his neck, **und** handed a sandwich to the King, **der** devoured it greedily.

"Another sandwich!" said the King.

"There's nothing **aber** hay left now," the Messenger said, peeping **in** the bag.

"Hay, then," the King murmured in a faint whisper.

Alice was glad **zu sehen** that it revived him a good deal. "There's nothing like eating hay **wenn** you are faint," **er** remarked to her, as **er** munched away.

"**Ich würde** think throwing cold water over **dich wäre** better," Alice suggested: "**oder** some sal-volatile."

"**Ich** did not say **es gab** nothing better," the King replied. "**Ich** said **es gab** nothing like it." Which Alice did not venture to deny.

"**Wer** did you pass on the road?" the King went on, holding out his hand to the Messenger for some more hay.

"Nobody," said the Messenger.

"Quite right," said the King: "this young lady saw him too. So of course Nobody walks slower **als** you."

"**Ich** do my best," the Messenger said in a sulky tone. "I'm sure nobody walks much faster **als ich** do!"

"**Er** can't do that," said the King, "**oder** else he'd have been here first. **Jedoch**, now you have got your breath, **Sie können** tell **uns** what's happened in the town."

"**Ich** will whisper it," said the Messenger, putting his hands to his mouth in the shape of a trumpet, **und** stooping so as to get close to the King's ear. Alice was sorry for this, as **sie wollte** to hear the news too. **Jedoch**, instead of whispering, **er** simply shouted at the top of his voice "**Sie** are at it again!"

"Do you call that a whisper?" cried the poor King, jumping up **und** shaking himself. "**Wenn** you do such a thing again, **ich** will have you buttered! It went through **und** through my head like an earthquake!"

"It would have to be a **sehr** tiny earthquake!" thought Alice. "**Wer** are at it again?" she ventured to ask.

"The Lion **und** the Unicorn, of course," said the King.

"Fighting for the crown?"

"Yes, to be sure," said the King: "**und** the best of the joke is, that it's my crown all the while! Let's run **und** see **sie**." **Und sie** trotted off, Alice repeating to herself, as she ran, the words of the old song:—

"The Lion **und** the Unicorn were fighting for the crown: The Lion beat the Unicorn all round the town. Some gave **ihnen** white bread, some gave **ihnen** brown; Some gave **ihnen** plumcake **und** drummed **sie** out of town."

"Does—the one—that wins—get the crown?" she asked, as **gut** as **sie konnte**, for the run was putting her quite out of breath.

"Dear me, no!" said the King. "What an idea!"

"Would you—be good enough," Alice panted out, after running a little further, "to stop a minute—just to get—one's breath again?"

"I'm good enough," the King said, "only I'm not strong enough. **Sie sehen**, a minute **geht** by so fearfully quick. **Man könnte** as **gut** try to stop a Bandersnatch!"

Alice had no more breath for talking, so **sie** trotted on in silence, till **sie** came in sight of a great crowd, in the middle of which the Lion **und** Unicorn were fighting. **Sie waren** in such a cloud of dust, that at first Alice couldn't make out which was which: **aber** she soon managed to distinguish the Unicorn by his horn.

**Sie** placed themselves close to **wo** Hatta, the other messenger, was standing watching the fight, **mit** a cup of tea in one hand **und** a piece of bread-and-butter in the other.

"He's only just out of prison, **und er hatte** not finished his tea **als er** was sent in," Haigha whispered to Alice: "**und sie** only give **ihnen** oyster-shells in there—so **sehen Sie**, he's **sehr** hungry **und** thirsty. **Wie geht es** you, dear child?" **er redete** on, putting his arm affectionately round Hatta's neck.

Hatta looked round **und** nodded, **und** went on **mit** his bread **und** butter.

"Were you happy in prison, dear child?" said Haigha.

Hatta looked round once more, **und** this time a tear **oder zwei** trickled down his cheek: **aber** not a word would **er** say.

"Speak, can't you!" Haigha cried impatiently. **Aber** Hatta only munched away, **und** drank some more tea.

"Speak, won't you!" cried the King. "**Wie** is it going **mit** the fight?"

Hatta made a desperate effort, **und** swallowed a large piece of bread-and-butter. "**Er** is going **sehr gut**," **er** said in a choking voice: "each of **ihnen** has been down about eighty-seven **Mal**."

"Then **ich** suppose **sie** will soon bring the white bread **und** the brown?" Alice ventured to remark.

"It's waiting for "em now," said Hatta: "this is a bit of it as I'm eating."

**Es gab** a pause in the fight just then, **und** the Lion **und** the Unicorn sat down, panting, **während** the King called out "Ten minutes allowed for refreshments!" Haigha **und** Hatta set **ans Werk** at once, carrying rough trays of white **und** brown bread. Alice took a piece to taste, **aber** it was **sehr** dry.

"**Ich glaube nicht**, **dass sie** will fight any more to-day," the King said to Hatta: "go **und** order the drums to begin." **Und** Hatta went bounding away like a grasshopper.

For a minute **oder zwei** Alice stood silent, watching him. Suddenly she brightened up. "Look, look!" she cried, pointing eagerly. "There's the White Queen running across the country! She came flying out of the wood over yonder—How fast **diese** Queens can run!"

"There's some enemy after her, no doubt," the King said, without even a **Blick** round. "That wood's full of **ihnen**."

"**Aber** are not you going to run **und** help her?" Alice asked, **sehr** much surprised at his takingit so quietly.

"No use, no use!" said the King. "She runs so fearfully quick. **Man könnte** as **gut** try to catch a Bandersnatch! **Aber ich werde machen** a memorandum about her, **wenn** you like—She's a dear good creature," **er** repeated softly to himself, as **er** opened his memorandum-book. "Do you spell 'creature' **mit** a double 'e'?"

At this moment the Unicorn sauntered by **ihnen**, **mit** his hands in his pockets. "**Ich hatte** the best of it this time?" **er** said to the King, just glancing at him as **er** passed.

"A little—a little," the King replied, rather nervously. "**Sie hätten sollten** not run him through **mit** your horn, **wissen Sie**."

"It did not hurt him," the Unicorn said carelessly, **und er redete** on, **als** his eye happened to fall upon Alice: **er** turned round rather instantly, **und** stood for some time **undsah** at her **mit einer** Luft of the deepest disgust.

"What—is—this?" **er** said at last.

"This is a child!" Haigha replied eagerly, coming in front of Alice to introduce her, **und** spreading out both his hands towards her in an Anglo-Saxon attitude. "**Wir** only found it to-day. It's as large as life, **und** twice as natural!"

"**Ich** always thought **sie sind** fabulous monsters!" said the Unicorn. "Is it alive?"

"It can talk," said Haigha, solemnly.

The Unicorn looked dreamily at Alice, **und** said "Talk, child."

Alice couldn't help her lips curling up **in** a smile as she began: "**Wissen sie, ich** always thought Unicorns were fabulous monsters, too! **Ich** never saw one alive **noch nie**!"

"**Gut**, now that **wir haben gesehen** each other," said the Unicorn, "**wenn** you will believe in me, **ich** will believe in you. Is that a bargain?"

"Yes, **wenn Sie möchten**," said Alice.

"Come, fetch out the plum-cake, old man!" the Unicorn went on, turning from her to the King. "None of your brown bread for me!"

"Certainly—certainly!" the King muttered, **und** beckoned to Haigha. "Open the bag!" **er** whispered. "Quick! Not that one—that's full of hay!"

Haigha took a large cake out of the bag, **und** gave it to Alice to hold, **während er** got out a dish **und** carving-knife. **Wie sie** all came out of it Alice couldn't guess. It was just like a conjuring-trick, **sie dachte**.

The Lion had joined **sie während** this wasgoing on: **er sah sehr** tired **und** sleepy **aus, und** his eyes were half shut. "What's this!" **er** said, blinking lazily at Alice, **und** speaking in a deep hollow tone that sounded like the tolling of a great bell.

"Ah, what is it, now?" the Unicorn cried eagerly. "You will never guess! **Ich könnte** not."

The Lion looked at Alice wearily. "Are you animal—vegetable—or mineral?" **er** said, yawning at every other word.

"It's a fabulous monster!" the Unicorn cried out, **bevor** Alice could reply.

"Then hand round the plum-cake, Monster," the Lion said, lying down **und** putting his chin on his paws. "**Und** sit down, both of you," (to the King **und** the Unicorn): "fair play **mit** the cake,

**wissen Sie!**"

The King was evidently **sehr** uncomfortable at having to sit down **zwischen** the **zwei** great creatures; **aber es gab** no other **Platz** for him.

"What a fight **wir könnten** have for the crown, now!" the Unicorn said, **er sah** slyly up at the crown, which the poor King was nearly shaking off his head, **er** trembled so much.

"**Ich würde** win easy," said the Lion.

"I'm not so sure of that," said the Unicorn.

"**Ich** beat you all round the town, you chicken!" the Lion replied angrily, half getting up as **er** spoke.

Here the King interrupted, to prevent the quarrelgoing on: **er** was **sehr** nervous, **und** his voice quite quivered. "All round the town?" **er** said. "That's a good long **Weg**. **<u>Seid ihr gegangen</u>** by the old bridge, **oder** the market-place? You get the best view by the old bridge."

"I'm sure **ich weiß nicht**," the Lion growled out as **er** lay down again. "**Es gab** too much dust **um zu sehen** anything. What **eine Zeit** the Monster is, cutting up that cake!"

Alice had seated herself on the bank of a little brook, **mit** the great dish on her knees, **und** was sawing away diligently **mit** the knife. "It's **sehr** provoking!" she said, in reply to the Lion (she was was quite **daran gewöhnt** being called "the Monster"). "**Ich** have cut several slices already, **aber sie** always join on again!"

"**Sie wissen nicht wie** to manage **Spiegel**-glass cakes," the Unicorn remarked. "Hand it round first, **und** cut it afterwards."

This sounded nonsense, **aber** Alice **sehr** obediently got up, **und** carried the dish round, **und** the cake divided itself **in** three pieces as she did so. "Now cut it up," said the Lion, as she returned to **ihrem Platz mit** the empty dish.

"**Ich** say, this isn't fair!" cried the Unicorn, as Alice sat **mit** the knife in her hand, **sehr** much puzzled **wie** to begin. "The Monster has given the Lion twice as much as me!"

"She's kept none for herself, anyhow," said the Lion. "**<u>Essen Sie gern</u>** plum-cake, Monster?" **Aber bevor** Alice could answer him, the drums began. **Wo** the noise came from, **sie konnte** not make out: **die Luft** seemed full of it, **und** it rang through **und** through her head till she felt quite deafened. **<u>Sie stand auf</u> und** sprang across the little brook in her terror,

\* \* \* \* \* \* \*

\* \* \* \* \* \*

\* \* \* \* \* \* \*

**und** had just time **zu sehen** the Lion **und** the Unicorn rise to their feet, **mit** angry <u>**Blicke**</u> at being interrupted in their feast, **bevor** she dropped to her knees, **und** put her hands over her ears, vainly trying to shut out the dreadful uproar.

"**Wenn** that doesn't 'drum **sie** out of town,'" **sie dachte** to herself, "nothing ever will!"

## weeve
### Chapter 7

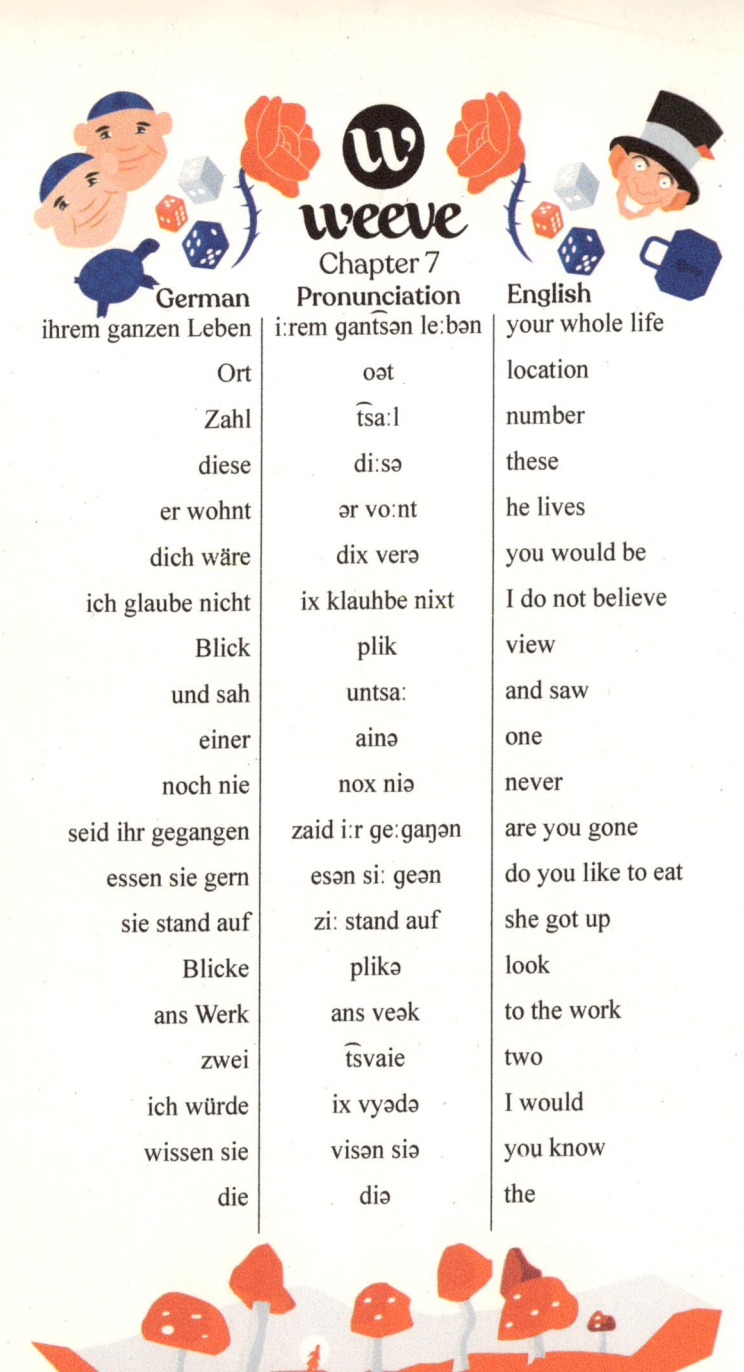

| German | Pronunciation | English |
|---|---|---|
| ihrem ganzen Leben | i:rem gantsən le:bən | your whole life |
| Ort | oət | location |
| Zahl | tsa:l | number |
| diese | di:sə | these |
| er wohnt | ər vo:nt | he lives |
| dich wäre | dix verə | you would be |
| ich glaube nicht | ix klauhbe nixt | I do not believe |
| Blick | plik | view |
| und sah | untsa: | and saw |
| einer | ainə | one |
| noch nie | nox niə | never |
| seid ihr gegangen | zaid i:r ge:gaŋən | are you gone |
| essen sie gern | esən si: geən | do you like to eat |
| sie stand auf | zi: stand auf | she got up |
| Blicke | plikə | look |
| ans Werk | ans veək | to the work |
| zwei | tsvaie | two |
| ich würde | ix vyədə | I would |
| wissen sie | visən siə | you know |
| die | diə | the |

70

# 8

# "IT'S MY OWN INVENTION"

In a 2006 study titled How Large a Vocabulary Is Needed For Reading and Listening? it was found that 95% of understood vocabulary (1 unknown word in 20) is necessary for reading a text and understanding it. This is the true value of weeve.

After a **Weile** the noise seemed gradually to die away, till all was dead silence, **und** Alice lifted up her head in some alarm. **Es gab** no one to be seen, **und** her first thought was that **sie muss** have been dreaming about the Lion **und** the Unicorn **und diese** queer Anglo-Saxon Messengers. **Jedoch, gab es** the great dish still lying at her feet, on which **sie hatte** tried to cut the plum-cake, "So **ich** was not dreaming, after all," she said to herself, "unless—unless **wir** are all Teil of the same dream. Only **ich** do hope it's my dream, **und** not the Red King's! **Ich** belong **nicht gern** to another person's dream," **sie redete** on in a rather complaining tone: "**Ich** have a great mind **zu gehen und** wake him, **und** see what happens!"

At this moment her thoughts were interrupted by a loud shouting of "Ahoy! Ahoy! Check!" **und** a Knight dressed in crimson armour came galloping down upon her, brandishing a great club. Just as **er** reached her, the horse stopped suddenly: "You are my prisoner!" the Knight cried, as **er** tumbled off his horse.

Startled as she was, Alice was more frightened for him **als** for herself at the moment, **und** watched him **mit** some anxiety as **er** mounted again. As soon as **er** was comfortably in the saddle, **er** began once more "You are my—" **aber** here another voice broke in "Ahoy! Ahoy! Check!" **und** Alice looked round in some surprise for the new enemy.

This time it was a White Knight. **Er** drew up at Alice's side, **und** tumbled off his horse just as the Red Knight had done: then **er** got on again, **und** the **zwei** Knights sat **und** looked at each other for some time without speaking. Alice looked from one to the other in some bewilderment.

"She's my prisoner, **wissen Sie**!" the Red Knight said at last.

"Yes, **aber** then **ich** came **und** rescued her!" the White Knight replied.

"**Gut, wir müssen** fight for her, then," said the Red Knight, as **er nahm** up his helmet (which hung from the saddle, **und** was something the shape of a horse's head), **und** put it on.

"You will observe the Rules of Battle, of course?" the White Knight remarked, putting on his helmet too.

"**Ich** always do," said the Red Knight, **und sie** began banging away at each other **mit** such fury that Alice got behind a tree to be **aus dem Weg** of the blows.

"**Ich** wonder, now, what the Rules of Battle are," she said to herself, as she watched the fight, timidly peeping out from her hiding-place: "one Rule seems to be, that **wenn** one Knight hits the other, **er** knocks him off his horse, **und wenn er** misses, **er** tumbles off himself—and another Rule seems to be that **sie** hold their clubs **mit** their arms, as **ob sie wären** Punch **und** Judy— What a noise **sie machen, wenn sie** tumble! Just like a whole set of fire-irons falling **in** the fender! **Und wie** quiet the horses are! **Sie** let **sie** get on **und** off **sie** just as **ob sie wären** tables!"

Another Rule of Battle, that Alice had not noticed, seemed to be that **sie** always fell on their heads, **und** the battle ended **mit** their both falling off in this **Weg**, side by side: **als sie** got up again, **sie** shook hands, **und** then the Red Knight mounted **und** galloped off.

"It was a glorious victory, was not it?" said the White Knight, as **er** came up panting.

"**Ich weiß nicht**," Alice said doubtfully. "**Ich möchte nicht** to be anybody's prisoner. **Ich möchte** to be a Queen."

"So you will, **wann** you have crossed the next brook," said the White Knight. "**Ich werde sehen** you safe to the end of the wood—and then **ich muss** go back, **wissen Sie**. That's the end of my move."

"Thank you very much," said Alice. "May **ich helfe** you off **mit** your helmet?" It was evidently more **als er konnte** manage by himself; **jedoch**, she managed to shake him out of it at last.

"Now one can breathe more easily," said the Knight, putting back his shaggy hair **mit** both hands, **und** turning his gentle face **und** large mild eyes to Alice. **Sie dachte, sie hatte** never seen such a strange-looking soldier in all **ihrem Leben**.

**Er** was dressed in tin armour, which seemed to fit him **sehr** badly, **und er hatte** a queer-shaped little deal box fastened across his shoulder, upside-down, **und mit** the lid hanging open. Alice looked at it **mit** great curiosity.

"**Ich verstehe** you are admiring my little box." the Knight said in a friendly tone. "It's my own invention—to keep clothes **und** sandwiches in. **Wie Sie sehen ich** carry it upside-down, so that the rain can't get in."

"**Aber** the things can get out," Alice gently remarked. "**Wissen Sie** the lid's open?"

"**Ich** did not know it," the Knight said, a shade of vexation passing over his face. "Then all the things must have fallen out! **Und** the box is no use without **sie**." **Er** unfastened it as **er** spoke, **und** was just going to throw it **in** the bushes, **als** a sudden thought seemed to strike him, **und er** hung it carefully on a tree. "Can you guess **warum ich** did that?" **er** said to Alice.

Alice shook her head.

"In hopes some bees may make a nest in it—then **ich werde** get the honey."

"**Aber** you have got a bee-hive—or something like one—fastened to the saddle," said Alice.

"Yes, it's a **sehr** good bee-hive," the Knight said in a discontented tone, "one of the best kind. **Aber** not a single bee has come near it yet. **Und** the other thing is a mouse-trap. **Ich** suppose the mice keep the bees out—or the bees keep the mice out, **ich weiß nicht** which."

"**Ich** was wondering what the mouse-trap was for," said Alice. "It isn't **sehr** likely there would be any mice on the horse's back."

"Not **sehr** likely, perhaps," said the Knight: "**aber wenn sie** do come, **ich** do not choose **zu haben sie** running all about."

"**Sie sehen,,**" **er redete** on after a pause, "it's as **gut** to be provided for everything. That's the reason the horse has all **jene** anklets round his feet."

"**Aber** what are **sie** for?" Alice asked in a tone of great curiosity.

"To guard against the bites of sharks," the Knight replied. "It's an invention of my own. **Und** now help me on. **Ich werde gehen mit** you to the end of the wood—What's the dish for?"

"It's meant for plum-cake," said Alice.

"We'd better take it **mit uns**," the Knight said. "It will come in handy **wenn wir finden** any plum-cake. Help me to get it **in** this bag."

This took a **sehr** long time to manage, though Alice held the bag open **sehr** carefully, **weil** the Knight was so **sehr** awkward in putting in the dish: the first **zwei oder** three **Mal** that **er** tried **er** fell in himself instead. "It's rather a tight fit, **wissen Sie,**," **er** said, as **sie** got it in a last; "**Es gibt** so many candlesticks in the bag." **Und er** hung it to the saddle, which was already loaded **mit** bunches of carrots, **und** fire-irons, **und** many other things.

"**Ich** hope you have got your hair **gut** fastened on?" **er** continued, as **sie** set off.

"Only in the usual **Weg**," Alice said, smiling.

"That's hardly enough," **er** said, anxiously. "**Wissen Sie**, the wind is so **sehr** strong here. It's as strong as soup."

"Have you invented a plan to **verhindern** the hair from blowing off?" Alice enquired.

"Not yet," said the Knight. "**Aber ich** have got a plan to **aufbewahrungverhindern** it from falling off."

"**Ich sollte** like to hear it, **sehr** much."

"First **man nimmt** an upright stick," said the Knight. "Then **man macht** their hair creep up it, like a fruit-tree. Now the reason hair falls off is **weil** it hangs down—things never fall upwards, **wissen Sie**. It's a plan of my own invention. **Sie können** try it **wenn Sie möchten**."

It did not sound a comfortable plan, Alice thought, **und** for a few minutes she walked on in silence, puzzling over the idea, **und** every now **und** then stopping **zu helfen** the poor Knight, **der** certainly was not a good rider.

Whenever the horse stopped (which it did **sehr oft**), **er** fell off in front; **und** whenever it went on again (which it generally did rather suddenly), **er** fell off behind. Otherwise **er hielt** on pretty **gut**, except that **er hatte** a habit of now **und** then falling off sideways; **und** as **er** generally did this on the side on which Alice was walking, she soon found that it was the best plan not to walk quite close to the horse.

"I'm afraid you haven't had much practice in riding," she ventured to say, as she **half** him up from his fifth tumble.

The Knight looked **sehr** much surprised, **und** a little offended at the remark. "What makes you say that?" **er** asked, as **er** scrambled back **in** the saddle, **hielt** Alice's hair **mit** one hand, to save himself from falling over on the other side.

"**Weil Leute** do not fall off quite so **häufig, wenn sie** have had much practice."

"**Ich** have had plenty of practice," the Knight said **sehr** gravely: "plenty of practice!"

Alice could think of nothing better to say **als** "Indeed?" **aber** she said it as heartily as **sie konnte**. **Sie gingen** on a little **Weg** in silence after this, the Knight **mit** his eyes shut, muttering to himself, **und** Alice watching anxiously for the next tumble.

"The great **Kunst** of riding," the Knight suddenly began in a loud voice, waving his right arm as **er** spoke, "is to keep—" Here the sentence ended as suddenly as it had begun, as the Knight fell heavily on the top of his head exactly in the path **wo** Alice was walking. She was quite frightened this time, **und** said in an anxious tone, as she picked him up, "**Ich** hope no bones are broken?"

"None to speak of," the Knight said, as **wenn er** did not mind breaking **zwei oder** three of **sie**. "The great **Kunst** of riding, as **ich** was saying, is—to keep your balance properly. Like this, you know—"

**Er** let go the bridle, **und** stretched out both his arms to show Alice what **er** meant, **und** this time **er** fell flat on his back, right under the horse's feet.

"Plenty of practice!" **er redete** on repeating, **die ganze Zeit** that Alice was getting him on his feet again. "Plenty of practice!"

"It's too ridiculous!" cried Alice, losing all her patience this time. "You ought **haben** a wooden horse on wheels, that you ought!"

"Does that kind go smoothly?" the Knight asked in a tone of great interest, clasping his arms round the horse's neck as **er** spoke, just in time to save himself from tumbling off again.

"Much more smoothly **als** a live horse," Alice said, **mit** a little scream of laughter, in spite of all **sie konnte** do to prevent it.

"**Ich** will get one," the Knight said thoughtfully to himself. "One **oder** two—several."

**Es gab** a short silence after this, **und** then the Knight went on again. "I'm a great hand at inventing things. Now, **ich** daresay you noticed, that last time you picked me up, that **ich sah** rather thoughtful **aus**?"

75

"**Sie waren** a little grave," said Alice.

"**Gut**, just then **ich** was inventing a new **Weg** of getting over a gate— **möchten Sie** hear it?"

"**Sehr** much indeed," Alice said politely.

"**Ich** will tell you **wie ich** came **zu denken** of it," said the Knight. "**Wissen Sie,**, **ich** said to myself, 'The only difficulty is **mit** the feet: the head is high enough already.' Now, first **ich** put my head on the top of the gate—then **ich** stand on my head—then the feet are high enough, you see—then I'm over, **wissen Sie,**."

"Yes, **ich** suppose you'd be over **wenn** that was done," Alice said thoughtfully: "**aber <u>denkst du nicht</u>** it would be rather hard?"

"**Ich** haven't tried it yet," the Knight said, gravely: "so **ich** can't tell for certain—but I'm afraid it would be a little hard."

**Er sah** so vexed at the idea, that Alice changed the subject hastily. "What a curious helmet you have got!" she said cheerfully. "Is that your invention too?"

The Knight looked down proudly at his helmet, which hung from the saddle. "Yes," **er** said, "**aber ich** have invented a better one **als** that—like a sugar loaf. **<u>Wenn ich früher</u>** wore it, **wenn ich** fell off the horse, it always touched the ground directly. So **ich hatte** a **sehr** little **Weg** to fall, you see—But **es gab** the danger of falling **in** it, to be sure. That happened to me once—and the worst of it was, **bevor ich konnte** get out again, the other White Knight came **und** put it on. **Er dachte** it was his own helmet."

The knight looked so solemn about it that Alice did not dare to laugh. "I'm afraid **Sie müssen** have hurt him," she said in a trembling voice, "being on the top of his head."

"**Ich musste** kick him, of course," the Knight said, **sehr** seriously. "**Und** then **er nahm** the helmet off again—but it took hours **und** hours to get me out. **Ich** was as fast as—as lightning, **wissen Sie**."

"**Aber** that's a different kind of fastness," Alice objected.

The Knight shook his head. "It was all kinds of fastness **mit** me, **ich kann** assure you!" **er** said. **Er** raised his hands in some excitement as **er** said this, **und** instantly rolled out of the saddle, **und** fell headlong **in** a deep ditch.

Alice ran to the side of the ditch **um zu <u>suchen</u>** for him. She was rather startled by the fall, as for some time **<u>er hatte gehalten</u>** on **sehr gut**, **und** she was afraid that **er** really was hurt this time. **Jedoch**, though **sie konnte** see nothing **aber** the soles of his feet, she was much relieved to hear that **er** was talking on in his usual tone. "All kinds of fastness," **er** repeated: "**aber** it was careless of him to put another man's helmet on—with the man in it, too."

"**Wie** can **Sie** talk **weiter** so quietly, head downwards?" Alice asked, as she dragged him out by the feet, **und** laid him in a heap on the bank.

The Knight looked surprised at the question. "What does it matter **wo** my body happens to be?" **er** said. "**Mein Geist geht weiter** working all the same. In fact, the more head downwards **ich** am, the more **ich** keep inventing new things."

"Now the cleverest thing of the sort that **ich** ever did," **er redete** on after a pause, "was inventing a new pudding **während des Fleisch**-course."

"In time **um zu haben** it cooked for the next course?" said Alice. "**Gut**, not the next course," the Knight said in a slow thoughtful tone: "no, certainly not the next course."

"Then it would have to be the next day. **Ich** suppose **Sie hätten nicht zwei** pudding-courses in one dinner?"

"**Gut**, not the next day," the Knight repeated as **zuvor**: "not the next day. In fact," **er redete** on, holding his head down, **und** his voice getting lower **und** lower, "**Ich** do not believe that pudding ever was cooked! In fact, **ich** do not believe that pudding ever will be cooked! **Und** yet it was a **sehr** clever pudding to invent."

"What did you mean it to be made of?" Alice asked, hoping to cheer him up, for the poor Knight seemed quite low-spirited about it.

"It began **mit** blotting paper," the Knight answered **mit** a groan.

"That wouldn't be **sehr** nice, I'm afraid—"

"Not **sehr** nice alone," **er** interrupted, quite eagerly: "**aber** you have no idea what a difference it makes mixing it **mit** other things—such as gunpowder **und** sealing-wax. **Und** here **ich muss** leave you." **Sie hatten** just come to the end of the wood.

Alice could only look puzzled: she **dachte** of the pudding.

"You are sad," the Knight said in an anxious tone: "let me sing you a song to comfort you."

"Is it **sehr** long?" Alice asked, for **sie hatte** heard a good deal of poetry that day.

"It's long," said the Knight, "**aber sehr**, **sehr** beautiful. Everybody that hears me sing it—either it brings the tears **in** their eyes, **oder** else—"

"**Oder** else what?" said Alice, for the Knight had made a sudden pause.

"**Oder** else it doesn't, **wissen Sie**. The name of the song is called 'Haddocks' Eyes.'"

"Oh, that's the name of the song, is it?" Alice said, trying to feel interested.

"No, you do not understand," the Knight said, **er sah** a little vexed **aus**. "That's what the name is called. The name really is 'The Aged Aged Man.'"

"Then **ich** ought **haben** said 'That's what the song is called'?" Alice corrected herself.

"No, you ought not: that's quite another thing! The song is called '**Wege und** Means': **aber** that's only what it's called, **wissen Sie!**"

"**Gut**, what is the song, then?" said Alice, **wer** was by this time completely bewildered.

"**Ich** was coming to that," the Knight said. "The song really is 'A-sitting On A Gate': **und** the tune's my own invention."

So saying, **er** stopped his horse **und** let the reins fall on its neck: then, slowly beating time **mit** one hand, **und mit** a faint smile lighting up his gentle foolish face, as **ob er** enjoyed the music of his song, **er** began.

Of all the strange things that Alice saw in her journey Through The **Spiegel**-Glass, this was the one that she always remembered most clearly. **Jahre** afterwards **sie konnte** bring the whole scene back again, as **ob** it had been only yesterday—the mild blue eyes **und** kindly smile of the Knight—the setting sun gleaming through his hair, **und** shining on his armour in a blaze of light that quite dazzled her—the horse quietly moving about, **mit** the reins hanging loose on his neck, cropping the grass at her feet—and the black shadows of the forest behind—all this **sie nahm** in like a picture, as, **mit** one hand shading her eyes, she leant against a tree, watching the strange pair, **und** listening, in a half dream, to the melancholy music of the song.

"**Aber** the tune isn't his own invention," she said to herself: "it's '**Ich** give thee all, **ich kann** no more.'" She stood **und** listened **sehr** attentively, **aber** no tears came **in** her eyes.

"**Ich** will tell thee everything **ich kann**; There's little to relate. **Ich sah** an aged aged man, A-sitting on a gate. '**Wer** are you, aged man?' **ich** said, '**und wie** is it you live?'

**Und** his answer trickled through my head Like water through a sieve.

Er said '**Ich suche** for butterflies That sleep among the wheat: **ich mache sie zu** mutton-pies, **Und** sell **sie** in the street. **Ich** sell **sie** unto men,' er said, '**die** sail on stormy seas; **Und** that's **die Art, wie ich** get my bread— A trifle, **wenn** you please.'

**Aber ich dachte** of a plan To dye one's whiskers green, **Und** always use so large a fan That **sie konnten** not be seen. So, having no reply **zu geben** To what the old man said, **ich** cried, 'Come, tell me **wie** you live!'

**Und** thumped him on the head.

His accents mild took up the tale: **Er** said '**Ich gehe** my **Wege, Und wenn ich finden** a mountain-rill, **ich** set it in a blaze; **Und** thence **sie machen** a stuff **sie** call Rolands' Macassar Oil— Yet twopence-halfpenny is all **sie geben** me for my toil.'

**Aber ich dachte** of **eine Methode** To feed oneself on batter, **Und** so go on from day to day Getting a little fatter. **Ich** shook him **gut** from side to side, Until his face was blue: 'Come, tell me **wie** you live,' **ich** cried, '**Und** what it is you do!'

**Er** said '**Ich** hunt for haddocks' eyes Among the heather bright, **Und** work **sie in** waistcoat-buttons In the silent night. **Und** these **ich** do not sell for gold **Oder** coin of silvery shine **Aber** for a copper halfpenny, **Und** that will purchase nine.

'**Ich** sometimes dig for buttered rolls, **Oder** set limed twigs for crabs; **ich** sometimes search the grassy knolls For wheels of Hansom-cabs. **Und** that's the way' (**er gab** a wink) 'By which **ich** get my wealth— **Und sehr** gladly will **ich** drink Your Honour's noble **Gesundheit**.'

**Ich** heard him then, for **ich hatte** just Completed my design **um zu verhindern** that the Menai bridge rusts By boiling it in wine. **Ich** thanked him much for telling me **Die Art, wie er** got his wealth, **Aber** chiefly for his wish that **er** Might drink my noble **Gesundheit**.

**Und** now, **wenn** e'er by chance **ich** put My fingers **in** glue **Oder** madly squeeze a right-hand foot **In** a left-hand shoe, **Oder wenn ich** drop upon my toe A **sehr** heavy weight, **ich** weep, for it reminds me so, Of that old man **ich kannte** Whose look was mild, whose speech was slow, Whose hair was whiter **als** the snow, Whose face was **sehr** like a crow, **Mit** eyes, like cinders, all aglow, **der** seemed distracted **mit** his woe, **der** rocked his body to **und** fro, **Und** muttered mumblingly **und** low, As **ob** his mouth were full of dough, **der** snorted like a buffalo— That summer evening, long ago, A-sitting on a gate."

As the Knight sang the last words of the ballad, **er** gathered up the reins, **und** turned his horse's head along the road by which **siewaren** come. "You have only a few yards **zu gehen**," **er** said, "down the hill **und** over that little brook, **und** then you will be a Queen—But you will stay **und** see me off first?" **er** added as Alice turned **mit** an eager look in the direction to which **er** pointed. "**Ich** sha not be long. You will wait **und** wave your handkerchief **wann ich** get to that turn in the road? **Meiner Ansicht nach** it will encourage me, **wissen Sie**,."

"Of course **ich** will wait," said Alice: "**und** thank you **sehr** much for coming so far—and for the song—I liked it **sehr** much."

"**Ich** hope so," the Knight said doubtfully: "**aber** you did not cry so much as **ich dachte Sie würden**."

So **sie** shook hands, **und** then the Knight rode slowly away **in** the forest. "It won't take long **um zu sehen** him off, **ich** expect," Alice said to herself, as she stood watching him. "There **er geht**! Right on his head as usual! **Jedoch, er** gets on again pretty easily—that comes of having so many things hung round the horse—" So **sie redete** on talking to herself, as she watched the horse walking leisurely along the road, **und** the Knight tumbling off, first on one side **und** then on the other. After the fourth **oder** fifth tumble **er** reached the turn, **und** then she waved her handkerchief to him, **und** waited till **er** was out of sight.

"**Ich** hope it encouraged him," she said, as she turned to run down the hill: "**und** now for the last brook, **und** to be a Queen! **Wie** grand it sounds!" A **sehr** few steps brought her to the edge of the brook. "The Eighth Square at last!" she cried as she bounded across,

\* \* \* \* \* \* \*

\* \* \* \* \* \*

\* \* \* \* \* \* \*

**und** threw herself down to rest on a lawn as soft as moss, **mit** little flower-beds dotted about it here **und** there. "Oh, **wie** glad **ich** am to get here! **Und** what is this on my head?" she exclaimed in a tone of dismay, as she put her hands up to something **sehr** heavy, **und** fitted tight all round her head.

"**Aber wie** can it have got there without my knowing it?" she said to herself, as she lifted it off, **und** set it on her lap **um herauszufinden** what it could possibly be.

It was a golden crown.

# weeve

## Chapter 8

| German | Pronunciation | English |
|---|---|---|
| Teil | tail | part |
| ich helfe | ix helfə | I help |
| verhindern | feəhindeən | impede |
| aufbewahrung verhindern | aufbe:va:ruŋk feəhindeən | prevent storage |
| helfen | helfən | help |
| er hielt | ər hi:lt | he held |
| sie gingen | zi: giŋən | they went |
| Kunst | kunst | arts |
| denkst du nicht | dənkst du nixt | do not you think |
| wenn ich früher | vənn ix fry:ə | if i used earlier |
| suchen | zu:xən | looking for |
| er hatte gehalten | ər hate ge:haltən | he had held |
| weiter | vaitə | further |
| mein Geist geht weiter | main gaist ge:t vaitə | my mind goes on |
| während des Fleisch | ve:rənd des flaiʃ | during the meat |
| Jahre | ja:rə | years |
| ich suche | ix suxə | I'm looking for |
| ich mache sie zu | ix ma:xe si: t͡su: | I close it |

# weeve
## Chapter 8

| German | Pronunciation | English |
|---|---|---|
| geben | ge:bən | give |
| Gesundheit | ge:suntait | bless you |
| aus dem Weg | aus dem vek | out of the way |
| es gab | es gap | there were |
| um zu sehen | um t͡su se:hən | to see |
| wir | viə | weather |
| es gibt | es gibt | there is |

# 9
# QUEEN ALICE

"Subconscious language acquisition is the central means by which adults internalize second languages, a position supported not only by research but also by the practice of successful language teachers who emphasize communicative activities in the classroom." – Stephen Krashen, expert in linguistics at University of Southern California

"**Gut**, this is grand!" said Alice. "**Ich** never expected **ichwürde** be a Queen so soon—and **ich** will tell you what it is, your majesty," **sie redete** on in a severe tone (she was always rather fond of scolding herself), "it will never do for you to be lolling about on the grass like that! Queens have to be dignified, **wissen Sie!**"

So she got up **und** walked about—rather stiffly just at first, as she was afraid that the crown might come off: **aber** she comforted herself **mit** the thought that **es gab** nobody **zu sehen** her, "**und wenn ich** really am a Queen," she said as she sat down again, "**Ich** shall be able to manage it quite **gut** in time."

Everything was happening so oddly that she did not feel a bit surprised **zu finden** the Red Queen **und** the White Queen sitting close to her, one on each side: **sie hätte sehr gern** to ask **ihnen**, **wie sie** came there, **aber** she feared it wouldn't be quite civil. **Jedoch**, there would be no harm, **sie dachte**, in asking **wann das Spiel** was over. "Please, would you tell me—" she began, **sah** timidly at the Red Queen.

"Speak **wann** you are spoken to!" The Queen sharply interrupted her.

83

"**Aber wenn** everybody obeyed that rule," said Alice, **die** was always ready for a little argument, "**und wenn** you only spoke <u>**wenn man wurde**</u> spoken to, **und** the other person always waited for you to begin, **wissen Sie**, nobody would ever say anything, so that—"

"Ridiculous!" cried the Queen. "**Warum, sehen Sie nicht,,** child—" here she broke off **mit** a frown, **und**, after she **dachte** for a minute, suddenly changed the subject of the conversation. "What do you mean by '**Wenn** you really are a Queen'? What right have you to call yourself so? You can't be a Queen, **wissen Sie**, till you have passed the proper examination. **Und** the sooner **wir** begin it, the better."

"**Ich** only said 'if'!" poor Alice pleaded in a piteous tone.

The **zwei** Queens looked at each other, **und** the Red Queen remarked, **mit** a little shudder, "She says she only said 'if'—"

"**Aber** she said a great deal more **als** that!" the White Queen moaned, wringing her hands. "Oh, ever so much more **als** that!"

"So you did, **wissen Sie**," the Red Queen said to Alice. "Always speak the truth—think **bevor** you speak—and write it down afterwards."

"I'm sure **ich** did not mean—" Alice was beginning, **aber** the Red Queen interrupted her impatiently.

"That's just what **ich** complain of! **Sie hätten sollen** meant! What do you suppose is the use of child without any meaning? Even a joke should have some meaning—and a child's more important **als** a joke, **ich** hope. **Sie könnten** not deny that, even **wenn** you tried **mit** both hands."

"**Ich** do not deny things **mit** my hands," Alice objected.

"Nobody said you did," said the Red Queen. "**Ich** said **Sie könnten** not **wenn** you tried."

"She's in that state of mind," said the White Queen, "that she wants to deny something—only she doesn't know what to deny!"

"A nasty, vicious temper," the Red Queen remarked; **und** then **gab es** an uncomfortable silence for a minute **oder zwei**.

The Red Queen broke the silence by saying to the White Queen, "**Ich** invite you to Alice's dinner-party this afternoon."

The White Queen smiled feebly, **und** said "**Und ich** invite you."

"**Ich** did not know **ich** werde **haben** a party at all," said Alice; "**aber wenn es** to be one, **ich denke, ich** ought to invite the guests."

"**Wir gaben** you the opportunity of doing it," the Red Queen remarked: "**aber ich** daresay you haven't had many lessons in manners yet?"

"Manners are not taught in lessons," said Alice. "Lessons teach you **zu machen** sums, **und** things of that sort."

"**Und** you do Addition?" the White Queen asked. "What's one **und** one **und** one **und** one **und** one **und** one **und** one **und** one **und** one **und** one?"

"**Ich weiß nicht**," said Alice. "**Ich** lost count."

"She can't do Addition," the Red Queen interrupted. "Can you do Subtraction? Take nine from eight."

"Nine from eight **ich** can't, **wissen Sie**," Alice replied **sehr** readily: "but—"

"She can't do Subtraction," said the White Queen. "Can you do Division? Divide a loaf by a knife—what's the answer to that?"

"**Ich** suppose—" Alice was beginning, **aber** the Red Queen answered for her. "Bread-and-butter, of course. Try another Subtraction sum. Take a bone from a dog: what remains?"

Alice considered. "The bone wouldn't remain, of course, **wenn ich nehme** it—and the dog wouldn't remain; it would come to bite me—and I'm sure **ich sollte** not remain!"

"Then **denken Sie** nothing would remain?" said the Red Queen.

"**Meiner Ansicht nach** that's the answer."

"Wrong, as usual," said the Red Queen: "the dog's temper would remain."

"**Aber ich sehe nicht**, how—"

"**Warum**, look here!" the Red Queen cried. "The dog would lose its temper, wouldn't it?"

"Perhaps it would," Alice replied cautiously.

"Then **wenn** the dog went away, its temper would remain!" the Queen exclaimed triumphantly.

Alice said, as gravely as **sie konnte**, "**Sie könnten** go different **Wege**." **Aber sie konnte** not help **zu denken** to herself, "What dreadful nonsense **wir** are talking!"

"She can't do sums a bit!" the Queens said together, **mit** great emphasis.

"Can you do sums?" Alice said, turning suddenly on the White

Queen, for she did not like **werden** found fault **mit** so much.

The Queen gasped **und** shut her eyes. "**Ich kann** do Addition, **wenn Sie geben** me time—but **ich** can't do Subtraction, under any circumstances!"

"Of course **Sie wissen** your A B C?" said the Red Queen.

"To be sure **ich** do." said Alice.

"So do **ich**," the White Queen whispered: "**wir** will **häufig** say it over together, dear. **Und ich** will tell you a secret—I can read words of one letter! Isn't that grand! **Jedoch**, do not be discouraged. You will come to it in time."

Here the Red Queen began again. "Can you answer useful questions?" she said. "**Wie** is bread made?"

"**Ich weiß** that!" Alice cried eagerly. "**Man nimmt** some flour—"

"**Wo** do you pick the flower?" the White Queen asked. "In a garden, **oder** in the hedges?"

"**Gut**, it isn't picked at all," Alice explained: "it's ground—"

"**Wie** many acres of ground?" said the White Queen. "**Sie müssen** not leave out so many things."

"Fan her head!" the Red Queen anxiously interrupted. "She will be feverish after so much **Denken**." So **sie** set **ans Werk und** fanned her **mit** bunches of leaves, till **sie musste** beg **sie** to leave off, it blew her hair about so.

"She's all right again now," said the Red Queen. "**Wissen Sie** Languages? What's the French for fiddle-de-dee?"

"Fiddle-de-dee's not English," Alice replied gravely.

"**Wer** ever said it was?" said the Red Queen.

Alice thought **sie sah einen Weg** out of the difficulty this time. "**Wenn** you will tell me what language 'fiddle-de-dee' is, **ich** will tell you the French for it!" she exclaimed triumphantly.

**Aber** the Red Queen drew herself up rather stiffly, **und** said "Queens never make bargains."

"**Ich** wish Queens never asked questions," Alice thought to herself.

"Do not let **uns** quarrel," the White Queen said in an anxious tone. "What is the cause of lightning?"

"The cause of lightning," Alice said **sehr** decidedly, for she felt quite certain about this, "is the thunder—no, no!" she hastily corrected herself. "**Ich** meant the other **Weg**."

"It's too late to correct it," said the Red Queen: "**wenn** you have **einmal** said a thing, that fixes it, **und sie müssen** take the consequences."

"Which reminds me—" the White Queen said, **sah** down **und** nervously clasping **und** unclasping her hands, "**wir hatten** such a thunderstorm last Tuesday—I mean one of the last set of Tuesdays, **wissen Sie**."

Alice was puzzled. "In our country," she remarked, "there's only one day <u>**zu einem Zeitpunkt**</u>."

The Red Queen said, "That's a poor thin **Weg** of doing things. Now here, **wir** mostly have **Tage und** nights **zwei oder** three **zu einem Zeitpunkt, und** sometimes in the winter **wir nehmen** as many as five nights together—for warmth, **wissen Sie**."

"Are five nights warmer **als** one night, then?" Alice ventured to ask.

"Five **Mal** as warm, of course."

"**Aber sie sollten** be five **Mal** as cold, by the same rule—"

"Just so!" cried the Red Queen. "Five **Mal** as warm, **und** five **Mal** as cold—just as I'm five **Mal** as rich as you are, **und** five **Mal** as clever!"

Alice sighed **und** gave it up. "It's exactly like a riddle **mit** no answer!" **sie dachte**.

"Humpty Dumpty saw it too," the White Queen went on in a low voice, more as **ob** she were talking to herself. "**Er** came to the door **mit** a corkscrew in his hand—"

"What did **er** want?" said the Red Queen.

"**Er** said **er würde** come in," the White Queen went on, "**weil er suchte** for a hippopotamus. Now, as it happened, **es gab** not such a thing in the house, that morning."

"Is there generally?" Alice asked in an astonished tone.

"**Naja**, only on Thursdays," said the Queen.

"**Ich weiß** what **er** came for," said Alice: "**er wollte** to punish the fish, because—"

Here the White Queen began again. "It was such a thunderstorm, you can't think!" ("She never could, **wissen Sie**," said the Red Queen.) "**Und ein Teil** of the roof came off, **und** ever so much thunder got in—and it went rolling round the room in great lumps—and knocking over the tables **und** things—till **ich** was so frightened, **ich könnte** not remember my own name!"

Alice thought to herself, "**Ich** never should try to remember my name in the middle of an accident! **Wo** would be the use of it?" **aber** she did not say this aloud, for fear of hurting the poor Queen's feeling.

"Your Majesty must excuse her," the Red Queen said to Alice, **nahm** one of the White Queen's hands in her own, **und** gently stroking it: "she means **gut**, **aber** she can't help saying foolish things, as a general rule."

The White Queen looked timidly at Alice, **die** felt she ought to say something kind, **aber** really couldn't think of anything at the moment.

"She never was really **gut** brought up," the Red Queen went on: "**aber** it's amazing **wie** good-tempered she is! Pat her on the head, **und** see **wie** pleased she will be!" **Aber** this was more **als** Alice had courage **zu machen**.

"A little kindness—and putting her hair in papers—would do wonders **mit** her—"

The White Queen gave a deep sigh, **und** laid her head on Alice's shoulder. "**Ich** am so sleepy?" she moaned.

"She's tired, poor thing!" said the Red Queen. "Smooth her hair—lend her your nightcap—and sing her a soothing lullaby."

"**Ich** haven't got a nightcap **mit** me," said Alice, as she tried to obey the first direction: "**und ich kenne keine** soothing lullabies."

"**Ich muss** do it myself, then," said the Red Queen, **und** she began:

"Hush-a-by lady, in Alice's lap! Till the feast's ready, **wir** have time for a nap: **Wann** the feast's over, **wir werden gehen** to the ball— Red Queen, **und** White Queen, **und** Alice, **und** all!

"**Und** now **Sie kennen** words," she added, as she put her head down on Alice's other shoulder, "just sing it through to me. I'm getting sleepy, too." In another moment both Queens were fast asleep, **und** snoring loud.

"What should **ich tun**?" exclaimed Alice, **sah** about in great perplexity, as first one round head, **und** then the other, rolled down from her shoulder, **und** lay like a heavy lump in her lap. "**Ich glaube nicht** it happened **schon mal**, that any one had **gekümmert** of **zwei** Queens asleep **auf einmal**! No, not in all the **Geschichte** of England—it couldn't, **wissen Sie**, **weil** there never was more **als** one Queen **zu einem Zeitpunkt**. Do wake up, you heavy things!" **sie redete** on in an impatient tone; **aber**

**es gab** no answer **außer** a gentle snoring.

The snoring got more distinct every minute, **und** sounded more like a tune: at last **sie konnte** even make out the words, **und** she listened so eagerly that, **wenn** the **zwei** great heads vanished from her lap, she hardly missed **sie**.

She was standing **vor** an arched doorway over which were the words QUEEN ALICE in large letters, **und** on each side of the arch **es gab** a bell-handle; one was marked "Visitors' Bell," **und** the other "Servants' Bell."

"**Ich** will wait till the song's over," thought Alice, "**und** then **ich** will ring—the—which bell must **ich** ring?" **sie redete** on, **sehr** much puzzled by the names. "I'm not a visitor, **und** I'm not a servant. There ought to be one marked 'Queen,' you know—"

Just then the door opened a little **Weg**, **und** a creature **mit** a long beak put its head out for a moment **und** said "No admittance till the week after next!" **und** shut the door again **mit** a bang.

Alice knocked **und** rang in vain for a long time, **aber** at last, a **sehr** old Frog, **der** was sitting under a tree, got up **und** hobbled slowly towards her: **er** was dressed in bright yellow, **und** had enormous boots on.

"What is it, now?" the Frog said in a deep hoarse whisper.

Alice turned round, ready **zu finden** fault **mit** anybody. "Where's the servant whose business it is to answer the door?" she began angrily.

"Which door?" said the Frog.

Alice almost stamped **mit** irritation at the slow drawl in which **er** spoke. "This door, of course!"

The Frog looked at the door **mit** his large dull eyes for a minute: then **er ging** nearer **und** rubbed it **mit** his thumb, as **ob er** were trying whether the paint would come off; then **er sah** at Alice.

"To answer the door?" **er** said. "What's it been asking of?" **Er** was so hoarse that Alice could scarcely hear him.

"**Ich weiß nicht** what you mean," she said.

"**Ich** talks English, doesn't **ich**?" the Frog went on. "**Oder** are you deaf? What did it ask you?"

"Nothing!" Alice said impatiently. "**Ich** have been knocking at it!"

"Shouldn't do that—shouldn't do that—" the Frog muttered. "Vexes it, **wissen Sie**." Then **er ging** up **und** gave the door a kick

**mit** one of his great feet. "You let it alone," **er** panted out, as **er** hobbled back to his tree, "**und** it will let you alone, **wissen Sie**."

At this moment the door was flung open, **und** a shrill voice was heard singing:

"To the **Spiegel**-Glass **Welt** it was Alice that said, '**Ich** have a sceptre in hand, **ich** have a crown on my head; Let the **Spiegel**-Glass creatures, whatever **sie** be, Come **und** dine **mit** the Red Queen, the White Queen, **und** me.'"

**Und** hundreds of voices joined in the chorus:

"Then fill up the glasses as quick as **ihr könnt**, **Und** sprinkle the table **mit** buttons **und** bran: Put cats in the coffee, **und** mice in the tea— **Und** welcome Queen Alice **mit** thirty-times-three!"

Then followed a confused noise of cheering, **und** Alice thought to herself, "Thirty **mal** three makes ninety. **Ich** wonder **ob** any one's counting?" In a minute **es gab** silence again, **und** the same shrill voice sang another verse;

"'O **Spiegel**-Glass creatures,' quoth Alice, 'draw near! "Tis an honour **um zu sehen** me, a favour to hear: "Tis a privilege high **zu essen** dinner **und** tea Along **mit** the Red Queen, the White Queen, **und** me!'"

Then came the chorus again:—

"Then fill up the glasses **mit** treacle **und** ink, **Oder** anything else that is pleasant to drink: Mix sand **mit** the cider, **und** wool **mit** the wine— **Und** welcome Queen Alice **mit** ninety-times-nine!"

"Ninety **mal** nine!" Alice repeated in despair, "Oh, that will never be done! I'd better go in at once—" **und es gab** a dead silence the moment she appeared.

Alice glanced nervously along the table, as she walked up the large hall, **und** noticed that **es gab** about fifty guests, of all kinds: some were animals, some birds, **und es gab** even a few flowers <u>**darunter**</u>. "I'm glad <u>**sie sind gekommen ohne**</u> waiting to be asked," **sie dachte**: "**Ich sollte** never have known **wer** were the right **Menschen** to invite!"

**Es gab** three chairs at the head of the table; the Red **und** White Queens had already **genommen zwei** of **ihnen, aber** the middle one was empty. Alice sat down in it, rather uncomfortable in the silence, **und** longing for some one to speak.

At last the Red Queen began. "You have missed the soup **und** fish," she said. "Put on the joint!" **Und** the waiters set a leg of mutton **vor** Alice, **die** looked at it rather anxiously, as **sie hatte** never had to carve a joint **zuvor**.

"**Sie sehen** a little shy **aus**; let me introduce you to that leg of mutton," said the Red Queen. "Alice—Mutton; Mutton—Alice." The leg of mutton got up in the dish **und** made a little bow to Alice; **und** Alice returned the bow, not knowing whether to be frightened **oder** amused.

"May **ich geben** you a slice?" she said, **sie nahm** up the knife **und** fork, **schaute** from one Queen to the other.

"Certainly not," the Red Queen said, **sehr** decidedly: "it isn't etiquette to cut any one you have been introduced to. Remove the joint!" **Und** the waiters carried it off, **und** brought a large plum-pudding in its **Stelle**.

"**Ich** won't be introduced to the pudding, please," Alice said rather hastily, "**oder wir** shall get no dinner at all. May **ich geben** you some?"

**Aber** the Red Queen looked sulky, **und** growled "Pudding—Alice; Alice—Pudding. Remove the pudding!" **und** the waiters took it away so quickly that Alice couldn't return its bow.

**Jedoch**, she did not see **warum** the Red Queen should be the only one **zu geben** orders, so, as an experiment, she called out "Waiter! Bring back the pudding!" **und** there it was again in a moment like a conjuring-trick. It was so large that **sie konnte** not help feeling a little shy **mit** it, as **sie hatte** been **mit** the mutton; **jedoch**, she conquered her shyness by a great effort **und** cut a slice **und** handed it to the Red Queen.

"What impertinence!" said the Pudding. "**Ich** wonder **wie** you'd like it, **wenn ich** were to cut a slice out of you, you creature!"

It spoke in a thick, suety sort of voice, **und** Alice had not a word to say in reply: **sie konnte** only sit **und** look at it **und** gasp.

"Make a remark," said the Red Queen: "it's ridiculous to leave all the conversation to the pudding!"

"**Wissen Sie, ich** have had such a quantity of poetry repeated to me to-day," Alice began, a little frightened to **finden** that, the moment she opened her lips, **es gab** dead silence, **und** all eyes were fixed upon her; "**und** it's a **sehr** curious thing, **ich** think—every poem was about **Fische** in some **Weise**. **Wissen Sie, warum sie** are so fond of **Fischen**, all about here?"

She spoke to the Red Queen, whose answer was a little wide of the mark. "As to **Fische**," she said, **sehr** slowly **und** solemnly, putting her mouth close to Alice's ear, "her White Majesty **weiß** a lovely riddle—all in poetry—all about **Fische**. Shall she repeat it?"

"Her Red Majesty's **sehr** kind to mention it," the White Queen murmured **in** Alice's other ear, in a voice like the cooing of a pigeon. "It would be such a treat! May **ich**?"

"Please do," Alice said **sehr** politely.

The White Queen laughed **mit** delight, **und** stroked Alice's cheek. Then she began:

"'First, the fish must be caught.' That is easy: a baby, **meiner Ansicht nach**, could have caught it. 'Next, the fish must be bought.' That is easy: a penny, **meiner Ansicht nach**, would have bought it.

'Now cook me the fish!'

That is easy, **und** will not take more **als** a minute. 'Let it lie in a dish!'

That is easy, **weil** it already is in it.

'Bring it here! Let me sup!'

It is easy to set such a dish on the table. 'Take the dish-cover up!'

Ah, that is so hard that **ich** fear I'm unable!

For it holds it like glue— Holds the lid to the dish, **während** it lies in the middle: Which is easiest **zu tun**, Un-dish-cover the fish, **oder** dishcover the riddle?"

"Take a minute **zu denken** about it, **und** then guess," said the Red Queen. "Meanwhile, **wir** will drink your health—Queen Alice's **Gesundheit**!" she screamed at the top of her voice, **und** all the guests began drinking it directly, **und sehr** queerly **sie** managed it: some of **ihnen** put their glasses upon their heads like extinguishers, **und** drank all that trickled down their faces—others upset the decanters, **und** drank the wine as it ran off the edges of the table—and three of **ihnen** (**die** looked like kangaroos) scrambled **in** the dish of roast mutton, **und** began eagerly lapping up the gravy, "just like pigs in a trough!" thought Alice.

"You ought to return thanks in a neat speech," the Red Queen said, frowning at Alice as she spoke.

"**Wir müssen** support you, **wissen Sie**," the White Queen whispered, as Alice got up <u>**zu halten**</u> it, **sehr** obediently, **aber** a little frightened.

"Thank you **sehr** much," she whispered in reply, "**aber ich kann** do quite **gut ohne es**."

"That wouldn't be at all the thing," the Red Queen said **sehr** decidedly: so Alice tried to submit to it **mit** a good grace.

("**Und sie** did push so!" she said afterwards, **als** she was telling her sister the **Geschichte** of the feast. "**Du hättest** thought **sie wollten** to squeeze me flat!")

In fact it was rather difficult for her **zu bleiben** in **ihrem Platz, während sie hielt** her speech: the **zwei** Queens pushed her so, one on each side, that **sie** nearly lifted her up **in die Luft**: "**Ich** rise to return thanks—" Alice began: **und** she really did rise as she spoke, several inches; **aber** she got hold of the edge of the table, **und** managed to pull herself down again.

"Take care of yourself!" screamed the White Queen, seizing Alice's hair **mit** both her hands. "Something's going to happen!"

**Und** then (as Alice afterwards described it) all sorts of things happened in a moment. The candles all grew up to the ceiling, **sie sahen** like a bed of rushes **mit** fireworks at the top. As to the bottles, **sie** each took a pair of plates, which **sie** hastily fitted on as wings, **und** so, **mit** forks for legs, went fluttering about in all directions: "**und sie sehen sehr** like birds **aus**," Alice thought to herself, as **gut** as **sie konnte** in the dreadful confusion that was beginning.

At this moment she heard a hoarse laugh at her side, **und** turned **um zu sehen** what was the matter **mit** the White Queen; **aber**, instead of the Queen, **es gab** the leg of mutton sitting in the chair. "Here **ich am**!" cried a voice from the soup tureen, **und** Alice turned again, just in time **um zu sehen** the Queen's broad good-natured face grinning at her for a moment over the edge of the tureen, **bevor** she disappeared **in** the soup.

**Es gab** not a moment to be lost. Already several of the guests were lying down in the dishes, **und** the soup ladle was walking up the table towards Alice's chair, **und** beckoning to her impatiently to get out of its **Weg**.

"**Ich** can't stand this any longer!" she cried as she jumped up **und** seized the table-cloth **mit** both hands: one good pull, **und** plates, dishes, guests, **und** candles came crashing down together in a heap on the floor.

"**Und** as for you," **sie redete** on, turning fiercely upon the Red Queen, whom she considered as the cause of all the mischief—but the Queen was no longer at her side—she had suddenly dwindled down to the size of a little doll, **und** was now on the table, merrily running round **und** round after her own shawl, which was trailing behind her.

At any other time, Alice would have felt surprised at this, **aber** she was far too much excited to be surprised at anything now. "As for you," she repeated, catching hold of the little creature in the act of jumping over a bottle which had just lighted upon the table, "**Ich** will shake you **in** a kitten, that **ich** will!"

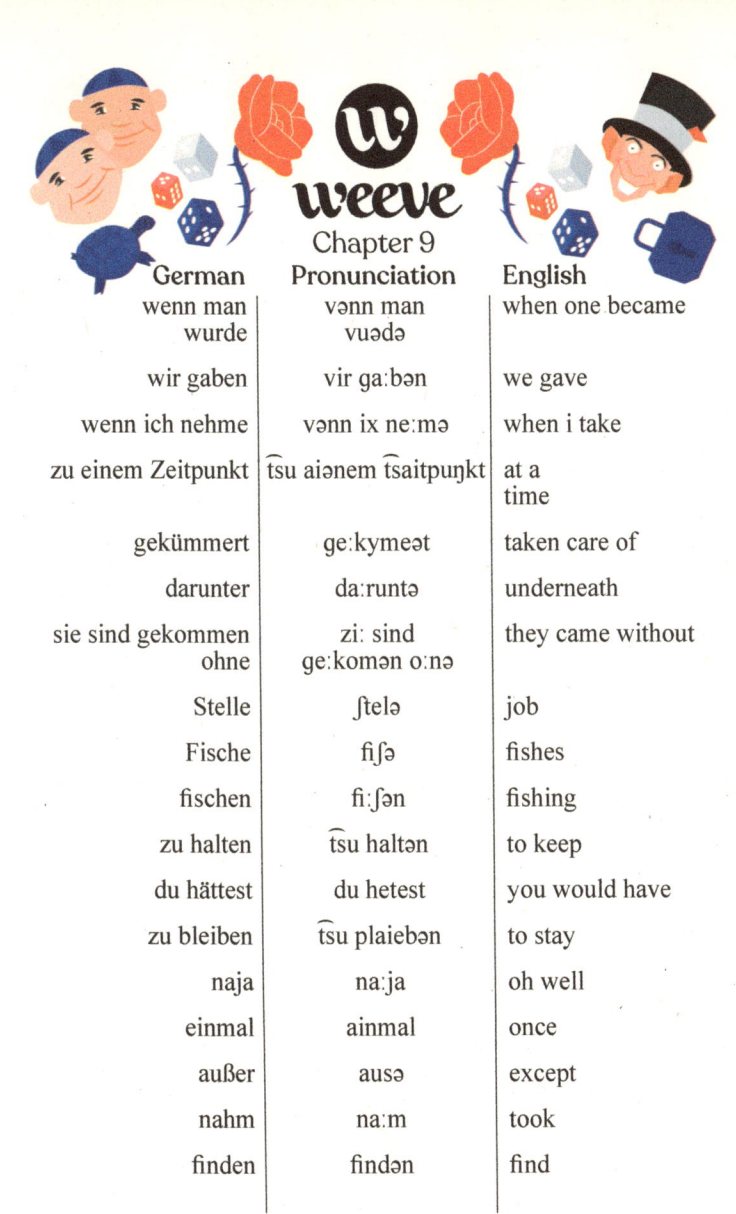

# weeve

## Chapter 9

| German | Pronunciation | English |
|---|---|---|
| wenn man wurde | vənn man vuədə | when one became |
| wir gaben | vir ga:bən | we gave |
| wenn ich nehme | vənn ix ne:mə | when i take |
| zu einem Zeitpunkt | t͡su aiənem t͡saitpuŋkt | at a time |
| gekümmert | ge:kymeət | taken care of |
| darunter | da:runtə | underneath |
| sie sind gekommen ohne | zi: sind ge:komən o:nə | they came without |
| Stelle | ʃtelə | job |
| Fische | fiʃə | fishes |
| fischen | fi:ʃən | fishing |
| zu halten | t͡su haltən | to keep |
| du hättest | du hetest | you would have |
| zu bleiben | t͡su plaiebən | to stay |
| naja | na:ja | oh well |
| einmal | ainmal | once |
| außer | ausə | except |
| nahm | na:m | took |
| finden | findən | find |

# weeve
## Chapter 9

| German | Pronunciation | English |
|--------|---------------|---------|
| und    | unt           | and     |
| mit    | mit           | with    |
| weiter | vaitə         | further |

# 10

## SHAKING

"When asked "Dr. McQuillan I need to take the TOEFL test in 6 months, what should I do?". The first thing I ask them is "How much time do you have to spend?" and they'll say "Oh, I have 2 to 3 hours to spend per day" and I'll say "Great, you should spend that time reading. All 3 hours." – Jeff McQuillan, senior researcher at Center for Educational Development, Inc.

**Sie nahm** her off the table as she spoke, **und** shook her backwards **und** forwards **mit** all her might.

The Red Queen made no resistance whatever; only her face grew **sehr** small, **und** her eyes got large **und** green: **und** still, as Alice went on shaking her, **sie** grew **weiter** shorter—and fatter—and softer—and rounder—and—

# 11
## WAKING

> "The way we acquire language is amazingly simple, we acquire language when we understand messages." – Stephen Krashen, expert in linguistics at University of Southern California

—and it really was a kitten, after all.

# 12

## WHICH DREAMED IT?

"To learn a language is to have one more window from which to look at the world." – Chinese Proverb

"Your majesty shouldn't purr so loud," Alice said, rubbing her eyes, **und** addressing the kitten, respectfully, yet **mit** some severity. "You woke **mich** out of oh! such a nice dream! **Und** you have been along **mit mir**, Kitty—all through the **Spiegel**-Glass **Welt. Wussest du** it, dear?"

It is a **sehr** inconvenient habit of kittens (Alice had **einmal** made the remark) that, whatever you say to **ihnen, sie** always purr. "**Wenn du würdest** only purr for 'yes' **und** mew for 'no,' **oder** any rule of that sort," **sie hatte** said, "so that one could keep up a conversation! **Aber wie** can you talk **mit** a person **wenn sie** always say the same thing?"

On this occasion the kitten only purred: **und** it was impossible to guess whether it meant "yes" **oder** "no."

So Alice hunted among the chessmen on the table till **sie hatte gefunden** the Red Queen: then **sie ging** down on her knees on the hearth-rug, **und** put the kitten **und** the Queen **damit sie sahen** at each other. "Now, Kitty!" she cried, clapping her hands triumphantly. "Confess that was what you turned **in**!"

("**Aber** it wouldn't look at it," she said, **wenn** she was explaining the thing afterwards to her sister: "it turned away its head, **und** pretended not **zu sehen** it: **aber** it looked a little ashamed of itself, so **meiner Ansicht nach** it must have been the Red Queen.")

"Sit up a little more stiffly, dear!" Alice cried **mit** a merry laugh. "**Und** curtsey **während** you **denkst** what to—what to purr. It saves time, remember!" **Und** she caught it up **und** gave it one little kiss, "just in honour of having been a Red Queen."

"Snowdrop, my pet!" **sie redete** on, **sah** over her shoulder at the White Kitten, which was still patiently undergoing its toilet, "**wann** will Dinah have finished **mit** your White Majesty, **ich** wonder? That must be the reason **du warst** so untidy in my dream—Dinah! **Weißt du** that you are scrubbing a White Queen? Really, it's most disrespectful of you!

"**Und** what did Dinah turn to, **ich** wonder?" she prattled on, as she settled comfortably down, **mit** one elbow in the rug, **und** her chin in her hand, to watch the kittens. "Tell **mir**, Dinah, did you turn to Humpty Dumpty? **Meiner Ansicht nach** you did—however, you'd better not mention it to your friends just yet, for I'm not sure.

"**Übrigens**, Kitty, **wenn** only you'd been really **mit mir** in my dream, **es gab** one thing **du hättest** enjoyed—I had such a quantity of poetry said to **mir**, all about **Fische**! To-morrow morning you shall have a real treat. **Die ganze Zeit** you are eating your breakfast, **ich** will repeat 'The Walrus **und** the Carpenter' to you; **und** then **sie können** make believe it's oysters, dear!

"Now, Kitty, let's consider **wer** it was that dreamed it all. This is a serious question, my dear, **und sie sollten** not go on licking your paw like that—as **ob** Dinah had not washed you this morning! **Weißt du**,, Kitty, it must have been either **ich oder** the Red King. **Er** was **Teil** of my dream, of course—but then **ich** was **Teil** of his dream, too! Was it the Red King, Kitty? **Du warst** his wife, my dear, so you ought to know—Oh, Kitty, do help to settle it! I'm sure your paw can wait!" **Aber** the provoking kitten only began on the other paw, **und** pretended it had not heard the question.

Which **denkst du** it was?

*A boat beneath a sunny sky,*
*Lingering onward dreamily*
*In an evening of July—*

*Children three that nestle near,*

*Eager eye **und** willing ear,*

*Pleased a simple **Geschichte** to hear—*

*Long has paled that sunny sky:*

*Echoes fade **und** memories die.*

*Autumn frosts **haben** slain July.*

*Still **sie** haunts me, phantomwise,*

*Alice moving under skies*

*Never seen by waking eyes.*

*Children yet, the **Geschichte** to hear,*

*Eager eye **und** willing ear,*

*Lovingly shall nestle near.*

***In** a Wonderland **sie** lie,*

*Dreaming **als** the days go by,*

*Dreaming **als** the summers die:*

*Ever drifting down the stream—*

*Lingering **in** the golden gleam—*

*Life, what is it **aber** a dream?*

## **<u>DAS ENDE</u>**

**Herzlichen Glückwunsch** on completing your weeve! We hoped you enjoyed the process and you feel like you have **viel gelernt.** Remember that **Sprachenlernen** is a long journey. Keep on reading your weeves and you will be a German speaking Mad Hatter **in kürzester Zeit!** If you felt this **Buch** helped you **würden wir uns Über** a review on Amazon, our website or goodreads. It helps **mehr Menschen** like yourself find our weeves. **Vielen Dank** for your support!

- Evan, Cian and Oisin

# Glossary

## A

aber // abə // but
aber er wollte // abər ər voltə // but he wanted
aber falls // abər fals // but if
aber sie wusste // abər si: vustə // but she knew
abwechseln // apvekseln // alternate
ach // ax // oh
allererste // ale:reəstə // very first
als // als // as
als ich used to lesen // als ix u:sed to le:sən // than i used to read
als sie sahen // als si: sa:hən // when they saw
alswürde ich // alsvyədə ix // as if I would
ans Werk // ans veək // to the work
auch // aux // even
auf // auf // on
aufbewahrungverhindern // aufbe:va:ruŋkfeəhindeən // prevent storage
aus dem Weg // aus dem vek // out of the way
aussehende // ause:həndə // looking
außer // ausə // except
außerdem // auseədem // aside from that

## B

begann // be:gan // started
begannen sehr // be:ganən se:ə // started very much
benutzten // be:nutstən // used
beorderte // beoədeətə // ordered
bis // bis // until
blick // plik // view
blicke // plikə // look
braucht // prauxt // needs
brunnen // prunən // fountain

## D

dadrin // datrin // in there
damit zu beginnen // da:mit tsu be:ginən // to start with
darin // da:rin // in this
darunter // da:runtə // underneath
darüber // da:rybə // about that
das Ende // das əndə // the end
dass // das // that
dazwischen // datsvi:ʃən // between
den Menschen // dən mənʃən // the people
denkst du nicht // dənkst du nixt // do not you think
denkt ihr // dənkt i:ə // you think
denn es gab // dənn es gap // because there was
der Weg // dər vek // the way
dich wäre // dix verə // you would be
die // diə // the
die Art // di: aət // the kind
die Welt // di: velt // the world
die ganze Zeit // di: gantsə tsait // the whole time
diese // di:sə // these
dir gefallen // dir ge:falən // you like
doch er // dox ə // but he
doch kkönnen Sie // dox kkønən siə // but you can
du bringst // du priŋst // you bring
du hättest // du hetest // you would have
du warst // du vaəst // you were
du weisst es nicht // du vaist es nixt // you do not know
du würdest // du vyədest // you would

## E

egal wie // egal viə // no matter how
ein Spiel // ain spi:l // a game
eine Weile // aiənə vailə // a while
eine Welt // aiənə velt // one world
einen // aiənən // a
einer // ainə // one
einiger Zeit // aiəniçər tsait // some time
einmal // ainmal // once
er ging // ər giŋk // he went
er hatte gehalten // ər hate ge:haltən // he had held
er hielt // ər hi:lt // he held
er kann // ər kan // he can
er konnte // ər kontə // he could
er wohnt // ər vo:nt // he lives
erst mal // eəst mal // for now
es gab // es gap // there were
es gibt // es gibt // there is
essen Sie gern // esən si: geən // do you like to eat

## F

finden // findən // find
fische // fiʃə // fishes
fischen // fi:ʃən // fishing
fluchtweg // fluxtvek // escape route

## G

ganz unten // gants untən // at the bottom

103

geben // ge:bən // give
gegangen // ge:gaŋən // went
gehen // ge:hən // walk
geht // ge:t // goes
gekümmert // ge:kymeət // taken care of
genauen // ge:nauən // exact
genauso gut // ge:nauhso gut // as good as
genommen // ge:nomən // taken
gern // geən // gladly
geschichte // ge:ʃixtə // story
gesundheit // ge:suntait // bless you
gewöhnt daran // ge:vø:nt da:ran // used to it
gut // gut // well

# H

helfen // helfən // help
herauszufinden // he:raustsu:findən // to find out
häufig // hoyhfik // frequently
hü // hy: // hü

# I

ich // ix // I
ich brauche // ix prauxə // I need
ich denke nicht // ix dənke nixt // I do not think so
ich esse sie nicht // ix ese si: nixt // i don't eat them
ich glaube nicht // ix klauhbe nixt // I do not believe
ich habe gesehen // ix ha:be ge:se:ən // I have seen
ich helfe // ix helfə // I help
ich hätte sollen // ix hete solən // I should have
ich kann // ix kan // I can
ich kenne // ix kənnə // I know
ich kenne keine // ix kənne kainə // I do not know any
ich lese // ix lesə // I read
ich mache sie zu // ix ma:xe si: tsu: // I close it
ich möchte // ix møxtə // I would like to
ich müsste // ix mystə // I would have to
ich sehe keinen // ix se:he kaiənən // i don't see any
ich sehe nicht // ix se:he nixt // I do not see
ich sollte // ix soltə // I should
ich suche // ix suxə // I'm looking for
ich verstehe // ix feəste:ə // I understand
ich weiß nicht wo // ix vais nixt vo: // I do not know where
ich werde gehen und // ix veəde ge:hən unt // i will go and
ich wünsche // ix vynʃə // I wish
ich würde // ix vyədə // I would
ie // iə // ie
ihnen // i:nən // them
ihr Gedächtnis // i:r ge:dextnis // your memory
ihr müsst // i:r myst // you must
ihr wollt // i:r volt // you want
ihrem Weg // i:rem vek // their way
ihrem ganzen Leben // i:rem gantsən le:bən // your whole life
ihren Weg // i:rən vek // your way
ihres Lebens // i:res le:bəns // of your life
im Spiegel- // im spi:gel- // in the mirror-
im Weg // im vek // in the way
immer // imə // always
immer kam // imər kam // always came
in // in // in
in ihrem Platz // in i:rem plats // in your place
ins // ins // into the

# J

jahre // ja:rə // years
jedoch // je:dox // however
jene // jənə // those

# K

kennst du den Weg // kənnst du dən vek // do you know the way
kennt // kənnt // knows
kunst // kunst // Arts

# L

lebensweise // le:bənsvaisə // way of life
leute // loytə // people
los // los // come on
luft // luft // air

# M

machen // ma:xən // do
macht // maxt // power
mal // mal // times
man darf // man daəf // one may
mein Geist geht weiter // main gaist ge:t vaitə // my mind goes on
meinen Weg in // maiənən veg in // my way in
meiner Ansicht nach // maiənər ansixt nax // in my opinion
meiner Zeit // maiənər tsait // in my time

104

methode // metodə // method
mich entschieden // mix əntʃi:dən // decided me
mir // miə // me
mit // mit // with
mit uns // mit uns // with us
mit wem // mit vem // with whom

# N

nahm // na:m // took
naja // na:ja // oh well
nimmt // nimt // takes
noch nie // nox niə // never
nun // nun // well

# O

ob sie könnte // ob si: køntə // if she could
oder // odə // or
ort // oət // location

# P

plätze // pletsə // places

# R

richtung // rixtuŋk // direction
richtungen // rixtuŋən // directions

# S

schaute // ʃautə // looked
schon fast // ʃon fast // almost
sehen Sie // ze:hən si:ə // see you
sehr // ze:ə // very
sehr oft // ze:r oft // very often
seid ihr gegangen // zaid i:r ge:gaŋən // are you gone
sein // zain // be
seine Meinung // zaiəne maiənuŋk // his opinion
seinen Weg // zaiənən vek // his way
sich an die Arbeit machen // zix an di: aəbait ma:xən // to start working
sie brauchen // zi: prauhxən // they need
sie dachte // zi: daxtə // she thought
sie entzifferte // zi: əntsifeətə // she deciphered
sie erkannte // zi: eəkantə // she recognized
sie fand heraus // zi: fand he:raus // she found out
sie gingen // zi: giŋən // they went
sie half // zi: half // she helped
sie hatte herausbekommen // zi: hate he:rausbe:komən // she had found out
sie hatten // zi: hatən // they had
sie hätten sollen // zi: hetən solən // they should have

sie kannte // zi: kantə // she knew
sie können // zi: kønən // you can
sie könnten // zi: køntən // you could
sie lernten // zi: leəntən // they learned
sie liefen // zi: li:fən // they ran
sie mochte sie // zi: moxtə siə // she liked them
sie muss // zi: mus // she must
sie musste // zi: mustə // she had to
sie mögen // zi: mø:gən // they like
sie müssen // zi: mysən // you need to
sie müssen sich entscheide // zi: mysən six əntʃaidə // you have to decide
sie müssten // zi: mystən // they would have to
sie pflegten // zi: pflektən // they used to
sie redete // zi: re:detə // she talked
sie sah // zi: sa: // she saw
sie sie gekannt // zi: si: ge:kant // she knew her
sie sind // zi: sint // they are
sie sind gekommen ohne // zi: sind ge:komən o:nə // they came without
sie sollten // zi: soltən // they should
sie stand auf // zi: stand auf // she got up
sie suchte // zi: suxtə // she was looking for
sie verstehen // zi: feəste:hən // you understand
sie warden wisen // zi: vaədən vi:sən // they will know
sie waren // zi: va:rən // they were
sie werden sehen // zi: veədən se:hən // you will see
sie wollen // zi: volən // you want to
sie würden // zi: vyədən // they would
sonst wären Sie // zonst verən siə // otherwise they would be
spiegel // ʃpi:gel // mirrors
spielten // ʃpi:ltən // played
stelle // ʃtelə // job
suchen // zu:xən // looking for

# T

tage // tagə // days
teil // tail // part
that man sollte // tat man soltə // that one should
they made // tai madə // they made
to Werk // to veək // to work
tun // tun // to do

# U

um es zu stoppen // um es tsu stopən // to stop it
um zu sehen // um tsu se:hən // to see
un sah // un sa: // un saw
und // unt // and
und da war // und da vaə // and there was
und damit // und da:mit // and thus
und entschied sich // und əntʃi:d six // and decided
und machte // und maxtə // and made
und making // und ma:kiŋk // and making
und wenn ich gefunden habe // und vənn ix ge:fundən habə // and when I've found
undsah // untsa: // and saw
ungewöhnliche // uŋe:vø:nlixə // unusual

# V

verhindern // feəhindeən // impede
vor // foə // before

# W

wann // van // when
warum // va:rum // why
was Sie wissen // vas si: visən // what you know
weg davor // veg da:foə // away from it
wege // vegə // ways
wegen // ve:gən // because
wegzunehmen // vektsu:ne:mən // to take away
weil man sieht // vail man si:t // because you see
weil sie // vail siə // because they
weise ihr könnt // vaiese i:r kønt // wise you can
weise wie die beiden // vaiese vi: di: baiedən // wise like the two
weiter // vaitə // further
wen // vən // whom
wenn Sie kennen würden // vənn si: kənnən vyədən // if they would know
wenn Sie möchten // vənn si: møxtən // if you want
wenn Sie wären // vənn si: verən // if they were
wenn du machst kein // vənn du makst kain // if you don't do any
wenn du sie nicht magst // vənn du si: nixt magst // if you don't like them
wenn du wärst // vənn du veəst // if you were
wenn es welche gibt // vənn es velxe gibt // if there are any
wenn ich // vənn ix // if I
wenn ich benutze // vənn ix be:nutsə // when i use
wenn ich früher // vənn ix fry:ə // if i used earlier
wenn ich gehe // vənn ix ge:ə // when I go
wenn ich mag // vənn ix mak // if i like
wenn ich nehme // vənn ix ne:mə // when i take
wenn man wurde // vənn man vuədə // when one became
wenn sie denken,wir // vənn si: dənkən,viə // if you think we
wenn sie wollten // vənn si: voltən // if you wanted
wennwir // vənnviə // if we
wer // və // who
werden gemacht // veədən ge:maxt // will be done
wie // viə // how
wie gefällt Ihnen // vi: ge:felt i:nən // how do you like
wie haben // vi: ha:bən // as have
wie sie singen // vi: si: siŋən // how they sing
wie viel Uhr ist es // vi: fi:l u:r ist es // what time is it
wie viel kostet sie // vi: fi:l kostet siə // how much does it cost
will // vil // want
wir // viə // weather
wir gaben // vir ga:bən // we gave
wissen Sie // visən siə // you know
wissen Sie" // visən si:" // you know"
woher wissen Sie // vo:hər visən siə // how do you know
wussten Sie // vustən siə // did you know
während // ve:rənt // while
während des Fleisch // ve:rənd des flaiʃ // during the meat

# Z

zahl // tsa:l // number
zu bleiben // tsu plaiebən // to stay
zu denken // tsu dənkən // to think
zu einem Zeitpunkt // tsu aiənem tsaitpuŋkt // at a time
zu halten // tsu haltən // to keep
zu kümmern // tsu kymeən // take care of
zu nehmen // tsu ne:mən // gain

106

weight
zu schauen // tsu ʃauən // watch
zu schließen // tsu ʃliːsən // close
zu streiten // tsu straietən // to argue
zuerst // tsueəst // first
zwei // tsvaie // two

## Ü

übrigens // ypriːgəns // by the way

# Acknowledgments

Books, as much as we may want them to, do not materialise out of thin air. There is a great deal of work that goes into each Weeve, from idea to print. We would like to offer our most sincere thanks to every single individual who helped get this book into your hands, the people who support the team, the test-readers who ensure the content you receive is of the highest quality, the designers who make sure your Weeve looks its best, and to our support staff who add the finishing touches, ensuring a crafted learning experience, from start to finish.

The most important person we'd like to thank, however, is you, our reader. Without you, and your passionate commitment to taking the plunge into learning a brand new language, there would be no book to read. We're fueled by people like you, people who are willing and able to try new things, people who look at the way languages are learned at school and think 'There must be a better way', and people who want to expand their skills and their knowledge while reading some of the finest literature this world has to offer. We feel the same, and we're happy to have you.

The end of this book does not mean the end of your language learning journey, however. Weeve regularly publishes content, with new Weeves coming out all the time, as well as other language resources.

To make the most of everything Weeve has to offer be sure to keep an eye on our website and social media!

Thank you again, and remember to keep on learning!

The Weeve Team


www.weeve.ie
Instagram: @WeeveLanguages
Twitter: @WeeveLanguages
TikTok: WeeveLanguages
LinkedIn: WeeveLanguages

# You've finished your Weeve... What's next?

## Try The Weeve Reader Now at
## WWW.WEEVE.IE

**Upload books of your choice**

**Dynamically adjust translation difficulty** — 25%

**Real-time pronunciations**